Mrs. Chard's Almanac
C O O K B O O K
HOLLYHOCKS & RADISHES

Bonnie Stewart Mickelson

Illustrations by Ann Schuler Santo
Cover Illustration by Jim Hays

Pickle Point Publishing Bellevue, Washington

First printing

Copyright © 1989 by Bonnie Stewart Mickelson

Illustrations © 1989 by Pickle Point Publishing

Printed and bound in the United States of America.

Library of Congress Catalog Card Number: 89-90856

ISBN 0-9622412-1-0.

Photographic assistance: Harry Harris and Peter Mikkelsen

Cover and Book Design by Sam Payne & Associates
Creative Director: Sam Payne   Designer: Anne Thomas

Pickle Point Publishing, P.O. Box 4107, Bellevue, Washington 98004

To the memory of

Catherine

Seiberling

Stewart

1906 - 1988

*...and the song
of the white throat*

CONTENTS

ACKNOWLEDGEMENTS

with grateful recognition of our dear friends and family...

Jean Abner
Beatrice Allen
Barbara Barr
Doris Beach
Oliver Birge
Betty Birkmeier
Gerry Bishop
Alesha Brown
Yvonne Brown
Jean Carr
Elaine Chard
Stephanie Chard
Verneita Chard
Claudette Connor
Ella Cope
Dorothy Currie
Shirley Dailey
Jack Daugherty
Beth Denney
Carol Duncan
Ollie Elliot
Marie Escola
Marilyn Evert
Ann Falor
Sally Flenniken
Dick Flynn
Ethel Fox
Ann Friedman
Ann Galbraith
Leona Gingrich
Annegret and
    Gordon Goehring
Sally Gordon
Marie Gregg

Joan Hagey
Arnie Hamel
Beulah Hansen
Helen and
    Harry Harris
Eunice Hefferan
Eileen Hensley
Paula Hoy
Neal Hutson
Mildred and
    Kenneth Jerew
Kay and Dirk Jongejan
Ruth Kester
Linda Larsen
Marie Lemond
Rozalia Lofdahl
Wanda and
    Wayne Long
Bill Madigan
June and Jim Maher
Karen McDermott
Millie McFadden
Bill McLeod
Pat McMillan
Jack Mertaugh
Marcia Mitchell
Thelma Nordberg
Thelma Nosek
Dorothy Nye
Edna Nye
Elda Nye
Geanna Nye
Ruth Nye
Sadie Nye

Ruth Patrick
Vickie Patson
Lois Pflueger
Bertha Phillips
Elgie Pollard
Bonnie Ratliff
Margaret Ratliff
Olive Ratliff
Eleanora Richards
Joan Romine
Cindy Roy
Sue Rye
Lida Rynearson
Omar Sanderson
Pat Sheppard
Frances Shoberg
Helen Shoberg
Betty Smith
Jane Spencer
Beverly Spodeck
Ethel Stansfield
Charlene and
    Randy Steir
Linda Storey
Meg Sullivan
Kelley Thon
Linda Vlasic
Bernice and
    Charles Weiss
Carol Welsh
Bonnie Wilson
Verna Windsor
Grace Wixom

PROLOGUE

Along the northern reaches of Lake Huron, lie the remarkably beautiful Les Cheneaux Islands. Etched by the glaciers of the Ice Age and steeped in the early history of America, they still shelter a way of life that prompts those who discover them to hide their existence.

Many believe this land to have been the home of Hiawatha. When one ventures into its dense woods, the air so fragrant of cedar and balsam, it's easy to imagine the moccasined feet of Chippewa Indians moving silently along the elusive trails of wild things. As you paddle the very channels that were crossed by the coureurs de bois and Father Marquette and LaSalle, you can feel so close to history that there is little sense of time's intervention.

The Islands protect two tiny but deeply rooted communities, Hessel and Cedarville. First settled by Scandinavian, Irish, and Italian immigrants during the burgeoning of the timber and fishing industries, they now reflect two diverse existences...that of the native who loves his environment with such intensity that seemingly no economic struggle could uproot him, and that of the summer visitor who briefly brings with him a bit of the very things he is trying to escape...the demands and pressures of modern life. Each respects, understands, and appreciates the different worlds, knowing that, in the case of the Islands, one could not be sustained without the other.

There are several factions of summer people. Among them, the steady trickle of tourists, with outboards in tow, who come each year in campers, or who inhabit what few resorts there are for a week or so, to fish and enjoy the low-keyed beach life. Families return year after year after year, and, at their vacations' end, reserve the same cabins for the next year, wondering as they do why they never seek another spot; then realizing that change is the very thing they don't want. And nothing ever seems to change in The Snows, as the island area is colloquially called.

Then, there are those who come by water in neatly rigged sailboats or opulent cruisers, tying up at the marinas or anchoring in nearby bays, to bide a few days between somewhere and nowhere. And always there are the Islanders...the families that have cherished the Les Cheneaux as their summer residence since as far back as the late 1800s. From affluent areas of Ohio, Illinois, and southern Michigan, they represent understated sophistication. Their so-called cottages and camps are tucked obscurely among the trees; sturdy, well-aged docks are often the only hints of habitation. They maintain the facilities as their forebears had...again, nothing changes.

Sleek, beautiful, wooden ChrisCrafts travel the channels...boats practically extinct to the rest of the world. The Mertaugh family of Hessel held the first franchise for ChrisCraft, and, to this day, maintains them with well-deserved pride. Thus, every August, "the largest antique wooden boat show in the world" is held at the Hessel docks, bringing thousands of tourists, like the proverbial swarm of locusts, to stun the community for one day of fun-filled madness.

The summer season is brief. Mid-September returns the towns to their quiet, simple pace; and the islands once again lie serene. The locals prepare for the long, dark, winter months, stashing their gardens' bounties in freezers or on pantry shelves, and looking forward to the hunting seasons to complete their larders. Economically, many must stretch last summer's profits to support them until next summer's commerce.

The Chards, Marv and Judy, are in their 65th year of marriage. Their lives have been filled with no more, no less joy and sadness than most anyone else's, but they have maintained an exceptionally clear sense of values that, to me, typifies the character of the Les Cheneaux people. Hard, hard working, but always looking toward the sunny side of life, they find great pleasure in the simplest of things and continually respect each other and their fellow man, no matter what his walk of life.

Judy Chard started sharing her garden with us summer people ten or so years ago. Word spread fast that one could find the youngest, freshest, most unusual variety of vegetables two and a half miles north of Hessel at "Mrs. Chard's." From the beginning

though, much of the appeal has been due to the Chards' warm, delightful personalities and the charming setting of their stand.

Intentionally or not, Marv built the tiny, roofed structure to resemble a wishing well, devising a simple watering system to sprinkle down on the produce like a gentle rain. Nestled in the shade of maple and tamarack trees, the stand is so inviting that robins nest yearly in its eaves.

Mrs. Chard gives no pretense to being artistic or creative, and yet each summer day she designs arrays of glistening, richly colorful vegetables and fruits, interspersed with hollyhocks and marigolds, that produce a visual treat that no formal farmers' market display could ever approach in beauty. Long before "miniature" vegetables came into vogue, she was providing them for her customers, suggesting how to uniquely display and serve them as hors d'oeuvres or in appealing salads.

This is what initially inspired this book. As Mrs. Chard would share her recipes, her delighted customers did so in return. I've included many of them herein, along with those of other good cooks in the Snows; and, granted, a goodly number of my own. They are to reflect the Les Cheneaux area, its history, and its unaffected approach to cooking, using all that its soil and pure lake waters have to offer. Every one of the recipes has been tested by me at least once, and, when appropriate, adapted to today's health-conscious modes.

Frequently I have used poetic license, such as in the recipes' introductions, in order to convey Mrs. Chard's warm-hearted, generous nature. But, the letters that wend their way through the chapters are collections of excerpts from the many she has written me over the four and a half years that this book has been nurtured. They are genuine reflections of her and her Marvin.

Through this book and the vehicle of the Chards' personalities, I hope to portray the timelessness of the Les Cheneaux region and all the good things in the simple life of yesteryear that can still be found and valued today to enrich our future.

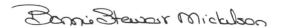

BEGINNINGS

beverages, appetizers, and sandwiches

Dear Bonnie,

Oh, I am so happy! Spring is finally here! The sap in the maple trees is running, although there are still great patches of snow. They're boiling it down in the sugar shacks. Just think... 40 to 50 gallons of sap to make just one gallon of syrup. Depends on how sweet the tree is.

We're waiting and watching for the ice to clear the bays and the smelt to start running... up stream, at night, by the thousands. What fun it is! There will be fires on the banks of the creek to give light and warmth while everyone goes crazy scooping them up with anything scoopable... nets, baskets, wastebaskets.

The suckers will follow soon after the smelt... they by day... when the leaves on the popple trees are the size of a squirrel's ear, so the old-timers say.

We are starting our seeds in the house... you know how short the growing season is here. Some got a little too eager (like Marv), and have plants growing big enough to move into greenhouses. We have to heat our greenhouse since the temperature still is dipping below freezing at night... good for maple sap but bad for young, tender plants.

Must check the garden to see what's been left in the ground all winter. Carrots are so sweet and crisp when they've been forgotten in the fall. Parsley should be starting up from old roots of last year... maybe dill from fallen seeds.

God bless you,

Judy Chard

SUNSHINE TEA

Yield: 6-8 tall glasses
Prepare: 5 minutes
Steep: 10 minutes
Cool

As clear as an "up north" day will be tea steeped in sunshine. In the warm summertime, I'll set a pitcher of this on the back stoop to await afternoon callers.

2 long stems of mint
Grated rind of ½ lemon
Grated rind of ½ orange
4 tea bags (or 2 table-
   spoons loose tea)

2 cups boiling water
⅓ cup sugar
3¾ cups cold water
Juice of ½ orange
Juice of ½ lemon

Garnish: thin slices of lemon and orange, mint sprigs

☐ Place stems of mint, grated rinds, and tea in a heat-proof pitcher or teapot. Pour 2 cups boiling water over all. Steep 10 minutes.

☐ Put remaining ingredients (except garnish) in a large pitcher or jar. Strain steeped tea mixture into it and blend.

☐ Let cool then pour into tall glasses of ice, and garnish with thin slices of lemon or orange and sprigs of mint.

▨ Note: This tea may be refrigerated for a day or two without becoming cloudy.

SWEET DANDELION WINE

Yield: 1 quart
Steep: 2 days
Prepare: 30 minutes
Ferment: 4 weeks
Age: 5 months

"Is there anything so fine as dandelion wine?" On an early spring day, pick young blooms in bright sunshine for December's pleasures.

2 quarts dandelion blossoms, tightly packed	4 quarts boiling water

☐ It is important that the blooms be young and fully open, and picked of as much green stem as possible. As soon as you have attained 2 quarts, place them in a very clean, large, stoneware or plastic container(s) and pour boiling water over. Cover and let steep 2 days.

4 oranges	½ cake of yeast
1 lemon	(or ½ envelope dry)
6 cups sugar	1 slice rye toast (that's right!)

☐ After the blossoms have steeped 2 days, peel the rind from the oranges and lemon (be careful not to include any pith) and place in a large kettle. Squeeze the juices from the fruit and set aside.

☐ Place the steeped blossoms, undrained, in the kettle with the rinds. Bring to a boil, and simmer 10 minutes. Strain through a sieve, lined with fine cheesecloth, into a large saucepan, squeezing flowers dry then discarding along with rinds. Stir sugar into dandelion liquid to dissolve, then add the juice of the oranges and lemon. Cool to lukewarm.

☐ Return mixture to the stoneware pot or plastic container(s). Crumble or sprinkle yeast on top of rye toast, and float on top. (If you need to use 2 containers, divide yeast and rye toast accordingly; do not increase amounts.) Cover with a cloth, and keep at room temperature (65°-70°) for a week.

☐ Strain into a clean, 1-gallon jug and plug loosely with a ball of cotton. Store in a cool, dark place for 3 weeks.

☐ Gently pour into bottles; cap or cork tightly. Age 5 months. Serve at your Christmas dinner!

RASPBERRY SHRUB

Yield: 4 drinks
Cook: 20 minutes
Cool
Prepare: 5 minutes

A mid-summer cooler...pretty as a picture.

2 cups fresh raspberries
(or 1 10-ounce package
frozen)
2 tablespoons sugar
(optional)*
2 cups water

Cracked ice
1 cup light rum or soda
water
2 teaspoons lime juice
Mint sprigs and raspberries
(optional)

We just had kids come by selling Halloween Carnival tickets...bought a bunch of them, although I think we'll be staying home this year. Too bad. We'll be missing all that fun and the good punch!

☐ In a saucepan, simmer raspberries, sugar, and water, uncovered, for 20 minutes.*(Omit sugar if using berries frozen with sugar.)

☐ Pour through a sieve, pressing to attain at least 2 cups of juice. Cool.

☐ Place cracked ice in 4 tall glasses. To each, add ½-cup juice, then 2 ounces (¼-cup) rum or soda water and ½ teaspoon lime juice. Stir. Garnish with mint springs and a few fresh raspberries.

HALLOWEEN PUNCH

Yield: 1 gallon
Prepare: 5 minutes

Around here, Halloween isn't Halloween without apple cider. This is how we dress it up for a party.

½ gallon apple cider
2 quarts ginger ale
Juice of 2 lemons
Juice of 2 oranges

Ice (optional)
1 lemon, thinly sliced
1 orange, thinly sliced

☐ In a large punch bowl, combine cider, ginger ale, and juices. Add ice if you wish, and garnish with fruit slices.

SMOKED WHITEFISH PÂTÉ

Serves: 6
Prepare: 5 minutes

We don't know anyone who doesn't rave about this. Serve it with small, thin slices of French bread or simple crackers for spreading, or with dry bread sticks for dipping.

1 pound smoked whitefish
¼ cup heavy cream
¼ cup mayonnaise
¼ cup lemon juice
⅛ teaspoon cayenne
   pepper
Finely chopped parsley
   or chives

☐ Remove any skin or bones from fish. Process with remaining ingredients, except parsley or chives, in a food processor or blender until smooth. Chill.

☐ Serve in a small pâté dish or bowl, garnished with chopped parsley or chives.

PICKLE POINT POACHED TROUT

Serves: 6-10
Prepare: 5 minutes
Bake: 1 hour
Chill

An unusual way to serve fish as an appetizer, and it is wonderful.

1 whole trout or baby
   salmon (about ¾ to
   1 pound)
½ cup red wine vinegar
½ cup water
2 teaspoons pickling spices
1 bay leaf
Bacon-flavored crackers

☐ Preheat oven to 250°.

☐ If necessary, clean trout, but do not bone or skin. Place in an ungreased, shallow, glass baking dish. Combine vinegar, water, spices, and bay leaf. Pour over trout, then cover dish with foil and bake 1 hour, turning fish over after first 30 minutes. Chill in same dish at least 2 hours or overnight.

☐ To serve, skin and bone fish, then arrange it attractively on a bed of leaf lettuce or watercress. Surround with crackers, and have small forks at hand. If you'd like, offer a small bowl of Green Goddess or Cool Cuke Dip to spoon over the fish.

DARLING POTATOES

Serves: 6 plus
Prepare: 15 minutes

So named by one of my customers, these are baby potatoes that I start putting out on the stand in mid-June. Sometimes they aren't any bigger than your thumbnail. Everyone loves them for hors d'oeuvres.

1 pint tiny new potatoes
2-3 tablespoons bacon fat
    or butter

Chopped parsley

☐ Scrub, then boil potatoes until barely fork-tender; about 2-3 minutes. In a large frying pan, over medium-high heat, sauté potatoes in a couple tablespoons or so of bacon fat or butter, shaking pan to evenly brown.

☐ Add chopped parsley and sauté about 10 seconds more, but not so long that parsley changes color. Spear with toothpicks to serve.

Those darling, little potatoes that our customers like so much will be ready soon. The beans have a little time to go, and it will be another couple weeks for the beets. Of course, no tomatoes 'til the very end of this month.

RED-SKINNED POTATOES
with CAPER SAUCE

Yield (sauce): 1¾ cups
Prepare: 5 minutes
Chill: 2 hours

This is for when those little red-skinned potatoes get to be about 1 to 1½ inches in diameter, and you want to serve something fancy before dinner or to dress up a picnic. Boil the potatoes until tender, drain well and chill. Slightly hollow-out tops of potatoes, then dress with small dollops of this sauce.

1½ cups mayonnaise
2 teaspoons curry powder
1 tablespoon grated onion
3-4 tablespoons drained
    capers

2-3 drops Tabasco sauce
¼ cup finely chopped
    parsley

☐ Combine all ingredients. Chill for 2 hours or more. This will keep at least a week in the fridge.

▣ Note: It's a wonderful sauce for cold salmon.

TOMATO DEVILS

Yield: 25
Serves: 10-12
Prepare: 15 minutes
Bake: 5 minutes

A hearty canapé that will disappear before your eyes. If you'd like, you can toast the bread rounds and prepare the filling several hours ahead.

25 small, bread rounds or cocktail rye slices
1 cup grated cheddar, Jarlsberg, or jack cheese
2 bunches green onions, finely chopped
½ green pepper, finely chopped
1 cup mayonnaise
½ teaspoon garlic salt
⅛ teaspoon cayenne pepper
1 pint baby yellow or cherry tomatoes, sliced
8 slices bacon, cooked and crumbled

☐ Toast only one side of bread slices under broiler. Cover to keep fresh and set aside.

☐ Combine cheese, onions, and green pepper with ⅔-cup of the mayonnaise. Season with garlic salt and cayenne pepper. Refrigerate if making in advance.

☐ Shortly before serving time, preheat oven to 350°. Spread untoasted sides of bread with remaining ⅓-cup mayonnaise. Top with tomato slices, then cheese mixture. Sprinkle with bacon.

☐ Bake 3-5 minutes, until bubbly and lightly browned. Serve immediately.

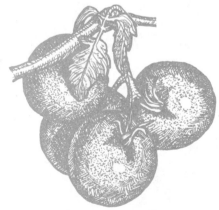

RACHEL's DIP

Yield: 2½ cups
Prepare: 10 minutes

Bacon and green onions always work well together. This is not only good with raw vegetables, but as a filling in a round, hollowed-out loaf of bread, surrounded by chunks of the bread for dipping.

1 pint sour cream
1 heaping tablespoon real mayonnaise
1 tablespoon horseradish
10-12 green onions
1 pound bacon, chopped

☐ Combine sour cream, mayonnaise, and horseradish. Finely chop the white part of the green onions and add to sour cream mixture. Chop the green tops and set aside. Sauté the bacon until crisp and drain on paper towels.

☐ When ready to serve, fill bowl with sour cream mixture. Decorate center with bacon and sprinkle chopped onion tops around the edge.

Green Goddess Dip can be made several days ahead. It's an excellent sauce for cold salmon or whitefish, or you may thin it with a splash or two of milk to dress a salad.

GREEN GODDESS DIP

Yield: 2 cups
Prepare: 10 minutes
Chill

Line a pretty, willow basket with bright red napkins then handsome leaves of kale; fill with broccoli and cauliflower florets, blanched Sugar Snap peas, green onions, cherry tomatoes, cubes and strips of sweet red, green, and yellow peppers; accent with leaves from half of a small, red cabbage. Hollow out the other cabbage-half, then fill with Green Goddess Dip and tuck into the basket...a simply breath-taking appetizer or buffet salad.

1 2-ounce can anchovy fillets
⅔ cup chopped parsley
3 tablespoons chopped chives or green onion tops
1 clove garlic
1 tablespoon tarragon vinegar
1 cup mayonnaise
½ cup sour cream
Salt and freshly ground pepper to taste

☐ Combine ingredients in a food processor or blender. Chill. For best flavor, remove from refrigerator a half-hour before serving.

MILLIE's VEGIE DIP

Yield: 1 ¼ cups
Prepare: 5 minutes
Chill

This does not have to be prepared ahead of time, but doing so will intensify the flavors. You'll love it as a dip for all sorts of pretty things from the garden.

1   cup mayonnaise
2   tablespoons Durkee's dressing
1   heaping tablespoon horseradish
½ small clove garlic, crushed

1   teaspoon celery seed
1   teaspoon curry powder
1   teaspoon seasoned salt
½ teaspoon Worcestershire sauce
Dash of Tabasco sauce

☐ Combine and chill.

COOL CUKE DIP

Yield: 2 cups
Prepare: 5 minutes
Marinate: 24 hours
Prepare: 5 minutes

It's important that the cucumber marinate overnight...that's what makes this so refreshing in taste.

1   large cucumber
¼ cup vinegar

1   teaspoon salt

☐ Peel and grate cucumber by hand or with a food processor. Combine with vinegar and salt. Cover and refrigerate 24 hours.

1   8-ounce package cream cheese, softened
⅓ cup mayonnaise

1   small clove garlic, minced
Salt to taste (optional)

☐ Drain and press all liquid from marinated cucumber. Combine cucumber and remaining ingredients. Serve as a dip for fresh vegies or chips.

HOT PECAN DIP

Yield: 3 cups
Prepare: 20 minutes
Bake: 15 minutes
20 minutes

Like rabbits in the lettuce patch, your guests won't leave this alone.

¾ cup chopped pecans
2 tablespoons butter, melted
½ teaspoon salt
1 8-ounce package cream cheese, softened
2 tablespoons milk
2½ ounces dried beef, chopped

¼ cup finely chopped green pepper
½ small onion, grated
½ teaspoon garlic powder
Freshly ground pepper to taste
½ cup sour cream

☐ Preheat oven to 350°.

☐ Combine pecans, butter, and salt, and spread out in a pie plate. Bake 15 minutes. Cool several minutes.

☐ Combine remaining ingredients in given order. Pour into an ungreased, shallow 8 to 9-inch baking dish. Cover with prepared nuts. At this point, the dip may be set aside or refrigerated until baking time.

☐ Bake 20 minutes. Serve hot with crackers or pumpernickel bread for dipping.

Marv is making ball bats for three of our great-grandsons for Christmas. He picked up some left-over teak at the boatyard for chip-and-dip bowls. They're going to be beautiful. He's good at anything like that...he's good at everything.

BEER-CHEESE DIP

Yield: 3 cups
Prepare: 10 minutes

If in a hurry, serve simply with chips or large pretzel sticks. Sometime, though, try surrounding a bowl of the dip with sliced, unpeeled apples and sticks of raw, peeled parsnips...yes, parsnips...they're great!

8 ounces cream cheese, softened
½ - ¾ cup beer or ale
8 ounces sharp cheddar cheese, cubed

1 clove garlic
12 small, sweet gherkins
1 teaspoon poppy seeds

☐ Combine cream cheese and a ½-cup of the beer in an electric blender for a few seconds. Add cheddar cheese cubes, garlic, and rest of beer, if you wish a thinner consistency. Blend until smooth. Add gherkins and poppy seeds; blend 3 seconds.

PEPPERONI DIP

Yield: 3 cups
Prepare: 5 minutes
Chill: 2 days

It's a must that the pepperoni mixture be prepared two days ahead for the flavors to mellow and the sausage to soften. Serve in a hollowed-out loaf of bread, surrounded by chunks of the bread for dipping. Men LOVE this recipe!

8 ounces pepperoni sausage
1 pint sour cream

1 round bread loaf (optional)
Garnish: chopped chives or parsley

☐ If necessary, remove casing from sausage. Finely chop sausage, then combine with sour cream. Cover and store in refrigerator for 2 days.

☐ Serve as suggested or with simple crackers, garnishing the dip with chopped chives or parsley.

JUDY's MEATBALLS

Serves: 24
Prepare: 30 minutes
Bake: 1 hour

Men rave about these. They are so tender and tasty, and, best of all, there is no need to brown them before baking.

For a delicious main dish, double the size of the meatballs and serve them over noodles for six to eight persons.

2 pounds lean ground beef
1 egg, beaten
1 cup crushed cornflakes
½ cup applesauce
1 onion, finely chopped
1 clove garlic, crushed
1½ teaspoons salt
Freshly ground pepper to taste

☐ Preheat oven to 350°.

☐ Gently, but thoroughly, combine the above ingredients and form into bite-size meatballs, placing them in one layer in a large, shallow baking dish. Note that the more tenderly you handle the meatballs, the tenderer they will be!

1 medium onion, finely chopped
¼ cup butter
¼ cup flour
⅓ cup tomato paste
¼ cup chili sauce or catsup
3 cups beef bouillon or broth
2 tablespoons beef concentrate (i.e. "beef tea")
1 tablespoon Worcestershire sauce
2 tablespoons chopped parsley
1 clove garlic, crushed
1 bay leaf
1 teaspoon basil
4 peppercorns
12-14 button-size mushrooms
½ cup dry white wine

☐ In a 12-inch skillet, over medium heat, sauté onion in butter until soft. Add flour and cook until golden brown, stirring with a flat whisk. Add remaining ingredients, except mushrooms and wine, and cook slowly until thickened, stirring from time to time.

☐ Place mushrooms and wine in a small saucepan, and cook over high heat for 5 minutes. Stir into sauce. Pour sauce over meatballs and bake, uncovered, for 1 hour. Serve in a chafing dish, if you'd like.

■ Note: These freeze beautifully.

SAUERKRAUT BALLS

Yield: 4 dozen
Prepare: 25 minutes
Chill
Deep-fry: 30 minutes

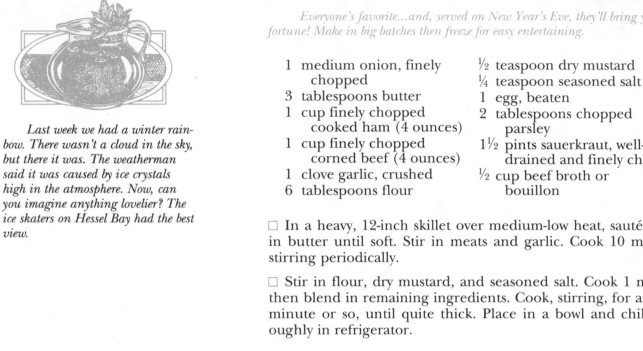

Last week we had a winter rainbow. There wasn't a cloud in the sky, but there it was. The weatherman said it was caused by ice crystals high in the atmosphere. Now, can you imagine anything lovelier? The ice skaters on Hessel Bay had the best view.

Everyone's favorite...and, served on New Year's Eve, they'll bring you good fortune! Make in big batches then freeze for easy entertaining.

1 medium onion, finely chopped	½ teaspoon dry mustard
3 tablespoons butter	¼ teaspoon seasoned salt
1 cup finely chopped cooked ham (4 ounces)	1 egg, beaten
1 cup finely chopped corned beef (4 ounces)	2 tablespoons chopped parsley
1 clove garlic, crushed	1½ pints sauerkraut, well-drained and finely chopped
6 tablespoons flour	½ cup beef broth or bouillon

☐ In a heavy, 12-inch skillet over medium-low heat, sauté onion in butter until soft. Stir in meats and garlic. Cook 10 minutes, stirring periodically.

☐ Stir in flour, dry mustard, and seasoned salt. Cook 1 minute, then blend in remaining ingredients. Cook, stirring, for another minute or so, until quite thick. Place in a bowl and chill thoroughly in refrigerator.

4 cups light vegetable oil	2 eggs, beaten
Flour	2 cups fine, dry bread crumbs

☐ Shape chilled meat mixture into walnut-size balls (about 1¼-inches).

☐ Heat oil in a deep-frying pan to 375°. Roll balls in flour, then, using 2 table forks, dip in beaten egg and roll in bread crumbs.

☐ Fry only 6 at a time in frying basket, shaking well when first immersing. When nicely browned (about 1½ minutes), remove to drain on paper towels.

☐ At this point, the kraut balls may be refrigerated or frozen. Reheat in oven before serving.

■ Note: A handy hint is to freeze balls on cookie sheets, then place in plastic bags for easy freezer storage. To serve, wrap desired number of frozen balls in foil and heat in a 400° oven for 20 minutes, opening foil for last 5 minutes.

SAUSAGE BITES
in APPLESAUCE

Serves: 8-10
Prepare: 5 minutes
Bake: 1½-2 hours

A nothing-to-it appetizer with lots-to-it appeal.

2 pounds lean kielbasa (Polish sausage)
4 cups chunky applesauce
½ cup brown sugar
1 tablespoon dried onion flakes

☐ Preheat oven to 325°.

☐ Slice sausage into ½-inch pieces. Combine with remaining ingredients in a 2½-quart, deep casserole. Bake, uncovered, 1½ to 2 hours.

☐ Serve warm in casserole or a chafing dish, with toothpicks and small napkins at hand.

CUCUMBER CHEESE SPREAD

Yield: 1⅔ cups
Prepare: 10 minutes

You can keep this in the refrigerator for special snacks and tea time sandwiches.

8 ounces cream cheese, softened
⅔ cup peeled, grated cucumber

1 tablespoon minced chives
1 good pinch each of onion salt, salt, and pepper

☐ Combine well.

FRESH SPINACH and BACON SANDWICHES

Yield: 4 sandwiches
Prepare: 10 minutes

Pluck the spinach from the garden for a nice, light sandwich on a hot, summer day, and serve with Sunshine Tea.

8 slices crisp bacon
¼ pound fresh spinach
8 slices sandwich bread

3 tablespoons mayonnaise
3 tablespoons butter, softened

☐ Fry bacon until crisp, and drain. Wash spinach and dry well. Spread 4 bread slices with mayonnaise. Top each with spinach leaves, then 2 slices of bacon. Spread remaining bread with butter, and close sandwiches.

PATRICK's SANDWICH

Yield: 4
Prepare: 10 minutes

The crunch of the cabbage and bacon make this a surprisingly tasty sandwich. Nice with hot soups such as Mushroom Zucchini.

8 slices bacon, slivered
2 cups finely shredded
   cabbage
¼ teaspoon salt
3 tablespoons mayonnaise

½ teaspoon prepared
   mustard
⅛ teaspoon Tabasco sauce
4 hamburger buns or
   sandwich rolls, split

☐ Sauté bacon until crisp. Drain. Combine with cabbage in a mixing bowl, and sprinkle with salt. Mix together mayonnaise, mustard, and Tabasco. Blend into cabbage mixture. Fill buns.

MACKINAC SUB

Serves: 3-4
Prepare: 15 minutes

You don't have to fight the summer crowds on Mackinac Island to enjoy a good "submarine." The secrets here are the lightly cooked vegies and the zip of the vinegar.

1 green pepper, cut in
   thin strips
2 medium-large onions,
   thinly sliced
1½ tablespoons olive oil
3 tablespoons white vinegar
Salt and freshly ground
   pepper to taste

1 10-ounce, long loaf of
   French bread
Butter, softened
6 ounces thinly sliced
   salami or ham
8 ounces thinly sliced
   mozzarella or jack cheese
2 tomatoes, thinly sliced

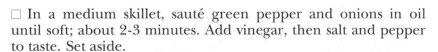

☐ In a medium skillet, sauté green pepper and onions in oil until soft; about 2-3 minutes. Add vinegar, then salt and pepper to taste. Set aside.

☐ Split bread lengthwise and generously butter both halves. On bottom half, layer meat and cheese, then green pepper/onion mixture. Add tomatoes, then sprinkle with more salt and pepper if you wish. Top with other bread half, and cut into serving portions.

What did we talk about at T-time today? The dance our neighbors, the Douds, had ever so long ago...when we were living between Trout Lake and Rudyard back in the early thirties. The music was home-style...anyone who could play an instrument did...fiddle, drums, harmonica. We had the best bean sandwiches ever! Can't remember exactly how they were made except they were on homemade bread. They were Michigan northern white beans that had been cooked in ham or bacon, then mashed. We had such a good time!

HEARTY CORNED BEEF and CABBAGE SANDWICHES

Yield: 6
Prepare: 15 minutes

This will pack a wallop of a lunch for the outdoorsmen in your family!

1½ cups finely shredded cabbage
3 tablespoons mayonnaise
1 tablespoon horseradish
½ teaspoon caraway seeds
6 tablespoons butter, softened

3 tablespoons yellow or Dijon mustard
12 large slices rye bread
10 ounces corned beef, thinly sliced
6 ounces Swiss cheese, thinly sliced

☐ Blanch cabbage in lightly salted boiling water until barely limp; about 1-2 minutes. Immediately rinse in cold water, then drain very well. Mix with mayonnaise, horseradish, and caraway seeds. Blend together butter and mustard, and spread on one side of bread slices. Divide corned beef among 6 of the slices. Top with cabbage mixture, cheese slices, and remaining bread. (These are very good grilled.)

SLOPPY SNOW-JOES

Serves 4-6
Prepare: 15 minutes
Cook: 15 minutes

Different parts of the country have their own versions of Sloppy Joes. Ours of the Les Cheneaux (the Snows) is unique because we include carrots, which add a natural sweetness.

1 onion, chopped
2 cloves garlic, minced
2 carrots, grated
2 tablespoons light cooking oil
1 pound lean ground beef
1 cup tomato sauce
3 tablespoons catsup
2 tablespoons vinegar

1 tablespoon molasses
1 teaspoon paprika
1 teaspoon chili powder
1 teaspoon Worcestershire sauce
Salt and freshly ground pepper to taste
4-6 hamburger buns

☐ In a large, heavy skillet, sauté onion, garlic, and carrots in oil until soft. Add meat and cook just until no longer pink. Stir in remaining ingredients (except buns!). Cover and gently simmer 15 minutes. Serve on broiler-toasted buns.

SOUPS

chilled or hot, light or hearty

Dear Bonnie,

My days are never long enough... especially in the spring.

I've just come from the garden... found a few things that wintered through... some carrots, garlic, green onions, parsley.

The temperature is 26° F. this a.m. There are still snowbanks in the yard and garden, but the rhubarb and asparagus should soon be up. Marv's trimmed the raspberry bushes and grapevines.

It's time to check the hives to see if the honey bees made it through the winter. We know some people who had to put an electric fence around their hives to keep the bears away. Did you hear about the bear running around Cedarville last fall? Helen and Harry Harris had one climb a tree right by their house down on Flower Creek.

By the way, Harry's real busy putting up his hundreds and hundreds of tree swallow houses. Everyone loves seeing them, in their pretty colors, dotting the marshes and bays. Isn't it wonderful that he cares that much?

I've ordered and received most of our seeds. Some are taking root in flats on top of the wood furnace. The plants in the south window are waiting to be transplanted and moved to the greenhouse.

Trout season came in this weekend, so lots of tourists around. Buds are showing up on the birch trees, and we hear that the smelt are running. Already people are checking their favorite spots for mushrooms.

Best of all, the spring peepers are peeping!

Love,
Judy Chard

WILD LEEK or ONION SOUP

Serves: 4
Prepare: 30 minutes
Bake: 1 hour

This is wonderfully satisfying to the tummy as well as the tastebuds. If leeks are not available, substitute 3 to 4 thinly sliced onions.

1½ to 2 cups split leek bulbs
2 tablespoons butter
1 teaspoon sugar
Freshly ground pepper to taste

4 cups hot beef bouillon*
⅓ loaf potato or French bread, sliced
6 ounces Swiss cheese, thinly sliced
3 tablespoons butter

☐ Preheat oven to 350°.

☐ In a large saucepan, gently sauté leeks in 2 tablespoons butter for 10 to 15 minutes. Sprinkle with sugar and pepper, then add hot bouillon. Simmer another 10 minutes.

□ Cut the bread slices in half. In a Dutch oven or 2½-quart, deep casserole, layer the bread slices, topping each with a slice of cheese. Slowly pour onion mixture over all. Dot with remaining butter. Bake, uncovered, for 1 hour.

■ Note: *This makes a very thick soup; thus, you may wish to offer extra bouillon on the side.

LEMON SPINACH SOUP

Serves: 8
Prepare: 20 minutes

Just as pretty as can be with the orange touches of carrot against the rich green of the spinach in a deliciously creamy, lemony broth.

8 cups chicken broth
3 small carrots, thinly sliced
1 stalk celery, finely chopped
1 pound fresh spinach
3 tablespoons butter
3 tablespoons flour
3 egg yolks
3 tablespoons lemon juice
Salt and freshly ground pepper to taste

□ Bring 7 of the 8 cups of broth to a boil in a large saucepan or pot. Add carrots and celery. Cover and simmer until tender; about 5 minutes.

□ Wash spinach, removing coarse stems. Tear into bite-size pieces. Add to soup and simmer, covered, 3-5 minutes, or just until tender. You want the leaves to retain their lovely color.

□ Over medium heat, melt the butter in a small saucepan. Blend in flour with a whisk and cook 1 minute, stirring. Whisk in the reserved cup of broth, and stir until smooth. Add to the soup pot as soon as the spinach is ready. Simmer, uncovered, just until thickened, stirring with a slotted spoon.

□ In a small bowl, beat egg yolks and lemon juice together. Add a ½-cup of soup broth to the bowl and blend well. Stir mixture into hot soup with slotted spoon.

□ Bring just to point of boiling, but do not boil or it will curdle. Season to taste with salt and pepper, if necessary.

Dessert may be for the sweet tooth, but soup is for the soul.

MINT CUCUMBER SOUP

Serves: 4-6
Prepare: 25 minutes
Chill

Cooking the cucumbers increases the flavor. This is the perfect summer soup.

1 medium onion, chopped
1 clove garlic, chopped
3 tablespoons butter
3 medium cucumbers, peeled and thinly sliced*
3 tablespoons flour
2 cups chicken broth
2 tablespoons chopped fresh mint
1 cup plain yogurt
1 cup light cream
Salt and white pepper to taste

☐ In a large skillet, over medium heat, sauté onion and garlic in butter until soft. Add cucumbers and cook until soft; about 5-8 minutes.

☐ Stir in flour, cooking 1 minute. Add broth, increase heat to medium-high, and bring to a boil. Reduce heat and simmer 5 minutes.

☐ Purée cucumber mixture in blender in batches. Pour into a bowl with the chopped mint. Cover and chill.

☐ Before serving, blend in yogurt and cream. Season with salt and white pepper. Garnish with mint sprigs or chopped mint leaves.

■ Note: *If you would like to use English cukes, you'll need only 1½, and you won't have to peel them, which will add much color. Our ordinary garden cukes give the most flavor, though.

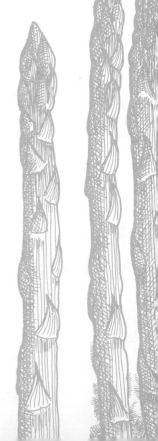

ASPARAGUS TOMATO SOUP

Serves: 8
Prepare: 20 minutes

Like so many good soups, this came about by gambling on what was in the larder. It has unusual but wonderful flavor...the touch of cloves is magical.

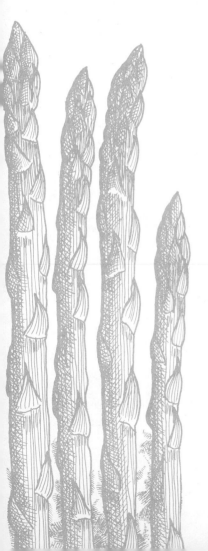

1 medium onion, coarsely chopped
1 carrot, coarsely chopped
2 tablespoons butter
2 tablespoons flour
2 cups canned tomatoes
5 cups chicken broth
½ teaspoon sugar
1 tablespoon chopped parsley

1 bay leaf
½ teaspoon thyme
⅛ teaspoon ground cloves
Salt and freshly ground pepper to taste
1½ pounds fresh asparagus
Garnish: sour cream and chopped chives or parsley

☐ In a large, heavy saucepan, sauté onion and carrot in butter until soft. Sprinkle with flour, and cook another minute, stirring. Add remaining ingredients except asparagus and garnish. Simmer, covered, 10 minutes or so.

☐ In the meantime, cook asparagus until fork-tender but still a pretty green. (See index for method.) Drain, then cut stalks into thirds.

☐ Discard bay leaf. Purée tomato mixture and asparagus in an electric blender in several batches.

☐ Reheat to serve, garnishing each bowl with a dollop of sour cream and a sprinkling of chopped chives or parsley.

23

SUMMER TOMATO SOUP

Serves: 4-6
Prepare: 10 minutes
Chill

About as fresh as can be...from the vine to the blender to the soup cup.

5-6 large tomatoes, peeled
3-4 green onions, chopped
1 teaspoon salt
½ teaspoon sugar
1 teaspoon each fresh
    marjoram and thyme

1 tablespoon lemon or lime
    juice
½ cup light sour cream
Chicken broth (optional)
Chopped chives, parsley,
    or dill

☐ Coarsely chop enough tomatoes to yield 4 cups puréed. Whirl in blender with onions, salt, sugar, herbs, and lemon juice. Pour into a bowl, then whisk in sour cream. Chill.

☐ The mixture may thicken with standing. If so, thin with broth. Serve garnished with chopped chives, parsley, or dill.

TOMATO RICE SOUP

Serves: 4-6
Prepare: 15 minutes
Cook: 1 hour

This is about as wholesome a soup as can be, and equally as good. It takes only a jiffy to prepare if you are using left-over rice.

1 onion, chopped
2 celery stalks, chopped
1 carrot, finely chopped
    or grated
1 clove garlic, minced
1 tablespoon butter
1 tablespoon oil
2 tablespoons whole wheat
    or unbleached flour

1½ cups cooked brown rice
1 quart fresh tomatoes
1 tablespoon brown sugar
½ teaspoon basil
½ teaspoon oregano
2 cups chicken broth
Salt and freshly ground
    pepper to taste
1 cup light cream

☐ In a pot or Dutch oven, sauté onion, celery, carrot, and garlic in butter and oil until onion is golden. Stir in flour and rice, and continue to sauté until rice is lightly browned. Add remaining ingredients except cream. Simmer, covered, 1 hour.

☐ Stir in cream; check seasoning. Do not boil if reheating.

MUSHROOM ZUCCHINI SOUP

Serves: 8-10
Prepare: 15 minutes

A wonderful combination...serve hot or cold. For fancy times, you can add a dollop of sour cream and a sprinkling of chives to each soup bowl.

6 cups chicken broth
1½ pounds zucchini
2 pounds fresh mushrooms
2 3-ounce packages cream
  cheese with chives

Salt and pepper to taste
1 teaspoon curry powder
  (optional)

☐ Bring chicken broth to boil in a large saucepan. Slice zucchini 1-inch thick. Clean then break mushrooms in half. Add the vegetables to the boiling broth. Cover and simmer 7-8 minutes.

☐ Purée with cream cheese in a blender or food processor. Add salt and pepper to taste, and curry powder if desired.

Must check the garden to see what's been left in the ground all winter. Carrots are so sweet and crisp when they've been forgotten in the fall.

HEAVENLY CARROT SOUP

Serves: 6
Prepare: 15 minutes
Cook: 30 minutes

Better tasting than carrots! The secret?...the cooking method and the fact that coriander and carrots do special things for each other. Serve hot, cold, or even room temp...it's just great and the color dazzling.

1 cup chopped onion
4 tablespoons butter
½ cup dry white wine
1 pound carrots, finely
  chopped

1½ teaspoons ground
  coriander
4 cups chicken broth
Salt and freshly ground
  pepper to taste

☐ In a large, heavy saucepan, sauté onion in butter until soft. Add wine and carrots. Cover tightly, and cook over very low heat for 30 minutes. Check a couple times, stirring to keep from browning (although a little bit adds something).

☐ Place carrot mixture in electric blender with coriander and some of chicken broth. Purée, then return to saucepan and whisk in remaining broth and salt and pepper to taste. If serving hot, reheat but do not boil.

The channels that etch the Les Cheneaux Islands, prompting the name given the lands by the coureurs de bois of the 17th century, provide extraordinary beauty and tranquility for those who seek a replete experience with nature.

In the 1890s, the first summer people discovered the Islands. Among them were a doctor and his bride from northern Ohio on their honeymoon.

Looking for adventure yet solitude, they had originally planned a canoe trip along the inland waterways, starting in Cheboygan. While buying a sweater at a general store in Ann Arbor, they were persuaded by the young salesman, who had just returned from a camping trip in the north with his father, to continue on to the Upper Peninsula and the idyllic Les Cheneaux. There, he promised, they could paddle from one lovely, misty cove to another with nary a soul intruding upon their paradise.

In the western group of the Islands lies Kauk-ge-nah-gwah Minishe, a mile's stretch of dense cedar and spruce, so named by the Chippewas for its minnow-like shape. It was here that the young couple beached their canoe on a moon-slip of white sand...the mouth of the minnow...and built their campfire; the first of ninety-some years of campfires there for them and their children and grandchildren and, now, great-grandchildren.

They called their safe harbor, "Camp Wildwood." Within the next few years, two brothers and a sister followed to build their own campsites...Cedar Lodge on the opposite tip of Kauk-ge-nah-gwah, then Lakanwood and Sun Sands, nearby on Marquette Island.

Today the camps are still much as they were, reflecting the unique character and personalities of the strong families that have dwelled within them. Time, in lending its patina, has fortified the memories and deep feelings of heritage that we, the descendants, feel so blessed to have.

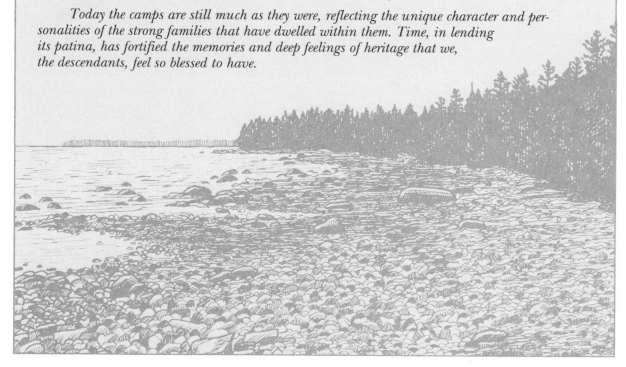

KAUK-GE-NAH-GWAH
LENTIL SOUP

Yield : 6-8 quarts
Soak
Prepare: 30 minutes
Simmer: 1½ to 2 hours

For many, many summers at Camp Wildwood, Uncle Doc and Aunt Grace Chase cooked their evening meals over open-fires built within the same circle of rocks they had placed there on their honeymoon in 1896.

Now, as then, this richly flavored lentil soup suits warm-hearted suppers in the cool, balsam-scented air.

1   pound lentils
4   strips bacon, chopped
2   large onions, chopped
6   stalks celery, chopped
6   carrots, chopped
1½ pounds smoked ham hocks, scored to bone
1   28-ounce can tomatoes, undrained
3   chicken bouillon cubes

¼   cup brown sugar
3   tablespoons cider vinegar
½   teaspoon thyme
2   bay leaves
1   teaspoon salt
Freshly ground pepper to taste
3   quarts water
2   unpeeled raw potatoes, grated or shredded

☐ Wash and drain lentils. Soak according to package directions.

☐ In a large pot or soup kettle, sauté bacon until just beginning to brown. Add onions, celery, and carrots, and cook until onions are soft, stirring periodically.

☐ Add remaining ingredients, including lentils. Simmer, covered, 1½ to 2 hours. Remove hocks. Pick the meat from the bones and return to soup. Check seasoning. You may wish to add more brown sugar and/or salt.

☐ As a next-day soup, this only gets better!

RED RED-HOT
VEGETABLE CHILI

Serves: 4
Prepare: 20 minutes
Cook: 20 minutes
10 minutes

Even our hottest summer days can end with chilly evenings, when the wind turns to the northwest. So, get a crackling fire going and treat everyone to this super-good chili. All that's needed to complete the meal is warm, crusty bread.

1 medium onion, cut in chunks
2 cloves garlic, minced
1 red bell pepper, coarsely chopped
2 tablespoons olive oil
2 medium tomatoes, cut in chunks
1 15-ounce can diced tomatoes in purée
½ cup water
2 tablespoons chopped parsley

1 tablespoon chili powder (hotter, the better!)
1½ teaspoons ground cumin
1½ teaspoons dried oregano
1½ teaspoons dried basil
½ teaspoon fennel seeds
½ teaspoon salt
Generous grinding of black pepper

☐ In a large, heavy saucepan, over medium heat, sauté the onion, garlic, and red pepper in oil until they just begin to soften; about 10 minutes.

☐ Add remaining ingredients. Bring to a simmer, then cook slowly, uncovered, for 20 minutes. Stir periodically.

☐ At this point, the chili may be set aside until 15 minutes or so before serving time.

1 cup of canned pinto, navy, or butter beans, drained
1 cup canned kidney beans, drained
¾ pound sliced summer squash (i.e. zucchini, crookneck, patty pan)

1 tablespoon chopped fresh dill
1 cup sour cream
6 green onions, chopped

☐ Stir beans, squash, and dill into chili. Cover and simmer 10 minutes, or until squash is just tender. Ladle into large soup bowls. Top with dollops of sour cream and garnish with green onions.

GRANDMA JUDY's VEGETABLE SOUP

Serves: 8-10
Prepare: 30 minutes
Cook: 1½ hours

The bacon gives this zip, and the zucchini, yellow squash, and tomatoes add the pretty summer colors. It's one of our very favorite soups when the garden's at its height.

3 slices bacon, chopped
1 medium onion, chopped
½ head of cabbage, chopped
2 unpeeled potatoes, diced
3½ cups chopped tomatoes (or 28 ounces canned)
3 carrots, sliced ½-inch thick
2 celery stalks, chopped
3 cloves garlic, minced (or ¼ teaspoon garlic powder)
6 cups water
1 tablespoon catsup
1 teaspoon Worcestershire sauce
4 drops Tabasco sauce
2 teaspoons salt
Freshly ground pepper to taste
1 18-ounce can tomato or vegetable juice
3 small zucchini, cubed or thickly sliced
3 small crookneck squash, cubed or thickly sliced

☐ In a large kettle, fry bacon until half-done. Stir in onion and sauté until lightly browned. Add remaining ingredients except tomato juice, zucchini, and squash. Simmer, covered, 10 minutes.

☐ Add tomato juice and simmer, covered, 1½ hours.

☐ A few minutes before serving, add the zucchini and crookneck. Simmer until just tender. Check seasoning.

■ Note: This is so good, it can be party fare. Just serve it buffet-style with cold cuts and a good, hearty bread.

FRESH CORN CHOWDER

Serves: 6
Prepare: 20 minutes
Cook: 30 minutes

You may use canned corn, but the real flavor comes from freshly picked. Boil the ears for only 3 minutes. After cutting off the kernels, be sure to scrape the cobs to get the best part of all.

1 medium onion, finely chopped	½ teaspoon dried basil
3 tablespoons butter	¼ teaspoon dried crushed sage
1 stalk celery, finely chopped	2 cups chicken broth
¼ green bell pepper, finely chopped	2 cups corn (about 4 ears)
¼ red bell pepper, finely chopped	1½ cups light cream
2-3 red-skinned potatoes, cubed	½ cup milk
2 tablespoons flour	Salt and freshly ground pepper to taste
½ teaspoon dried marjoram	Bacon bits and parsley (optional)

☐ In a kettle or Dutch oven over medium heat, sauté onion in butter until soft. Add celery, peppers, and potatoes. Cook 5 minutes, stirring periodically. Stir in flour, and cook 2 more minutes.

☐ Add herbs and chicken broth. Cover and simmer over low heat for 30 minutes, or until potatoes are tender.

☐ Stir in corn, cream, milk, and salt and pepper to taste. Reheat but do not allow to boil.

☐ If you have had to use canned corn, you may wish to garnish with bacon bits and parsley.

JACK MERTAUGH's
FISH CHOWDER

Serves: 4-6
Prepare: 30 minutes

Anyone around town will tell you that Jack's a great cook, but he cooks from the heart, not from the book, so it wasn't easy pulling together this recipe. A meal in itself, this is the best chowder of them all!

2 tablespoons butter
6 green onions, chopped
1 stalk celery, chopped
2 carrots, chopped
1 large, unpeeled potato, diced*
½ teaspoon thyme, crumbled
¼ teaspoon dill weed
1¼ teaspoons salt
¼ teaspoon freshly ground pepper

2 tablespoons flour
1 16-ounce can diced tomatoes in purée (or stewed)
3 cups milk
1-2 cups cooked or canned fish**
1 cup grated sharp cheddar cheese
2 tablespoons chopped parsley

☐ Melt butter in a large, heavy saucepan or Dutch oven. Gently sauté onions, celery, carrots, and potato until tender, stirring from time to time. This takes approximately 10 minutes. Cover the pot part of the time if you wish to speed things up.

☐ Add herbs, seasoning, and flour, stirring for a minute. Stir in tomatoes and simmer another minute or two. Add milk and fish.

☐ When well-heated but not boiling, stir in cheese and parsley. Correct seasoning. When cheese has melted, serve in warm bowls with one of the good breads or biscuits in this book.

◼ Notes: *If preparing in larger quantities, parboil the potato(es) until barely tender, instead of sautéing with rest of vegetables.

**If using canned fish, salmon or albacore tuna is best.

BEEF and KALE SOUP

Serves: 6-8
Prepare: 10 minutes
Cook: 1½ - 2 hours
30-40 minutes

At first glance, you may wonder about the seemingly hefty amount of wine, but it becomes quite subtle as the kale takes over in a wonderful way...particularly good the next day.

2-2½ pounds meaty beef chuck bones or shortribs	Salt and freshly ground pepper
2 onions, chopped	Water
3 cloves garlic, minced	1 bunch kale
2 cups dry red wine	5 red-skinned potatoes, diced ½-inch

☐ Place meat, onions, garlic, and wine in a heavy kettle or Dutch oven. Season lightly with salt and pepper, then add just enough water to cover. Bring to a boil and simmer, covered, until meat is falling off the bones, about 1½ to 2 hours.

☐ Discard bones and fat, returning meat to soup. At this point, you may wish to chill the soup in order to remove all fat.

☐ Chop only the leaves of the kale, discarding the stems. Add kale and potatoes to soup, and cook until tender; about 30-40 minutes. Correct seasoning.

☐ This is a full-bodied soup, so a good, crusty bread will complete a supper.

By the way, Harry Harris has been real busy putting up his hundreds and hundreds of tree swallow houses. Everyone loves seeing them, in their pretty colors, dotting the marshes and bays. Isn't it wonderful that he cares that much?

FLOWER BAY
CAULIFLOWER SOUP

Serves: 6
Prepare: 20 minutes
Cook: 15 minutes

Different and delicious in any season.

1 cauliflower
5 cups chicken broth
¼ lemon
4 tablespoons butter
1 onion, chopped
2 medium carrots, chopped
1 stalk celery with top,
   finely chopped

6 mushrooms, sliced
2 tablespoons flour
¼ cup pearl barley
Salt and white pepper
   to taste

☐ Trim florets from cauliflower. Finely chop core.

☐ Bring chicken broth to boil in a pot or large saucepan. Drop in florets, the chopped core, and lemon quarter. Cover and simmer until florets are tender; about 6 minutes. Discard lemon.

☐ Melt butter in a skillet. Gently sauté onion, carrots, celery, and mushrooms until onions are soft. With a flat whisk, stir in flour and cook 1 minute. Whisk in a cup or so of cauliflower broth. Stir just until smooth, then add all to pot.

☐ Add barley. Cover and simmer 15 minutes. Add salt and white pepper to taste. Serve piping hot.

This is a good soup to serve with Hearty Corned Beef and Cabbage Sandwiches.

CREAM of BRUSSELS SPROUTS SOUP

Serves: 6
Prepare: 30 minutes

If you were to taste this while blindfolded, we just know you would guess it to be broccoli soup. So, don't tell your diners and have some fun! It's very, very good and has lovely color.

1½ pounds Brussels
    sprouts
3 cups chicken broth
3 tablespoons butter
3 tablespoons flour
2 cups milk

Grating of nutmeg
½ cup heavy cream
    (optional)
3-4 drops Tabasco sauce
Salt and freshly ground
    pepper to taste

☐ Cut an x in the stem-end of each sprout, and trim away any tough, outer leaves. Bring the chicken broth to a boil in a large saucepan. Drop in the sprouts and simmer, covered, until tender; about 10 minutes.

☐ Purée sprouts in a blender or food processor, along with half of their broth. Set remaining broth aside.

☐ In large saucepan, melt butter then stir in flour with a whisk. Cook, stirring, for a minute or so. Stir in remaining broth, milk, puréed sprouts, and nutmeg. Simmer, uncovered, for 5 minutes. Add cream (if you wish), Tabasco, and salt and pepper to taste.

LUSCIOUS PARSNIP SOUP

Serves: 4-6
Prepare: 30 minutes

Parsnips get sweeter the longer they're stored in the root cellar. They give this really pretty and tasty soup its appearance of being rich and creamy, and yet it is low in calories and quite nutritious. Serve hot or cold.

4 tablespoons butter
1 pound parsnips, peeled
   and thinly sliced
1 cup chopped celery
3 tablespoons flour
¼ cup chopped parsley

⅛ teaspoon white pepper
4 cups chicken broth
Salt to taste
Freshly grated Parmesan
   cheese

□ In a large, heavy saucepan, melt butter then stir in parsnips and celery. Cover and cook over medium-low heat for 10 minutes, stirring several times.

□ Place the cooked vegetables in a blender with the flour, parsley, and white pepper. Add 3 cups of broth and blend at high speed.

□ Return to saucepan and whisk in remaining broth. Simmer over low heat a few more minutes. Salt to taste.

□ At serving time, sprinkle with Parmesan cheese.

▨ Note: This soup reheats nicely, but do not overcook.

When I can, I keep a bunch of parsley in my white cream pitcher right on our kitchen table. It'll keep a week like that if you don't let any of its leaves get in the water. Always there to chop up for soups and other good things, and it's so pretty.

BUTTERMILK BROCCOLI SOUP

Serves: 6-8
Prepare: 30 minutes

Buttermilk is the secret here. Wonderful served ice-cold in the summer or piping hot in the winter.

½ onion, chopped
2 tablespoons butter
4 cups chicken broth
1 bay leaf
1 pinch each of sage, basil,
    and thyme
¾ teaspoon salt
¾ teaspoon white pepper
Dash of cayenne pepper

1½ pounds broccoli,
    chopped
4 tablespoons butter
6 tablespoons flour
2 cups milk
1 cup buttermilk
Garnish: sour cream
    (optional)

☐ In a large saucepan, sauté onion in 2 tablespoons butter until soft. Add broth and seasonings. Bring to a boil, then add chopped broccoli. Simmer, covered, until tender.

☐ In a medium saucepan, melt remaining 4 tablespoons of butter over medium heat. Stir in flour with a whisk, and continue to stir for 1 to 2 minutes until bubbly and smooth. Whisk in milk and buttermilk. Stir just until thickened.

☐ Add to chicken broth and broccoli. Continue to stir until very hot but do not allow to boil. Check seasoning.

☐ Serve hot or cold, garnished with dollops of sour cream if you wish.

CABBAGE SOUP with CHEESE

Serves: 4-6
Prepare: 30 minutes
Cook: 30 minutes

Oh my, but this is good!

½ pound bacon, chopped
1 onion, chopped
1 bunch green onions, chopped
½ head of cabbage, coarsely chopped
2 potatoes, peeled and diced
5 cups chicken broth
1½ teaspoons fines herbes (see margin)

Salt and freshly ground pepper to taste
4 ounces Swiss or Jarlsberg cheese, shredded (1 cup)
2 ounces Gouda or sharp cheddar cheese, shredded (½ cup)
¾ cup heavy cream
½ teaspoon dried dill
⅛ teaspoon cayenne pepper

To create your own version of fines herbes, combine 1 tablespoon each marjoram, savory, and thyme with 1 teaspoon sweet basil and a pinch of crushed sage.

☐ Sauté bacon in a Dutch oven over medium heat until partially crisp. Pour off all but 3 to 4 tablespoons fat.

☐ Add the chopped onions and the cabbage to the pan. Sauté for 5 minutes, or until onions are soft.

☐ Stir in potatoes, then chicken broth, fines herbes, and salt and pepper. Bring to a boil. Immediately reduce heat, and simmer, uncovered, 30 minutes, or until potatoes are quite tender.

☐ Just before serving, slowly add cheeses, stirring until melted, but do not allow to boil. Add remaining ingredients and adjust seasoning.

Hearty enough to be a main-course soup, just serve with a good hot and crusty bread and a simple salad.

HEARTY CHICKEN and SAUSAGE SOUP

Serves: 8-10
Prepare: 30 minutes
Cook/Bake: 1½ hours
Prepare: 10 minutes

Unique and satisfying to the bone, this is definitely a soup for the hunting camp. It's a filler-upper that will hearten a group of shivering Nimrods, and they can add an unlucky rabbit to the pot, if they wish. This freezes well.

Elda Nye and our Ruth were up for a visit Sunday. Ruth was on her way back to the hunting camp in the woods to take supper for Betty Smith's crew of deer hunters because it's Betty's birthday.

3-4 pounds chicken, bone in	Freshly ground pepper to taste
5 cubes chicken bouillon	Water
2 bay leaves	

☐ Place above ingredients in a large pot with just enough water to cover chicken. Cover pot and simmer until chicken is quite tender; about 1 to 1½ hours.

3 onions, chopped	6 ounces packaged stuffing mix
4 stalks celery, chopped	4 teaspoons sage
3 tablespoons butter	1 tablespoon basil
1 tablespoon oil	1 cup grated Parmesan cheese
12 ounces pork sausage links, sliced ¾-inch thick	½ cup water

☐ Preheat oven to 300°.

☐ In the meantime, in a heavy, 10-inch skillet, sauté onions and celery in butter and oil until onions are soft. Remove with a slotted spoon to a large bowl. Brown sausage in same skillet, and transfer to bowl. Add stuffing mix, sage, basil, cheese, and water to bowl, and combine all. Place in a buttered, 9x13-inch pan or baking dish. Cover and bake 1½ hours.

1 teaspoon celery seed	Chopped parsley to taste
½ teaspoon crumbled rosemary leaves	

☐ After chicken has cooked, strain broth into another pot. Remove meat from bones, and cut into bite-size pieces. Add to broth along with celery seed, rosemary, and chopped parsley. When the stuffing mixture has finished baking, stir into the pot of chicken. Check seasoning, and serve piping hot.

HAMBURGER
with BARLEY SOUP

Serves: 8
Prepare: 25 minutes
Cook: 1 hour

Hearty and easy...the barley adds something.

1 pound lean ground beef
¼ cup chopped onion
1 cup chopped celery
1 cup chopped carrots
1 cup chopped cabbage
1 28-ounce can tomatoes, undrained
28 ounces water
⅓ cup uncooked barley
4 teaspoons beef bouillon base (concentrate)
½ teaspoon basil
½ teaspoon thyme
Salt and pepper to taste
1 tablespoon brown sugar
2 teaspoons vinegar

☐ In a kettle or Dutch oven, brown beef just until no longer pink. Add remaining ingredients, except brown sugar and vinegar. Cover, bring to a boil, and immediately reduce heat. Simmer 1 hour. Add brown sugar and vinegar. Check seasoning.

GOLDEN AUTUMN
BEEF POT

Serves: 8
Prepare: 20 minutes
Cook: 1-1½ hours

Here's proof of how unfair many of us have been to rutabagas. In this delicious, substantial soup, they add gorgeous color and subtle good flavor.

1 pound stew meat, cut in ½-inch cubes
1 tablespoon butter
1 tablespoon oil
2 medium onions, chopped
3 medium potatoes, cubed
2 cups cubed rutabaga
1½ cups chopped carrots
2 cups coarsely chopped cabbage
2 tablespoons chopped parsley
1 bay leaf
4 beef bouillon cubes
6 cups water
1 tablespoon vinegar
1 teaspoon sugar
1½ teaspoons salt
Freshly ground pepper to taste

☐ In a Dutch oven or heavy pot, brown meat in butter and oil in 2 batches. Set aside. Sauté onions in same pan until soft. Return meat to pan along with remaining ingredients. Simmer, covered, 1 to 1½ hours or until meat is tender. Correct seasoning.

OLD-FASHIONED BEEF and VEGETABLE SOUP

Serves: 8-12
Prepare: 15 minutes
Cook: 2 hours
1 hour
½ hour

This is what soup is all about! When one is heading back across the ice from a day in the fishing shanty, nothing cheers him more than the thought of going home to a big bowl of this hearty soup.

3 pounds lean short ribs or meaty beef chuck bones
4 onions, coarsely chopped
4-6 cups cold water
1 small head cabbage, cut up
3 stalks celery, chopped
8 carrots, diced
1 16-ounce can tomatoes or tomato bits
1 10½-ounce can tomato soup

1 bay leaf
1 tablespoon Worcestershire sauce
1 tablespoon sugar
4 medium potatoes, cut up (optional)
1 10-ounce package frozen peas
1 10-ounce package frozen lima beans
Salt and freshly ground pepper to taste

☐ Place meat and onions in a large pot or soup kettle. Add cold water to cover; about 6 cups if you will be adding potatoes, 4 cups otherwise. Cover and bring to a boil, then immediately reduce heat to barely simmer. Cook slowly for 2 hours.

☐ Remove meat, and skim fat. Add remaining ingredients to pot except potatoes, peas, and beans. Cover and cook slowly another hour.

☐ Trim meat of all fat and bone. Return to pot along with potatoes and cook 15 minutes. Add peas and beans; simmer another 10 minutes. Season to taste with salt and freshly ground pepper.

☐ It's a meal in itself...just serve with hunks of warm, fresh bread.

■ Note: Freezes well.

DR. WEISS's
BEAN SOUP

Serves: 6-8
Soak: overnight
Cook: 45 minutes
Prepare: 15 minutes
Cook: 2 hours

At first, this may look like any other bean soup, but there are subtle touches that make it different and wonderful. A very thick soup, all it needs with it is piping hot Johnny Cake and a good beer!

1 pound navy or small white beans	1 pinch saffron (optional)
7 cups cold water	Freshly ground pepper to taste
1 teaspoon salt	1 carrot, chopped
1 1-pound ham hock, cracked	2 stalks celery, chopped
1 large onion, chopped	1 clove garlic, minced
2 tablespoons chopped parsley	1 tablespoon butter
3 cloves	1 15-ounce can tomatoes, diced in puree
2 bay leaves	Chopped parsley

If a soup seems to have something missing, just add a couple pinches of sugar or a splash of vinegar...does wonders.

☐ Rinse and sort beans. Place in a Dutch oven or heavy soup pot, and add 7 cups cold water. Cover and let soak 12 hours or so. Do *not* pour off water.

☐ Add 1 teaspoon salt to beans and their water. Simmer, covered, until beans begin to feel soft; about 45 minutes.

☐ Add ham hock, onion, parsley, and seasonings, but do not be tempted to add more water! Cover and simmer while preparing remaining vegetables.

☐ Sauté carrot, celery, and garlic in butter until soft. Add to soup along with tomatoes. Cover and simmer 2 hours.

☐ Check seasoning, then serve soup, hock and all and garnished with chopped parsley, from a large tureen. Your diners can remove the meat from the hock as they serve themselves.

HAM HOCK and SAUSAGE SOUP

Serves: 12-14
Prepare: 15 minutes
Cook: 3 hours
20 minutes

A soup that will satisfy the biggest of appetites...an extra plus is that the beans do not need to be soaked!

2 ham hocks
2 cups dried beans (your choice), well-rinsed
2 onions, chopped
1 bunch celery, chopped (leaves and all!)
2 cups canned whole tomatoes, broken up
12 carrots, chopped

1-2 cups chicken broth
1 teaspoon basil
1 tablespoon salt
½ pound smoked Polish sausage, thinly sliced
2 zucchini, coarsely chopped (optional)
1 pint sour cream
Fresh parsley, chopped

☐ Place ham hocks, beans, onions, and celery in a large kettle. Add water to barely cover. Bring to a boil then immediately lower heat. Simmer, covered, until beans are tender; about 2½ to 3 hours.

☐ Remove ham hocks and set aside. Add tomatoes and carrots to soup, along with broth and seasonings. Simmer, covered, 15 minutes. During that time, remove meat from hocks, discarding all fat.

☐ Skim as much fat from soup as possible. (If making ahead, chilling will make the job easier.) Return meat to soup, along with sausage and zucchini. Simmer 5 minutes.

☐ To serve, top each steaming bowl of soup with a good dollop of sour cream and chopped parsley for color. The Iroquois's Cornsticks are wonderful with this!

MAIN DISHES

eggs, cheese, and chicken

Dear Bonnie,

I can't believe that it is almost mid-May. It's time to get everything but the tomado plants out of the greenhouse and into the garden.

We've planted the sunflower seeds... I love the way they set the stage for the garden... and a few strawberries, and Copenhagen cablage seeds. The crab apples are in bloom... a beautiful pale pink. They perfume the yard... and the birds and the bees are having a wonderful time.

Two miles to the northwest of us is a stand of hardwoods that leads you into a corner of heaven. This time of year, it's a big treat to spend an afternoon there, gathering leeks and hunting for morels.

The silky leaves of the leeks weave a lovely pattern in the thickest carpet of Dutchman's breeches, trillium, and violets you can imagine. The velvety-brown morels are so well hidden, you must be very careful where you step. I love the smell of leaf mold, meaning spring is underway.

Here, the warblers and the olive-back thrush and the white throat sing their sweetest songs... nothing else intrudes on the softness of the day. It's why we call this God's country.

We are having dandelion greens for dinner... spring tonic, you know! Will write down how I cook them... same with Lamb's quarters.

Love 'ya,

Judy Chard

SHIRRED EGGS with CORNED BEEF HASH

Serves: 3-6
Prepare: 10 minutes
Bake: 25 minutes

Our friend, "The Professor," who visits on Beavertail, gave this recipe to me. It makes a great breakfast or simple supper.

1 15½-ounce can corned beef hash
¼ cup finely chopped green pepper
2 tablespoons minced onion
1 tablespoon minced parsley
¼ cup catsup
6 eggs
6 teaspoons cream
Salt and freshly ground pepper to taste
2 tablespoons grated sharp cheddar cheese

☐ Preheat oven to 350°.

☐ Combine hash, green pepper, onion, parsley, and catsup. Turn into a 9-inch pie plate. With a spoon, make 6 indentations in hash then break an egg into each one. Top each egg with a teaspoon of cream, salt and pepper, and grated cheese.

☐ Bake until yolks have *just* set; about 25 minutes. Serve immediately.

HOME-STYLE OMELET

Serves: 3-4
Prepare: 15 minutes
Cook: 15 minutes

Brown eggs taste no differently than white eggs...only the layer is different. Rhode Island Reds give you brown eggs...the older the hen, the darker the egg.

The Chards are fun-loving people, and there are a lot of us. Each year, we have the Chard clan reunion for two days in Decker, north of Marlette. There are trailers, campers, tents...music, singing, eating...and we visit almost all night. Then a big, potluck dinner the next evening and fireworks.

Outdoors, in a beautiful grove by a creek, Bob Chard cooks breakfast for 50 or so...do we enjoy it! Here's his long-time recipe for home-style omelet.

½ pound bacon, chopped
1 1-pound package frozen
    hash browns
6 eggs
2 tablespoons milk

Salt and freshly ground
    pepper
6 ounces cheddar or
    processed cheese,
    shredded

☐ In a heavy, 10-inch skillet, fry bacon until crisp. Remove with a slotted spoon to drain on paper toweling.

☐ Pour off all but 1½ tablespoons bacon fat. Add frozen hash browns and cook over medium heat until thawed, stirring periodically; about 2 minutes. Press down with a spoon into an even layer.

☐ Beat eggs with milk, a pinch of salt, and freshly ground pepper to taste. Pour over potatoes. Top with cheese and reserved bacon.

☐ Cover and cook over medium-low heat until eggs have just set; about 15 minutes.

■ Note: Chopped green onions and sliced mushrooms, sautéed for a minute or two before adding the hash browns, make a nice variation.

MINUTE CHEESE SOUFFLÉ

Serves: 4
Prepare: 15 minutes
Bake: 1½ hours

If you think that soufflés are for only the "fancy" cook, give this another thought. The secret is the tapioca.

1½ cups milk
3 tablespoons Minute
   Tapioca
½ teaspoon salt

8-10 ounces sharp cheddar
   cheese, grated
6 eggs, separated

☐ Preheat oven to 300°.

☐ In a medium saucepan, combine milk, tapioca, and salt. Over medium heat, bring to a boil, stirring constantly with a whisk. Remove from heat. Stir in cheese until melted.

☐ In a medium bowl, beat egg yolks until thick and lemon-colored. Add cheese mixture and beat well.

☐ In a large bowl, beat egg whites until stiff but not dry. Fold in cheese mixture, gently but thoroughly.

☐ Pour into a 3 to 4-quart, ungreased, soufflé dish. With a teaspoon, draw a circle on the surface, an inch in from edge of dish. This will create the crown when the soufflé is baked.

☐ Bake until high and golden, about 1½ hours; but don't peek until near the very end.

JACK DAUGHERTY's
SPAGHETTI FRITTATA

Serves: 2
Prepare: 10 minutes
Broil

Jack comes all the way from Beavertail Bay just to get his fresh vegetables from us. Here is one of his creations...leave it to a man to figure out what to do with left-over spaghetti noodles!

1 small onion, chopped	Pinches of dried oregano
1 teaspoon oil	and basil
1 teaspoon butter	Salt and freshly ground
1 egg	pepper to taste
1 cup cold, cooked	1 teaspoon oil
spaghetti*	Grated Parmesan cheese
2 tablespoons freshly grated	
Parmesan cheese	

I'm sending you a whole bunch of recipes from all our thoughtful customers who are so generous about sharing. One of the nicest things about the Stand is the many new friends it brings us.

☐ Preheat broiler.

☐ In a 9-inch heavy or non-stick skillet, sauté onion in 1 teaspoon each oil and butter until soft.

☐ Beat egg in a medium-size bowl. With a fork, stir in spaghetti, 2 tablespoons grated cheese, herbs, and salt and pepper to taste. Add sautéed onion.

☐ Wipe out skillet with a paper towel. Over medium heat, heat 1 more teaspoon oil until sizzling. Pour in spaghetti mixture, and reduce heat to low to very-low. Do not stir, browning the one side only. Be careful not to let it stick.

☐ Sprinkle with a little more cheese, then run under broiler to lightly brown top. Serve at once.

■ Notes: *One-eighth pound uncooked spaghetti yields 1 cup cooked. Also, you can double this recipe; just use a larger skillet.

For variety, while sautéing the onion you may add crushed garlic, chopped green peppers, and/or chopped tomatoes.

THE BEST MAC and CHEESE

Serves: 4
Prepare: 15 minutes
Bake: 1 ½ hours

In our minds, this is the very best way to prepare "mac-and-cheese," as the children call it.

1 7-ounce package
   macaroni*
Salt and pepper
3 cups grated aged, sharp
   cheddar cheese
   (12 ounces)

Butter
3 cups milk
½ cup buttered fresh
   bread crumbs
Paprika

☐ Preheat oven to 350°. Butter a 1 ½-quart, deep casserole.

☐ Cook macaroni according to package directions, then rinse immediately in cold water to stop cooking process. Drain well.

☐ Layer in casserole ⅓ of macaroni, sprinkling lightly with salt and pepper, and ⅓ of cheese, dotting generously with slivers of butter. Repeat twice more. Pour milk over all. Cover with bread crumbs and sprinkle with paprika.

☐ Bake, uncovered, for 1 ½ hours.

■ Note: *The texture of Creamettes macaroni makes it the best brand for this recipe.

BAKED BROCCOLI
or SPINACH FONDUE

Serves: 6
Prepare: 20 minutes
Stand: 1-4 hours
Bake: 40-45 minutes

Because I was always looking for the ideal brunch or luncheon dish, my kitchen drawer used to be cluttered with all sorts of recipes for bread and cheese casseroles. When this one came along, I cleaned out the drawer!

2 cups broccoli florets or
    1 bunch (1 pound)
    spinach
3 cups (12 ounces) grated
    sharp cheddar cheese
3 tablespoons minced
    onion
1 tablespoon lemon juice
3 eggs

1½ cups milk
½ teaspoon salt
Freshly ground pepper
    to taste
8 slices day-old white or
    whole-grain bread
2-3 tablespoons butter,
    softened

☐ Cook broccoli or spinach until *just* tender. Drain well, then coarsely chop. Combine with cheese, onion, and lemon juice, and set aside.

☐ In a medium-size bowl, beat eggs, then beat in milk, salt, and pepper. Set aside.

☐ Trim crusts from bread and spread bread with butter. Place 6 slices in bottom of a buttered, 8x12-inch, shallow casserole. Cut remaining 2 slices into strips and set aside.

☐ Pour ½-cup of egg/milk mixture over bread in casserole. Top with all of broccoli/cheese mixture. Arrange bread strips on top of broccoli in spoke-fashion. Pour remaining egg/milk mixture over all.

☐ Cover and let stand 1-2 hours on counter, or 2-4 hours in refrigerator.

☐ Preheat oven to 350°. Bake, uncovered, 40-45 minutes, or until golden brown. You may serve immediately.

■ Note: A great buffet dish, it's also good with a standing rib roast or leg of lamb, and just a tossed salad.

CHICKEN with LEEKS

Serves: 4
Prepare: 15 minutes
Cook: 1 hour

One of my favorite cookbooks is The Cedar Chest, *put together some years back by the missionary society of The First Union Church in Cedarville. This is one of its recipes, donated by Frances Shoberg. In it, she called for green onions, but we love it with wild leeks.*

1 fryer chicken, cut up	1 cup chicken broth or water
3 tablespoons butter	Salt and freshly ground
1 tablespoon oil	pepper to taste
16 wild leeks (or green onions)	3 eggs, beaten
	Juice of 1 lemon

☐ In a 12-inch, heavy skillet, brown chicken in butter and oil. Cut leeks into 1-inch pieces. Add to chicken along with broth and salt and pepper. Cover and barely simmer for 1 hour. Skim fat.

☐ In a small bowl, combine eggs and lemon juice; then whisk in several tablespoons of broth from skillet. Stir mixture into pan and heat, but do not boil.

CHICKEN BREASTS in TOMATOES AND CREAM

Serves: 4-6
Prepare: 15 minutes
Cook: 20-25 minutes

An easy way to get fancy.

6 boned chicken breast halves	3 medium tomatoes, peeled and sliced
3 tablespoons butter	⅓ cup sour cream
1 onion, thinly sliced	3 tablespoons grated Parmesan cheese
1 clove garlic, minced	Salt to taste
1 tablespoon flour	

☐ In a large skillet, over medium-high heat, sauté chicken in butter until lightly browned. Remove. Reduce heat to medium and cook onion and garlic until soft. With a flat whisk, stir in flour and brown for a minute. Add tomatoes and return chicken to pan. Cover and simmer gently over low heat for 20-25 minutes.

☐ Stir in sour cream, Parmesan cheese, and salt to taste. Heat to serve, but do not allow to boil.

THELMA's OVEN-FRIED LEMON CHICKEN

Serves: 4-6
Prepare: 5 minutes
Marinate: 6-24 hours
Bake: 35-40 minutes

Thelma Nosek's three loves were her husband, the outdoors, and cooking. When she and Tony (an acclaimed architect) brought their trailer all the way from Tucson, Arizona, to live in while he designed the lodge at Pt. Brule, she treated it as a big adventure. She was real company for those of us who like to walk the woods and beaches, and she didn't let her tiny kitchen stop her from creating great meals and sharing the recipes.

3 chickens breasts, halved
½ cup lemon juice
½ cup olive oil
2-3 cloves garlic, minced
1-2 teaspoons Italian mixed
   herbs

1 teaspoon salt
Freshly ground pepper to taste
¼ cup freshly grated
   Parmesan cheese

☐ Place chicken in a shallow, glass baking dish. In a small bowl, combine remaining ingredients and pour over chicken, coating well. Cover and refrigerate overnight or a minimum of 6 hours, turning occasionally.

☐ Preheat oven to 325°. Bake chicken in same dish, uncovered, for 35-40 minutes, periodically basting with marinade.

Thelma liked serving this with barley cooked in chicken broth, broccoli florets tossed in lemon butter, and Baked Tomatoes in Cream.

BASQUE COUNTRY CHICKEN

Serves: 4
Prepare: 20 minutes
Bake: 45 minutes

Be brave...leave the eggplant in. It adds important flavor to the casserole, and yet no one will know it is there.

3 slices bacon, chopped
2 tablespoons butter
1 fryer chicken, quartered
8 small boiling onions (or 1 large onion, thinly sliced)
½ pound mushrooms, quartered
½ small eggplant, peeled and cut into fingers
2 medium tomatoes, peeled and quartered
1 small green pepper, cut into strips
1 clove garlic, crushed
1 bay leaf
1 teaspoon minced fresh thyme (¼ teaspoon dried)
2 teaspoons chopped fresh basil (½ teaspoon dried)
¼ cup dry white wine
Salt and freshly ground pepper to taste

☐ Preheat oven to 350°.

☐ In a large skillet, sauté bacon until partially browned. Remove with a slotted spoon to drain on a paper towel. Add butter to pan drippings, then brown chicken. Place in a 3-quart casserole.

☐ In same skillet, sauté onions until golden brown. Return bacon to pan along with mushrooms, eggplant, tomatoes, green pepper, garlic, and herbs. Sauté 3 minutes while gradually adding wine. Season with salt and pepper to taste. Place in casserole with chicken.

☐ Bake, covered, for 45 minutes.

Good with this are buttered rice with chopped parsley and Feather-Light Corn Fritters.

HONEY-BAKED CHICKEN

Serves: 4
Prepare: 10 minutes
Bake: 1 hour

Just as good as it sounds! The chicken takes on a rich glaze, and the soy sauce stays in the back seat.

3 chicken breasts, cut in
   half (or 1 3-pound
   chicken, cut up)
½ cup flour
½ teaspoon pepper

4 tablespoons butter
¼ cup honey
¼ cup lemon juice
1 tablespoon soy sauce

☐ Preheat oven to 350°.

☐ Wash and drain chicken. Combine flour and pepper in a paper bag, then add chicken pieces. Shake to coat well.

☐ In a small saucepan, melt butter. Pour half of it into a 9 x 13-inch, shallow baking dish. Place chicken in dish, turning to coat with butter, then leave skin-side down. Bake, uncovered, for 30 minutes.

☐ To the butter remaining in saucepan, add rest of ingredients. Warm, blending with a whisk.

☐ At end of 30 minutes, turn chicken and pour honey mixture over top. Bake another 30 minutes, basting several times with sauce.

Good with this: rice cooked in chicken broth then finished with sweet butter and a goodly amount of chopped chives or parsley, plus simply dressed sliced tomatoes, and Yellow Squash and Sweet Corn.

CHICKEN and APPLES in CIDER and CREAM

Serves: 4-6
Prepare: 30 minutes

When autumn's at our door, we look forward to this dish.

3 whole chicken breasts, split, skinned, and boned*
Flour seasoned with salt and pepper to taste
4 tablespoons butter
2 tart apples, cored and cut into rings

2 cups cider
2 tablespoons Dijon mustard
2 cups heavy cream
Salt and freshly ground pepper to taste

☐ Dredge chicken in seasoned flour, shaking off excess. In a large skillet, sauté chicken in 2 tablespoons butter until lightly browned and just cooked through; about 3-5 minutes per side. Remove and keep warm under foil.

☐ Add 2 more tablespoons butter to skillet. Sauté apple rings until browned; about 3-5 minutes. Set aside with chicken.

☐ Pour off any excess butter from skillet. Over medium-high heat, add cider, and boil down to half its original amount, loosening any browned bits with a flat whisk. Whisk in mustard, then cream. Boil down until thickened, then season to taste with salt and pepper.

☐ To serve, pour cream sauce over chicken and garnish with apple rings.

▉ Note: *If you wish to use this recipe for unboned chicken, leave chicken in skillet after browning and cover with a sheet of wax paper (this helps to keep it tender). Cover skillet tightly with lid, simmer 5 minutes, then remove chicken and proceed with recipe.

ROAST CHICKEN
with HERBS

Serves: 3-4
Prepare: 10 minutes
Roast: 1½ hours
Rest: 15 minutes

It's easy to forget how attractive a whole roasted chicken is, whether as picnic fare or for dinner. When prepared this way, it is superb warm or cold...crisp, yet moist and tender inside.

1 3-pound whole chicken	1 teaspoon salt
5 cloves garlic	½ teaspoon white pepper
1 bay leaf, coarsely crumbled	½ teaspoon each of thyme, marjoram, oregano, and basil
4 tablespoons butter, melted	¼ teaspoon rubbed sage

☐ Do *not* preheat oven.

☐ Wash and thoroughly dry chicken, inside and out. Split a clove of garlic and rub over chicken, inside and out. Place inside chicken, along with rest of garlic and crumbled bay leaf.

☐ Combine remaining ingredients. Brush a tablespoon or so inside chicken. Truss chicken to hold legs and wings close to body.

☐ Brush herb butter generously over outside of chicken. Set, breast side down, on a rack in a shallow baking dish or pan.

☐ Place in cold oven, then turn oven on to 425°. Roast 45 minutes without basting. Turn chicken over, and brush with herb butter. Roast another 45 minutes, brushing/basting periodically with remaining herb butter and pan drippings.

☐ Remove chicken from oven and place on carving tray. Cover loosely with a tent of foil. Let rest this way for at least 15 minutes before carving to serve. (Or cool completely, cover, and chill.)

Good with this are Baked Hominy with Cheese and Spinach with Sesame Seeds.

MOTHER RATLIFF's BRUNSWICK STEW

Serves: 4-5
Prepare: 30 minutes
Cook: 30-45 minutes

There probably is no such thing as an authentic recipe for Brunswick Stew. In olden days, it was the common way to prepare squirrel, with each cook creating his or her own version with what was at hand.

We've brought Mother Ratliff's recipe up to date...chicken taking the place of the once luckless squirrel, sausage instead of salt pork, fresh tomatoes in place of canned, and some wine for the fun of it...a nutritious, full-flavored meal that improves with time.

Our family history is kept in our bible. Did you know that I was the oldest of three girls and had ten brothers? I was born Julia Beatrice Ratliff on August 2, 1905, and grew up in South Ironton, Ohio. I recall the flood of 1913 there, and how we all headed for the roof...the first floor ended up under water.

- 1 2½-3 pound chicken, cut up
- 1 tablespoon butter
- 1 tablespoon oil
- ½ pound link sausages, cut in thirds
- 1 onion, halved then thinly sliced
- 2 carrots, thinly sliced
- ½ stalk celery, finely chopped
- 1 clove garlic, minced
- 2-3 tomatoes, skinned and coarsely chopped
- 1 bay leaf
- 2 dried red pepper pods (Japanese chilies)
- ½ teaspoon dried thyme (2 teaspoons fresh)
- 2 tablespoons chopped parsley
- Juice of ½ lemon
- 2 cups chicken broth
- 1 cup dry white wine
- Salt and freshly ground pepper to taste
- 1 10-ounce package frozen lima beans or Brussels sprouts, thawed
- 1 12-ounce can Shoe Peg corn, drained (or fresh corn)
- Cooked rice

☐ In a heavy Dutch oven, quickly brown chicken in butter and oil over high heat. Set aside. Brown sausages and set aside.

☐ Pour off all but 1 tablespoon of fat. Reduce heat to medium, then sauté onion, carrots, celery, and garlic until onion is soft.

☐ Return chicken and sausages to pot. Add remaining ingredients except frozen vegetables, corn, and rice.

☐ Cover, bring to a boil, then immediately reduce heat and simmer gently until chicken is tender; about 20-30 minutes. (At this point, the stew may be set aside until about 15 minutes before serving time.)

☐ Add lima beans or Brussels sprouts and corn. Simmer until beans or sprouts are heated through but have not lost their color. Check seasoning, then serve in shallow soup bowls over hot rice.

JEAN's CHICKEN DINNER CASSEROLE

Serves: 6-8
Prepare: 10 minutes
Bake: 35-50 minutes

My daughter, Jean, gave me this recipe for those special times when we want drop-in friends to stay for dinner with no fuss nor bother. It's a full meal by itself, and always a success.

4 whole chicken breasts, skinned and split (bone in or out)
6 ounces Jarlsberg, Amish, or jack cheese, sliced
1 medium zucchini, thinly sliced*
1 can cream of mushroom soup

¼ cup dry white wine
Salt and pepper (optional)
Garlic powder (optional)
1 8-ounce package (2 cups) Pepperidge Farm herbed stuffing mix (not the cubes)
3 tablespoons melted butter

☐ Preheat oven to 350°. Butter a shallow 9x13-inch baking dish. Arrange chicken breasts in dish. Top with cheese slices, then zucchini.

☐ Combine soup and wine. Pour over zucchini. If you'd like, sprinkle lightly with salt, pepper, and garlic powder. Top with stuffing mix, then drizzle with butter.

☐ Bake, uncovered, for 35 minutes for boned chicken, up to 50 minutes for bone-in. Chicken should be cooked through and the casserole bubbling.

■ Note: *As a substitute for zucchini, try 1 to 1½ cups of small florets of broccoli cooked barely tender.

ROAST TURKEY with CHESTNUT-BREAD STUFFING

Serves: 12
Prepare: 50 minutes
Roast: 5 hours
Rest: 30-45 minutes

Sure you can find how to roast a turkey in any basic cookbook, but we think our way is best of all! Skip the chestnuts if you wish, but they make it extra special. And don't turn up your nose at the commercial bread...in this case, it gives the right consistency.

1½ loaves (22½-ounce each) thin-slice Wonder bread	2 cups finely chopped celery, leaves and all
¾ pound butter	1½ tablespoons poultry seasoning
1½ cups chopped onion	1½ tablespoons salt
1 pound (30) raw chestnuts, peeled and coarsely chopped*	1½ teaspoons pepper
	1 18-pound turkey

☐ Cut bread, crusts and all, into ½ to ¾-inch cubes (should total about 16 cups). Place in a very large bowl.

☐ Melt butter in a large, heavy skillet. Add onions and chestnuts, sautéing until onion is soft, stirring periodically; about 3-4 minutes.

☐ Stir in about ¼ of bread cubes. Brown lightly over medium-high heat, stirring often.

☐ Mix remaining ingredients (except turkey!) in with bread cubes in bowl. Add sautéed bread mixture and gently toss.

▪ Note: *To peel chestnuts:* Fill a large saucepan ⅔-full of water and bring to a boil. With the tip of a sharp paring knife, cut an x into flat side of each chestnut. Drop no more than a handful of chestnuts into boiling water at a time. Boil 1-2 minutes. Remove with a slotted spoon. While still warm, quarter chestnuts then peel away shell and inner skins. For stuffing, coarsely chop in a food processor or by hand. (Preparation time is about 15 minutes per pound of chestnuts.)

TO ROAST TURKEY:

☐ Preheat oven to 325°. Remove giblets and neck from turkey, reserving for gravy preparation. Thoroughly wash and dry bird.

☐ Melt ½-cup butter. Lavishly brush half of butter inside neck and body cavities. Fill both cavities completely with stuffing mixture but do not pack tightly as it will swell while roasting.

☐ Pin cavities closed with trussing pins. Truss turkey and place breast-up in a large, shallow roasting pan. Brush remaining butter over *entire* turkey. Cover top of turkey *loosely* with a tent of foil.

☐ Roast about 5 hours, or until a fork-test proves thigh to be tender. (If you wish the breast to brown, remove foil for the last 30 to 45 minutes.)

☐ To guarantee a tender bird, let turkey sit, covered loosely with foil, 30 to 45 minutes before carving.

TO PREPARE GRAVY:

☐ Place giblets and neck in a large saucepan with at least 8 cups water. Cover, bring to a boil, reduce heat, and simmer 45-60 minutes. Cool.

☐ When turkey is done and has been removed to carving board to rest, skim fat from roasting pan, leaving about ¾-cup. Place pan over 2 stove burners set at medium heat.

☐ With a flat whisk, loosen browned bits and drippings in bottom of pan. Stir in ¾-cup flour (flour and fat should be equal amounts). Cook 1 minute, stirring constantly with whisk, then add 6-7 cups of the giblet broth. Continue stirring until smooth, thickened, and bubbling.

☐ For a richly colored gravy, add a splash or two of Kitchen Bouquet. Salt and pepper to taste.

☐ Reduce heat to barely simmer until serving time. Whisk in more broth at end, if necessary.

I've been quite busy washing windows and cleaning house. I never get a chance to in the summer. I want to have everything ready for Thanksgiving. We are expecting twenty for dinner...family...some we haven't seen for some time. Ruth's going to do a lot of the cooking. I'm fixing the potatoes and baking 2 to 3 pies and pumpkin cake. Ruth's stuffing the turkey, I'm roasting it, then we'll stuff ourselves.

TURKEY HASH

Serves: 2
Prepare: 10 minutes
Cook: 15-20 minutes

One of the best reasons to have some turkey left over! Good for brunch with poached eggs perched on top, or Sunday supper with Honeyed Carrots and a green salad.

2 cups diced or ground cooked turkey

1 raw or cooked potato, diced

¼ cup finely chopped onion

2-3 tablespoons finely chopped green pepper

1 good pinch poultry seasoning

Salt to taste

Generous grinding of black pepper

½ cup good, rich turkey or chicken broth

¼ cup heavy cream

2 tablespoons butter

☐ Toss together first 7 ingredients.* Stir in broth and cream.

☐ Over medium-high heat, melt butter in a heavy, 10-inch skillet until sizzling. Add hash, spreading out evenly in pan.

☐ Continue to cook over medium-high heat, without stirring, for 5-10 minutes or until liquid has evaporated and hash is browning nicely on bottom. Turn hash, scraping pan well, then spread out evenly. Reduce heat to medium, and cook another 5 minutes or until crusty on bottom.

☐ To serve, be sure to include all of those tasty, browned bits from the bottom of the pan...the best part!

■ Note: *If you have any left-over stuffing, you can add some to the hash mixture.

MAIN DISHES

. . . from the lake

Dear Bonnie,

Summer is almost here. We've been enjoying rhubarb and asparagus... they grow so well here. Did you know that they can get 6,000 asparagus roots per acre?

We've already had some green onions, radishes, and parsley from the garden. The long rows of sweet corn are beginning to show up in the field. It makes me think of when I was little. After my father had cultivated the cornfield, he would send my brothers and me out barefoot to knock the dirt off the young shoots with our toes.

We have planted lots of beans, beets, squash, spinach, etc., but it's still too early to set out the tomato plants.

It seems as if we have more birds than ever this year. The hummingbirds are at our window feeder from morning 'til dark... they fly backwards! Lots of robins but not sure where they're nesting yet,... we hope they'll choose the eave of the Stand again. We've turned the water on there so that they can take a bath.

The Harrises and Doris Beach and your mother went on a picnic up in the woods along the escarpment north of here. Doris said they had a fine time looking for rare ferns.

I hear that your mother counted seventeen great blue herons feeding off her south shore at Windswept. Now if that isn't something! Must mean the herring are coming in.

Love to you all.
Judy Chard

BEER BATTER FRIED SMELT

Serves: 4-6
Prepare: 20 minutes

I think this is the best batter to guarantee really crisp, fried fish. I use it for deep-frying perch and herring, too. You'll find that the longer it stands, the better it seems to get.

We serve the golden-brown, fried smelt as finger food with Aunt Lyla's Sauce for dipping.

2 pounds (16-24) smelt
Oil for deep frying
1 cup flour
¼ teaspoon paprika

½ teaspoon salt
⅛ teaspoon pepper
¾ cup beer

◻ Some people leave *everything* intact...heads, tails, fins, etc. I'm just not that brave. So, if you're like me, clean the smelt, using scissors to snip off the heads, tails, and fins. Rinse in cold water and wipe dry.

◻ Preheat oil in a deep-fryer, wok, or deep skillet to 375°.

◻ In a bowl, combine flour, paprika, salt, and pepper. Gradually stir in beer with a whisk, beating until smooth.

◻ Dip fish in batter, letting excess drip off, then gently lower into the hot fat, frying only a few at a time. Fry each batch 2 to 3 minutes, or until golden brown. Using tongs or a slotted spoon, remove to paper towels to drain. Serve immediately.

We're waiting and watching for the ice to clear the bays and the smelt to start running...up stream, at night, by the thousands. What fun it is! There will be fires on the banks of the creek to give light and warmth while everyone goes crazy scooping them up with anything scoopable... nets, baskets, wastebaskets.

PAN-FRIED PERCH
or ROCK BASS

Prepare: 10 minutes

Have you ever tried pan-fried fish for breakfast?...with eggs over-easy and crisp strips of bacon? For fishermen, it makes getting up at the crack of dawn well-worth it.

Whenever the catch is brought in, for the best meal on the lake the fish should be popped into the pan almost the moment they're cleaned.

Perch or rock bass, cleaned and skinned	Cornmeal
	Salt and pepper
Flour	Butter

◻ Roll the fish in equal amounts of flour and cornmeal seasoned with salt and pepper. Over medium-high heat, melt a generous amount of butter in a heavy skillet. When sizzling, quickly fry the fish. They should be nicely browned and crisp on both sides but quite moist inside.

◼ Note: If frying more than a ½-dozen fish, use clarified butter or ½ butter and ½ oil to prevent the butter turning black.

MUSKIE STEAKS

Serves: 6-8
Prepare: 15 minutes
Bake: 20-25 minutes

The whale of the pike family, record muskellunge have topped 80 pounds. Too large to cook whole, it is almost always cut into steaks. Because it tends to be dry, it should be cooked with a sauce. This preparation is very good.

3-4 pounds muskie	½ teaspoon sugar
Salt and pepper	1½ cups sour cream
3 tablespoons butter, softened	1 bay leaf
1 onion, minced	3 tablespoons grated Parmesan cheese
1 tablespoon butter	1 tablespoon horseradish
1 tablespoon flour	Chopped parsley or chives

☐ Preheat oven to 400°.

☐ Cut muskie into 1-inch thick steaks. Rub with salt and pepper and place in a shallow, buttered baking dish or pan in a single layer. Spread with softened butter. Bake 10 minutes.

☐ In a small skillet or saucepan, sauté onion in butter. Stir in flour and sugar. Remove from heat and combine with sour cream and bay leaf.

☐ Spoon sour cream mixture over steaks after the first 10 minutes of baking. Bake another 10 minutes. Baste, then sprinkle with Parmesan cheese. Bake until browned.

☐ Transfer the fish to a warm serving platter. Stir horseradish into sauce remaining in baking dish. Remove the bay leaf before pouring the sauce around the steaks. Garnish with chopped parsley or chives, if you wish.

Good with this are Fried Carrots, plus Romaine and Broccoli.

Thaw frozen fish in milk...the milk returns the fresh-caught flavor. For best taste and texture, do not completely thaw before cooking.

SIMPLY BROILED WHITEFISH

Serves: 6
Prepare: 10-15 minutes

In our minds, no fish can match the whitefish. Its delicate flavor and texture require only the simplest of preparation.

2 pounds whitefish filets	1 tablespoon chopped parsley
¼ cup melted butter	1 tablespoon sugar
¼ cup lemon juice	2 teaspoons salt
2 tablespoons minced onions or shallots	

☐ Place filets, skin-side down, on a foil-lined, rimmed cookie sheet or broiler pan. Combine remaining ingredients and generously baste the fish.

☐ Broil 10 minutes or until fish *just* begins to flake, basting periodically. Garnish with wedges of lemon, if you wish.

BAKED FILET of WHITEFISH

Prepare: 5 minutes
Bake: 15-20 minutes

Just a shake or two away from a very good fish dinner.

Whitefish filet(s)	Butter
Salt and white pepper	Paprika
Cracker meal	

☐ Preheat oven to 400°.

☐ Lay filet(s) skin-side down in a shallow pan lined with foil. Season with salt and white pepper to taste. Sprinkle with cracker meal and dot generously with butter, then finish with a few shakes of paprika.

☐ Place on top rack of oven and bake 10-15 minutes, or until fish just begins to flake.

WHITEFISH SALADS

Whitefish was so named for good reason...the princess of the Great Lakes, it is the whitest and most delicate of all fish. When properly cooked, nothing can compare. It is even a great treat as a left-over, especially in a salad.

Here are two salads we love to serve on warm, summer days...one with left-over fish, the other with smoked.

WILDERNESS BAY WHITEFISH SALAD

Serves: 4
Prepare: 10 minutes

1 pound chilled, poached whitefish
½ cup sliced cucumbers
½ red bell pepper, cut in thin strips (optional)
¼ cup finely chopped celery
¼ cup finely chopped green onions
¼ cup chopped parsley
1 tablespoon capers
Salt and freshly ground pepper to taste
⅓ cup mayonnaise dressing (see note)
Garnish: greens, hard-cooked egg wedges, cherry tomatoes

□ Cut fish into chunks. Gently toss with remaining ingredients. Serve on a bed of greens, garnished with hard-cooked eggs and cherry tomatoes.

SMOKED WHITEFISH SALAD

Serves: 4
Prepare: 10 minutes

½ pound smoked whitefish
4 cold, boiled, red-skinned potatoes (to yield 1 cup sliced)
¼ pound fresh green beans, cooked to tender-crisp, chilled
½ cup very thinly sliced onions
¼ cup chopped parsley
⅓ cup mayonnaise dressing (see note)
Garnish: greens and cherry tomatoes

☐ Flake fish into bite-size pieces. Slice enough potatoes to yield 1 cup or so. Cut beans to 1½-inches. Place all in a bowl with onions and parsley.

☐ Add mayonnaise dressing, and gently toss just to dress. Adjust seasoning if you wish, but the saltiness of the smoked fish is usually adequate.

☐ Serve on beds of greens, garnishing with cherry tomatoes.

■ Note: You can flavor mayonnaise with either 2 teaspoons chopped fresh tarragon or ½-teaspoon curry powder, or try Green Mayonnaise.

OVEN-FRIED WHITEFISH
or BASS

Serves: 4-6
Marinate: 20 minutes
Prepare: 5 minutes
Bake: 12-15 minutes

The high oven temperature gives your fish a beautifully browned, crisp exterior while leaving it wonderfully moist and tender inside.

2 pounds whitefish or bass filets	1 cup freshly grated Parmesan cheese
½ cup light vegetable oil	1 cup dry bread crumbs
1 teaspoon salt	Lemon wedges and/or tartare sauce
2 cloves garlic, minced	

☐ Cut fish into 6 equal portions. Marinate in oil, salt, and garlic in a shallow, glass baking dish for 20 minutes.

☐ Preheat oven to 500°. Line a baking sheet with foil.

☐ Remove fish from marinade, and roll first in cheese and then in bread crumbs. Place on prepared baking sheet.

☐ Bake 12 minutes, or until fish just begins to flake. Serve with lemon wedges and/or tartare sauce.

John Osogwin was a grandson of the last chief of the Chippewas in the Les Cheneaux Islands. He did not know his birthdate, for the Catholic church that had housed the only records, Our Lady of the Snows, burned down many years ago. It is believed, though, that he was in his mid-eighties when he died in 1964.

John never married, spending much of his life as a caretaker for our family's summer home, Sun Sands, in Coats Bay on Marquette Island. He was a central figure in our cherished memories of childhood up north.

He taught us how to fish, sharing his secret spots for finding prized bait such as stonefish and brown leeches. He knew the woods like no other, leading us on adventures that we still love to recall. His gentle ways, keen sense of humour, inborn understanding and appreciation of the outdoors, and enthralling tales of Indian lore deeply enriched our lives.

One of the longed-for events of each summer was John's planking of whitefish on the beach as his people had done for many lifetimes. To this day, it is still the most delicious dinner one can imagine, but it was always best when John prepared it.

The pleasure was in seeing John standing, hunch-shouldered, head bowed, intent upon tending his fire while he listened and watched for the little happenings of nature that were too subtle for our citified minds; and the broad smile that would cross his dark, handsome, high-cheekboned face as he sensed our delight when he placed the planked fish on the table, done to perfection.

PLANKED WHITEFISH

Serves 6-8
Prepare: 20 minutes
Barbecue: 1 hour

Start a fire of oak, maple, or birch logs* at least an hour in advance to establish good coals. Use a hickory or oak board, 1½ inches thick and large enough to accommodate the fish...18x30 inches is ideal. Have a goodly supply of finishing nails on hand, preferably copper since they will conduct the heat the best. *(On the Islands, where no hardwoods grow, birch is best for a good, hot fire.)

4 whitefish filets   Lemon wedges
1 pound bacon, thinly
   sliced

☐ Lay the filets lengthwise on the board, thickest portions toward center. Lay strips of bacon along the edges of the filets. With a hammer, gently tap the nails through the bacon strips and fish and into the board...just far enough to secure. They should be spaced about 2 inches apart.

☐ On the windward side of the fire, about 3-4 feet from its edge, lay 2 logs parallel to each other (about 2 feet apart) but pointing away from the fire. Using a third log or stick to steady its top edge, prop up the plank horizontally on the logs. The fish should be just close enough to the fire to cook slowly but steadily.

☐ Maintain the fire, turning the plank after 20-30 minutes for even basting from the bacon drippings. The filets should be golden brown but barely beginning to flake when done, since they will continue to cook on the hot board after leaving the fire. The usual cooking time is from 45 minutes to 1 hour.

☐ To present the planked fish, just wiggle the nails to loosen and remove, and serve the fish on its plank, bedecked with wedges of lemon.

Good with this: New Potatoes with Lemon-Chive Butter, Cherry or Yellow Tomato Salad, cole slaw, oven-warm Indian Bread, and Our Blueberry Pie á la mode.

BARBECUED STUFFED FISH

Serves: 6-8
Prepare: 15 minutes
Bake: 20-30 minutes

Walleye, pike, salmon, bass...fresh from the lake...stuffed whole and barbecued...roasted corn-on-the-cob, spinach salad, and warm garlic bread...what better dinner in late summer?

This is our favorite stuffing for fish. Sometimes I'll include a couple strips of bacon, fried crisp and crumbled.

The next best thing to eating a good dinner is reading about it.

1 whole fish, 3 to 4 pounds
1 small onion, chopped
3 tablespoons butter
1 cup chopped mushrooms
1 tomato, chopped
¾ cup fresh bread crumbs
1 tablespoon chopped chives
1 tablespoon chopped parsley
Salt and freshly ground pepper to taste
Crumbled bacon (optional)
4 bacon strips

☐ Clean and scale fish, then wash and dry. Season inside of fish with salt and pepper, if you wish.

☐ In a medium skillet, sauté onion in butter until soft. Add mushrooms and cook until softened. Add tomato and simmer several minutes. Stir in remaining ingredients except the 4 bacon strips.

☐ Stuff fish, skewering closed if necessary. Top with bacon strips and place on a sheet of heavy-duty foil on top of barbecue grill. Bake, lid down, as you would in oven: 400° for 20-30 minutes, or 350° for 30-40 minutes, or 300° for 40 minutes plus.

EASY BAKED FISH

Serves: 6
Marinate: optional
Prepare: 5 minutes
Bake: 30 minutes

A great recipe for any of the larger lake fish...salmon, pike, lake trout, muskie, bass. Notice the unusual baking method. The mayonnaise keeps the moisture and flavor in, and, if you use low-fat, the dish remains healthful.

1 filet, 2-3 pounds
Juice of 2 limes
Salt and freshly ground
    pepper to taste
Mayonnaise

¼ cup freshly grated
    Parmesan cheese
Garnish: chopped fresh
    herbs

☐ Preheat oven to 500°.

☐ Place the filet with the lime juice in a shallow, glass dish, turning the fish in the juice. If there's time, let marinate 30 minutes.

☐ Lay the filet on a cookie sheet lined with aluminum foil, seasoning with salt and pepper to taste. Spread mayonnaise generously over fish, to about ⅛-inch thickness. Top with grated cheese.

☐ Turn preheated oven off. Immediately place fish in oven and bake 30 minutes *without* opening door.

☐ Garnish with chopped parsley, dill, or chives, if you wish.

Well, the ice fishermen love this February weather! You should see Hessel and Musky Bays...honest-to-goodness shantytowns on the ice. They're catching perch, pike, and walleye. At night, closer in, you'll see the twinkling lights of lanterns where people are fishing without shanties, as late as they please.

SALMON on the GRILL

Serves: 6
Prepare: 5 minutes
Marinate: 1 hour
Barbecue: 15 minutes

To create a simply wonderful meal, gently sauté lots of sliced sweet onions in butter just until soft. Add a touch of nutmeg, then salt and freshly ground pepper to taste. Garnish the barbecued salmon with the onions, and serve with corn-on-the-cob, sliced garden tomatoes, and Mile High Biscuits hot out of the oven.

1 5-pound salmon filet,
    boned and butterflied
Garlic salt

Juice of 3 lemons or 4 limes
Butter

☐ Sprinkle filet with garlic salt to taste. Marinate in lemon or lime juice for 1 hour.

☐ Brush or spray hot barbecue grill generously with oil. Place fish flesh-side down on grill. In 5 minutes, use 2 broad spatulas to turn fish over in 1 piece. Dot with butter.

☐ Grill 10 minutes more (with lid on barbecue, if fire seems too low), until fish just begins to flake. Either transfer fish to serving platter or lower the grate of coals and serve directly from the grill, lifting the meat from the skin.

■ Note: A good rule of thumb is 7-8 minutes total cooking time per inch of thickest part of fish.

INDOOR BARBECUED SALMON

Serves: 6
Prepare: 10 minutes
Broil: 20-25 minutes

When the weather leaves you little choice, here's a delicious way to fake a barbecue!

5-6 pounds salmon filets	Butter
Hickory-smoked salt	Dried dill weed
Garlic powder	
Brown sugar	

☐ Preheat broiler.

☐ Place fish, skin-side down, on a piece of heavy-duty foil. Crimp the edges of the foil to form a rim.

☐ With a sharp knife, score the flesh in the direction of the grain in ½-inch deep rows, 1 inch apart. Lightly dust the fish with hickory-smoked salt, garlic powder, and brown sugar, then gently rub in with your fingers. Dot with butter.

☐ Place on lowest rack in oven. Broil with oven door slightly open. After 15 minutes, dust the fish with dried dill weed. Continue broiling until flesh just begins to brown; about 10 minutes. If fish has not begun to flake, turn off oven and close door for a few minutes. Be sure not to overcook.

Particularly good with this are Baked Shoe Peg Corn and Swiss Chard Italian-Style.

To some folks around here, the fishing shanty is as snug in the dead of winter as their own home. They've got their tiny stove and maybe a good toddy or two to keep them warm in the cozy darkness. Peering down through the eery light from the blue ice makes the fish look bigger and better than they ever do at the summer fishing hole.

MARINATED SALMON STEAKS

Serves: 4-6
Prepare: 5 minutes
Marinate: 1-2 hours
Grill: 10-15 minutes

Broil the steaks or grill them on your barbecue. Serve with Scalloped Onions and Broccoli Florets With Cherry Tomatoes...makes a great summer supper.

4-6 salmon steaks, about
    1-inch thick
½ cup olive oil
1 tablespoon Dijon mustard
Juice of 2 limes
3 green onions, finely
    chopped

¼ cup chopped dill
    (1 tablespoon dried)
Salt and freshly ground
    pepper to taste

☐ Place salmon steaks in a shallow dish. Combine remaining ingredients with a whisk, beating well. Pour over fish. Cover and marinate 1 to 2 hours, turning a couple of times.

☐ To broil, place steaks about 5 inches from element. Broil 4-5 minutes per side, basting with marinade.

☐ If grilling on the barbecue, when the coals are white, brush or spray grill with oil, then place steaks directly on grill. Cook 5 to 7 minutes, then turn carefully with a large spatula. Brush with marinade and grill another 5 to 7 minutes.

☐ Warm any extra marinade, and spoon a little over each steak when serving.

SALMON POACHED in FOIL

Prepare: 5 minutes
Bake: 12-15 minutes

This is another favorite way to prepare salmon, particularly when we plan to have some left over to serve cold.

Salmon filet
Salt and pepper to taste

Dried tarragon

☐ Preheat oven to 500°.

☐ Place salmon on a large sheet of heavy duty foil. Salt and pepper to taste, then sprinkle with a few pinches of tarragon. Loosely wrap salmon in foil but seal well. Place on a cookie sheet or in a shallow roasting pan.

☐ Bake 12-15 minutes, depending on size of filet. Fish should have *just* begun to flake.

FRESH SALMON HASH

Serves: 4
Prepare: 10 minutes

We know some people who will cook salmon just so they can have hash the next day!

½ pound cold, cooked salmon
1 tablespoon butter
1 tablespoon oil
1 medium onion, finely chopped
½ green pepper, finely chopped

1 clove garlic, minced
2-3 cold, boiled or baked potatoes (skins, too!), diced
Salt and freshly ground pepper to taste
Chopped parsley
Tabasco sauce (optional)

☐ Break salmon up into bite-size pieces, removing any bones and skin. Set aside.

☐ Heat butter and oil in a large, heavy skillet. Sauté onion, green pepper, garlic, and potatoes until potatoes begin to brown, turning frequently with a metal spatula. Add salmon, and season with salt and pepper. Continue to cook until salmon is heated through and hash is crusty.

☐ Serve garnished with chopped parsley, and offer Tabasco sauce for those who wish extra zest.

GREAT LAKES GRAVLAX

Serves: 12-50!
Prepare: 20 minutes
Marinate: 2-3 days

Gravlax is the Swedish name for salt-cured salmon or, as many of us know it, lox. Truly a delicacy, as an appetizer or for a smörgasbörd nothing can compare.

Serve it with thin slices of Russian rye, generously spread with sweet butter or cream cheese, and have a pepper grinder and wedges of lemon close at hand. Or offer as a main dish, with Dill Mustard Sauce on the side.

1 large salmon or lake trout, fileted but not skinned

½ cup non-iodized salt (fine sea salt or kosher is ideal)

½ cup sugar

2 large bunches fresh dill weed (¼-½ cup dried)

1 tablespoon coarsely ground peppercorns (white or black)

☐ Split fish in half lengthwise, if still whole. Pull out any wayward bones with pliers or tweezers. Do not rinse fish in water; just gently wipe clean with paper towels.

☐ Combine salt and sugar. Coarsely chop dill weed.

☐ Cut a sheet of heavy-duty aluminum foil larger than fish. Sprinkle the foil with some of salt/sugar mixture and chopped dill. Gently rub cut sides of filets with salt/sugar. Lay a filet, skin-side down, on foil. Sprinkle generously with more of salt/sugar mixture and *all* of ground peppercorns. Cover *entirely* with dill weed.

☐ Lay second filet over top, skin-side up, matching head and tail ends. Sprinkle outside of salmon with remaining salt/sugar and dill. Enclose with another sheet of foil, sealing well.

☐ Place the wrapped fish on a large platter or shallow pan. Lay a board or tray on top of fish, then weight down with bricks or heavy canned goods.

☐ Refrigerate this way for a minimum of 48 hours but preferably 3 days, turning the package over every 12 hours or so. Some of the leached liquid may accumulate in the container. If so, just pour off, then reseal foil more securely.

☐ Prior to serving, drain fish then gently brush off dillweed and seasoning from flesh. Place filets skin-side down to slice. Starting about 3 inches from the tail-end, slice diagonally toward the tail (almost parallel to the skin) as thinly as possible; working back toward the head-end as you go.

■ Notes: For a beautiful display, place 1 filet, unsliced, on the serving board. Garnish lavishly with feathery heads of dill, and surround with the slices cut from the other piece.

Any left-over gravlax will keep for 2 weeks if properly wrapped and refrigerated.

FRIED FISH PATTIES

Yield: 5 large patties
Prepare: 10 minutes

These make wonderful sandwiches served on buns with lettuce, tomatoes, onions, and mayonnaise; or fix as a main course with a cruet of malt vinegar and Aunt Lyla's Sauce to the side.

2 cups cooked salmon (or 16 ounces canncd)*	1 tablespoon chopped fresh parsley
6 soda crackers, crushed (¼ cup)	1 tablespoon flour
1 egg, slightly beaten	Salt to taste
⅓ cup milk	1-2 tablespoons light oil
1 small onion, grated	Flour

☐ Drain fish well, then place in a bowl and flake with a fork. Add crushed crackers.

☐ Combine egg with milk, onion, parsley, and 1 tablespoon flour. Mix into fish and cracker crumbs, then salt to taste. Gently form into 5 patties.

☐ Heat oil in a large, heavy skillet over medium to medium-low heat. Lightly dust patties with flour, then fry on both sides until nicely browned; about 5 minutes per side.

■ Note: *Almost any kind of left-over fish will do. Mock Salmon is very good prepared this way.

LAKE HURON SALMON LOAF

Serves 4
Prepare: 15 minutes
Bake: 1 hour

You'll like this version because it is so delicate. Sauce with Sweet and Sour Mustard or slightly diluted condensed tomato soup.

2 cups cooked or canned salmon, flaked
½ cup uncooked oatmeal
2 eggs, beaten
1 medium onion, finely chopped
¼ green pepper, finely chopped
2 tablespoons chopped parsley
1 tablespoon lemon juice
1 teaspoon Worcestershire sauce
½ teaspoon salt
¾ cup milk

☐ Preheat oven to 350°. Gently, but thoroughly, combine all of the above ingredients. Place in a buttered, small loaf pan or casserole. Bake, uncovered, 1 hour.

POOR MAN's LOBSTER

Serves: 6
Prepare: 15 minutes

Magically, this recipe gives fish the taste and texture of lobster, but it must be a very firm variety, such as pike.

3 quarts water
1 medium onion, quartered
3 stalks celery, cut up
½ cup lemon juice
3 tablespoons salt
3 pounds pike filets, skinned
¼ cup melted butter
Paprika
Lemon wedges and melted butter

☐ Preheat broiler, setting rack approximately 6 inches below. Fill a large pan with 3 quarts water. Add onion, celery, lemon juice, and salt. Bring to a boil.

☐ Cut pike filets into 2-inch pieces. Drop into boiling pot, and cook exactly 3 minutes, not 1 second longer. Drain immediately, discarding onion and celery. Place fish pieces on a foil-lined baking sheet. Brush with ¼ cup melted butter and sprinkle with paprika. Broil 2 minutes, or just until fish starts to turn golden. Serve with lemon wedges and little bowls of melted butter.

MAIN DISHES

pork, ham, and sausage

Dear Bonnie,

First we had crocuses and daffodils and iris, now peonies and lilacs. The lady-slippers are blooming in the woodlands and marsh marigolds along the creek.

I talked by phone with your mother this morning. She said she'd be coming over one day this week to have a cup of tea with me. Then I called Bess McFee... she said today is such a perfect day. You know what? It is for us too!

Marv and I just finished our "T-time"... as usual talking about our memories and the good life we have had.

"T-time isn't at everyone else's tea time... it's about 10:30 in the morning, when Marv comes in from the fields or the mill for a good cup of tea and maybe some apple or zucchini bread that I keep on hand in the freezer. All our friends and neighbors know that this is when they can come to visit, too. We sit at the kitchen window and watch our special world... there's always something new to see or chat about. It's kind of like a front porch brought inside.

Today we talked about our 50th wedding anniversary, when we went to Hawaii with Marv's brother and his wife, Harry and Verneita. All that summer they helped us with the garden, and the money we made at the Stand was saved just for the trip. We had free champagne on the plane... and got to see Pearl Harbor!

Sometime I'll write you about all our dear memories. I think it must be very hard for people to find a good, simple way of life in the bustling world that we hear about today. Marv and I are so lucky.

Marv is planting the last of the sweet corn. He always does two plantings, ten days apart, to be safe from the frost.

We have not opened the Stand yet. We had a frost scare last night. Covered the tomato plants and then the water system at the Stand, in case. But the wind came up and no frost.

we are busy, healthy, and happy,

Judy Chard

PORK CHOPS and
RHUBARB CASSEROLE

Serves: 6
Prepare: 20 minutes
Bake: 40 minutes
10 minutes

You'll love what each does for the other...don't miss this at rhubarb-time.

6 pork chops, 1 inch thick
1 tablespoon oil
1 tablespoon butter
Salt and freshly ground
    pepper to taste
2 cups fine, fresh bread
    crumbs

½ cup sugar
½ cup brown sugar
3 tablespoons flour
½ teaspoon cinnamon
¼ teaspoon salt
6 cups thinly sliced rhubarb

The temperature is 26 degrees this a.m. There are still snowbanks in the yard and garden, but the rhubarb and asparagus should soon be up.

☐ Preheat oven to 350°.

☐ Trim fat from chops. In a large, heavy skillet, quickly brown chops in oil and butter, and season with salt and pepper to taste. Set them aside, then pour any pan drippings over bread crumbs, mixing in with a fork.

☐ Combine remaining ingredients.

☐ Butter a shallow casserole, large enough to accommodate chops in one layer. Sprinkle bottom with half of bread crumbs, then cover with half of rhubarb mixture. Place chops on top, then rest of rhubarb (but not remaining crumbs).

☐ Tightly cover casserole, and bake 40 minutes. Remove cover, top with rest of bread crumbs, and bake another 10 minutes.

Nice with this are buttered brown rice and Dandelion Greens.

BON's STUFFED PORK CHOPS

Serves: 4-6
Prepare: 25 minutes
Cook: 1-1½ hours

These are easy, very satisfying, and stay moist and tender. Nice with this for an early fall dinner are Apple-Filled Acorn Squash and Spinach With Red Onions.

6 pork chops, at least 1½ inches thick	2 tablespoons finely chopped parsley
2 cups Pepperidge Farm seasoned bread cubes	½ teaspoon poultry seasoning
¼ cup water	½ teaspoon salt
½ cup finely chopped celery	Freshly ground pepper to taste
½ cup finely chopped onion	2 tablespoons butter, melted
	½ cup hot water

☐ Cut pockets into chops for stuffing (or persuade your butcher to).

☐ In a mixing bowl, toss together remaining ingredients except the ½-cup hot water. Stuff chops, but do not pack. Fasten openings with toothpicks, lacing with string.

☐ In a large skillet, over medium-high heat, sear fatty edges of chops to grease pan, then brown both sides. Reduce heat, and add ½-cup hot water. Lay a sheet of wax paper loosely over chops (this helps to keep the meat tender), then cover pan tightly. Simmer until tender; about 1-1½ hours.

ORANGE-CRANBERRY PORK CHOPS

Serves: 4-6
Prepare: 15 minutes
Bake: 45 minutes

This is cranberry country, so here's one of our favorite ways to enjoy them. Try this same recipe for cut-up chicken; just reduce the baking time to 30-35 minutes.

6 pork chops (½ to ¾-inch thick)	2 cups whole cranberry sauce
Salt and freshly ground pepper to taste	Juice and grated rind of 1 orange

□ Preheat oven to 325°.

□ Slightly warm then grease a large skillet with the fatty edges of the chops, then arrange chops in pan. Brown quickly on both sides over medium-high heat, seasoning with salt and freshly ground pepper to taste.

□ Remove chops to a shallow baking dish, large enough to accommodate them in 1 to 2 layers. Pour off any fat from skillet, but do not scrape.

□ Combine the cranberry sauce, orange juice and rind, saving a little rind for garnish, if you wish. Pour into still-hot skillet, and immediately stir with a flat whisk to loosen browned bits. Pour over chops.

□ Bake, covered, for 45 minutes or until tender.

Good with this are Sweet Potato Spoon Bread, buttered rice, and tiny green peas.

PORK CHOPS
and APPLES

Serves: 4
Prepare: 15 minutes
Bake: 1 ½ hours

A different approach to just plain-good food.

4 pork chops, ¾-1 inch thick	3 tablespoons butter
5 baking apples, pared, cored, and sliced	3 tablespoons flour
1 onion, thinly sliced	12 ounces beer
Salt and freshly ground pepper	Paprika

□ Preheat oven to 350°.

□ Trim any fat from pork chops. Layer apples, onions, and chops (in that order) in a well-buttered, 10-inch casserole, at least 2 inches deep. Season with salt and pepper to taste.

□ Melt the butter in a small saucepan. Whisk in flour and cook over medium heat for a minute, stirring. Add beer all at once, and stir constantly until thickened. Pour over chops. Sprinkle with paprika. Bake, uncovered, for 1 ½ hours.

SAUERKRAUT SMOTHERED with PORK CHOPS and SAUSAGE

Serves: 4
Prepare: 30 minutes
Cook: 30 minutes

6 slices bacon, coarsely chopped
1 medium onion, chopped
22-27 ounces sauerkraut, drained
2 carrots, thinly sliced
2 teaspoons brown sugar

¾ cup chicken broth
½ cup dry white wine
4-6 peppercorns
4-6 juniper berries
2-3 whole cloves
1 bay leaf, broken up
1 large sprig parsley

☐ In a 12-inch skillet or electric frying pan, cook bacon until it just begins to brown. Pour off fat, then add onion. Sauté until onion is transparent.

☐ Stir in sauerkraut, carrots, brown sugar, chicken broth, and wine.

☐ Tie up spices and herbs in small bag of cheesecloth. Bury in center of sauerkraut mixture. Cover and simmer 10 minutes.

2-3 bratwurst
4 small pork chops
4-8 smoked sausage links

2 potatoes, peeled and cut to bite-size

☐ Diagonally score 1 side of each bratwurst. In a separate skillet, brown the bratwurst and pork chops.

☐ After sauerkraut mixture has simmered 10 minutes, add potatoes, working them down into sauerkraut. Top with browned bratwurst and pork chops. Cover and simmer 15 minutes.

☐ Add smoked sausages. Simmer, covered, another 15 minutes. Remove the pouch of seasonings before serving.

■ Note: You can use smoked pork chops and regular link sausages or Polish sausage. Just allow 15 minutes cooking time for precooked meats; 30 minutes for uncooked, browning first.

BREAKFAST SAUSAGE and APPLES

Serves: 6
Stand: overnight
Prepare: 15 minutes

A must for Sunday brunches or winter holiday breakfasts.

8 large cooking apples
½ cup sugar
½ teaspoon cinnamon
2 pounds link and/or
   Italian sausage

4 tablespoons butter
1 cup raisins
½ cup red wine

☐ Peel and quarter apples. Combine sugar and cinnamon, then sprinkle over apples and toss. Cover and refrigerate overnight.

☐ In morning, in a large skillet, brown sausages until done. Drain and place in a heat-proof serving dish.

☐ Pour any fat from skillet, then add butter to melt. Lay in apples, juice and all, then raisins. Cook until apples are fork-tender, then add to sausages.

☐ Pour wine into skillet. Heat, then pour over apples and sausage. Serve.

Great with Waffled French Toast, or creamy scrambled eggs and Simply The Best Blueberry Muffins.

DUTCH POTATO SALAD

Serves: 6
Prepare: 30 minutes
Bake: 25 minutes
10 minutes

The sausage turns this into a great main dish, and it can be made up to a day ahead.

3 pounds red-skinned potatoes (about 8 medium)
½ pound bacon
⅓ cup bacon fat
2 tablespoons flour
2 tablespoons sugar
1 teaspoon dry mustard
⅔ cup cider vinegar
⅔ cup water
1 beef bouillon cube, crumbled

1 teaspoon salt
Freshly ground pepper to taste
½ cup diced celery
12 green onions, chopped (include some of tops)
½ pound kielbasa or knockwurst sausage, sliced

☐ Cook potatoes in salted water to cover until *just* tender. Slice no more than ¼-inch thick.

☐ Cut bacon into 1-inch pieces. In a medium skillet, fry until crisp. Remove bacon and drain, reserving ⅓-cup bacon fat in skillet.

☐ To fat in skillet, stir in flour, sugar, and mustard with a flat whisk. Over medium heat, cook for 1 minute, stirring. Whisk in vinegar, water, and bouillon cube. Stir until thickened, seasoning with salt and pepper. Remove from heat.

☐ Arrange half of the warm potatoes in a buttered, shallow, 8x12-inch baking dish. Sprinkle with half of the celery, green onions, and bacon. Pour over half of the cooked dressing. Repeat the layers of vegetables and bacon, finishing with rest of dressing. At this point, the dish may be covered and set aside.

☐ When ready, bake, uncovered, at 350° for 20-25 minutes, or until heated through. Top with sliced sausage, and bake another 10 minutes before serving.

KIELBASA, RED BEANS, and RICE

Serves: 4-6
Prepare: 20 minutes
Cook: 15-30 minutes

Summertime sailors who tie up at Hessel's marina while cruising the Islands, have come up with this recipe for suppers onboard because the ingredients can always be found in the little Hessel Grocery nearby. It's so good and easy, it's become popular with us landlubbers.

3 slices bacon, chopped
1 medium onion, sliced
½ green pepper, cut into 1 to 2-inch strips
3 cloves garlic, minced
2 15-ounce cans kidney beans, undrained
1 bay leaf
2 tablespoons catsup
1½ teaspoons Worcestershire sauce

1-2 teaspoons plain or seasoned salt
Freshly ground pepper to taste
1 Polish sausage (½ pound), sliced*
1 tablespoon vinegar
1 teaspoon sugar
Cooked rice

☐ In a large, heavy saucepan, sauté bacon until lightly browned. Remove all but 2 tablespoons fat. Add onion, green pepper, and garlic. Sauté until soft.

☐ Add remaining ingredients except vinegar, sugar, and rice. Simmer, uncovered, for 15-30 minutes. Stir in vinegar and sugar for last few minutes. Serve over cooked rice.

■ Note: *To serve as a side dish, omit the sausage.

GRATIN of HAM
and POTATOES

Serves: 4
Prepare: 15 minutes
Bake: 30-35 minutes

This can be the main course or a side dish. We like it for barbecues and picnics, because it prepares and totes easily.

¼ cup chopped onion	1 cup milk
¼ cup chopped green pepper (optional)	1 cup shredded sharp cheddar cheese
2 tablespoons butter	¼ cup mayonnaise
1 tablespoon flour	4 cups cubed cooked potatoes
Freshly ground pepper to taste	2 cups diced ham

□ Preheat oven to 350°. In a medium saucepan, gently sauté onion and green pepper in butter until tender. Whisk, in flour and ground pepper, then milk. Bring to a boil, stirring constantly, then reduce heat and add cheese and mayonnaise. Stir until cheese melts, then combine with potatoes and ham. Bake in a greased, 8 x 11-inch, shallow casserole, uncovered, for 30-35 minutes, until golden brown.

TENDER HAM LOAVES

Serves: 12
Prepare: 20 minutes
Bake: 1 hour

Individual, delicate ham loaves...so nice for the holidays, since they can be made ahead and frozen. Serve with Sweet and Sour Mustard.

2 pounds ground tenderized ham	1 cup milk
1 pound lean ground pork	3 eggs, beaten
1 cup uncooked oatmeal	Freshly ground pepper to taste

□ Preheat oven to 325°. Gently, but thoroughly, combine above ingredients. Form into 12 small loaves (tender handling guarantees tender loaves), and place on a foil-lined, rimmed, baking sheet.

1 cup catsup	2 teaspoons dry mustard
1 cup brown sugar	½ teaspoon nutmeg

□ Combine and spread over ham loaves. Bake 1 hour.

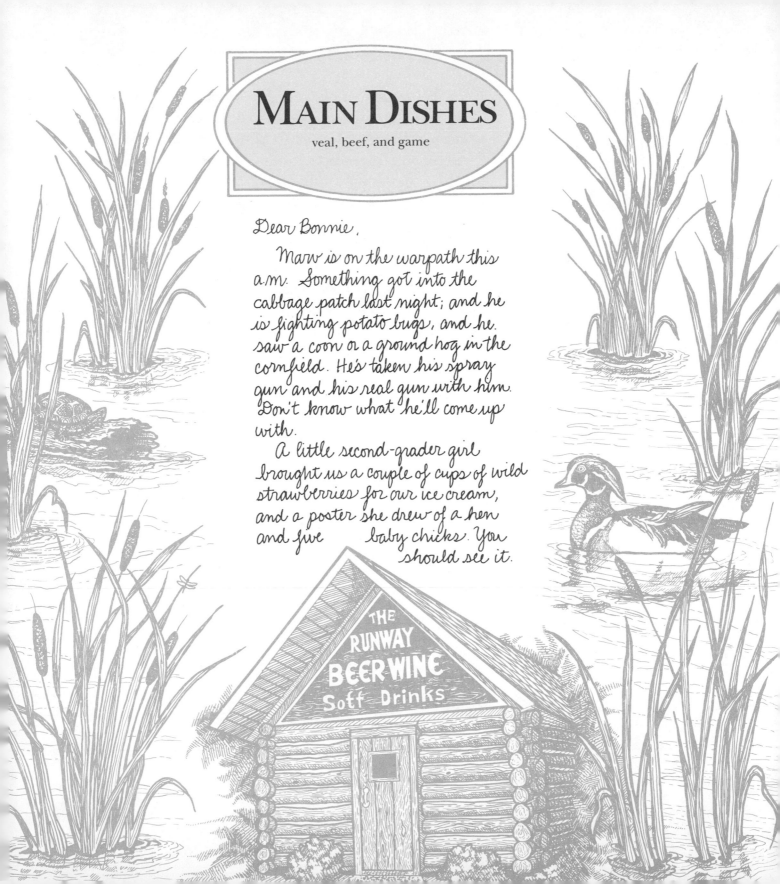

MAIN DISHES

veal, beef, and game

Dear Bonnie,

Maw is on the warpath this a.m. Something got into the cabbage patch last night; and he is fighting potato bugs, and he saw a coon or a ground hog in the cornfield. He's taken his spray gun and his real gun with him. Don't know what he'll come up with.

A little second-grader girl brought us a couple of cups of wild strawberries for our ice cream, and a poster she drew of a hen and five baby chicks. You should see it.

THE RUNWAY
BEER·WINE
Soft Drinks

The neighbor-children are always bringing us something... pressed flowers, poems, pictures. Or stopping by for bandaids... or to play dress-up in my old clothes. They all call me "Grandma Judy". Even lots of big people do... why don't you?

We had a deer on top of that high sawdust pile by the mill... just stood there waiting to get his picture taken, but Marv forgot that we had a loaded camera just inside the back door. I just know that it was that deer that got into the cabbage patch. They can mow everything down in sight.

A mourning dove kept calling to us from the big maple tree. We sat and listened to it for some time.

We have a friendly little chipmunk outside the kitchen window, and the hummingbirds never seem to leave. Aren't we lucky?

Love,

Grandma Judy

POLISH VEAL CUTLETS

Serves: 4-6
Prepare: 10 minutes
Cook: 25 minutes

Gently cooked, these are delicate and special.

1½ pounds ground veal
1-2 teaspoons lemon juice
½ teaspoon paprika
Salt and freshly ground
    pepper to taste
1 egg, slightly beaten
2 tablespoons water

1 cup dry bread crumbs
¼ cup butter
1 tablespoon flour
1 cup milk
1-2 teaspoons lemon juice
Salt and pepper to taste

☐ Gently combine veal, lemon juice, paprika, and salt and pepper to taste. Just as gently, form into 6 patties, ½-inch thick.

☐ Combine egg and water in a shallow dish. Place bread crumbs on a plate or sheet of wax paper. Dip patties into egg mixture, and then into bread crumbs.

☐ Over medium-high heat, melt butter in a heavy, 12-inch skillet. Brown patties on both sides. Reduce heat to medium-low, and cook gently for 20 minutes, turning several times.

☐ Remove patties and keep warm. To pan drippings, stir in flour with a flat whisk, cooking for a minute. Stir in milk, increase heat, and cook until thickened, stirring constantly. Add rest of lemon juice and salt and pepper to taste.

☐ Pour gravy over cutlets to serve with either buttered noodles or Spider Bread.

MUSHROOM-STUFFED FLANK STEAK

Serves: 4-6
Prepare: 15 minutes
Barbecue or Broil: 10-15 minutes

The next time you prepare flank steak, try stuffing it...really stuffing it, not just spreading it with something then rolling it up. You'll get a kick out of how easy it is and how nice to serve, especially with Butter-Wine Sauce.

This is good year 'round, barbecued or broiled, but we like it during morel season and particularly for Father's Day.

1 1½-pound flank steak	½ teaspoon dried basil
1 medium onion, chopped	¼ teaspoon hot pepper
2 cloves garlic, minced	flakes (optional)
4 tablespoons butter	¼ teaspoon salt
2-3 cups sliced morels or	Generous grinding of black
mushrooms	pepper
¼ cup chopped parsley	2 thin slices bread, finely cubed

☐ Place the steak on a cutting board. To make the pocket, with a sharp knife start cutting from the center of one long edge, parallel to the board and at mid-thickness. Work the knife throughout the inside of the steak without cutting through the opposite side or ends.

☐ In a large skillet, sauté the onion and garlic in butter until soft. Add mushrooms, and cook until they have just begun to soften. Stir in seasonings and bread cubes. Stir for 1 minute to incorporate bread.

☐ Fill the steak pocket with the stuffing. Secure the open part with round toothpicks, placed about 1 inch apart. Brush both sides of steak with oil.

☐ *To barbecue:* Plan about 5 minutes per side for rare to medium-rare, seasoning with salt and pepper as you turn it.

☐ *To broil:* Preheat the broiler to 375°. Fill a shallow roasting pan with ½-inch water. Place the steak on a rack over the pan. Set under broiler so that meat is 3 to 4 inches from element. Broil 7 minutes, season with salt and pepper to taste, and turn. Broil another 7-8 minutes for medium to medium rare. Do not overcook, for meat will toughen.

☐ Place meat on carving board, and remove toothpicks. Cover loosely with foil, and let sit 5 minutes. Carve diagonally across grain in ¾-inch thick slices. Serve with Butter-Wine Sauce.

BUTTER-WINE SAUCE

1 cup chopped green
   onions
1 cup red wine
4 tablespoons butter

2 tablespoons chopped
   parsley
Salt and freshly ground
   pepper to taste

☐ Place onions and wine in a saucepan. Bring to a boil. Add remaining ingredients, stirring until butter is melted. Serve warm over steak.

MARINATED FLANK STEAK
with PEACHES

Serves: 4
Prepare: 15 minutes
Marinate: 2-3 hours or overnight
Broil: 10-15 minutes

This is a wonderful dish for the deepest part of winter, for it makes summer seem just around the corner.

1 16-ounce can cling peach
   halves
4 tablespoons butter
1 cup chili sauce
½ cup vinegar

4 tablespoons Worcestershire
   sauce
2 beef bouillon cubes
2 cloves garlic, minced
1 1¾-pound flank steak

☐ To make marinade, drain the syrup from the peaches into a saucepan. Add remaining ingredients, except mcat and peaches. Whisk together and simmer 10 minutes.

☐ Lightly score both sides of steak diagonally to form a diamond pattern. Place in an 8x11-inch, shallow, glass baking dish with the peaches. Pour warm marinade over, and tightly cover. Let sit on your counter for 2-3 hours, or in refrigerator overnight. Turn several times.

☐ Preheat broiler. Place steak on broiling rack. Broil 2-3 inches from heat for 5-7 minutes, basting once with marinade. Turn. Add peaches, cut-side up, and baste all. Broil 5-7 minutes longer, basting once again.

☐ Let steak sit for a minute, then carve it on a slant into fairly thin slices. Drizzle with warm marinade and garnish with peaches.

Good with this is Simply Potato Casserole.

GADABOUT GOULASH

Serves: 3-4
Prepare: 15 minutes
Bake: 2 hours

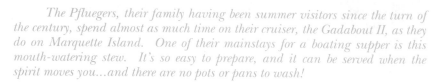

The Pfluegers, their family having been summer visitors since the turn of the century, spend almost as much time on their cruiser, the Gadabout II, as they do on Marquette Island. One of their mainstays for a boating supper is this mouth-watering stew. It's so easy to prepare, and it can be served when the spirit moves you...and there are no pots or pans to wash!

In the early 30s, a man named Mr. Graves started a tiny restaurant in his log cabin home about a mile and a half north of us. Did his own cooking and served coffee or beer...no bar, just 3 or 4 tables.

Then he sold it to Mr. Willis Taylor, a woodsman who lived near Nuns Creek. Mr. Taylor didn't cook and he liked his pie baked daily. Well, Marv was working in the woods then, making very little money, so I went to work for Mr. Taylor. I took care of the place and cooked, making soups, fried chicken, biscuits, sausage and milk gravy, beef stew and venison stew...and baked his pies. Pretty soon, I had drummed up a pretty good business.

1½ pounds boneless top round steak, cut into 3-4 pieces	Salt and freshly ground pepper to taste
4 carrots, sliced	½ packet dried onion soup mix
2 sweet green peppers, sliced	1 15-ounce can stewed tomatoes
1 large, unpeeled potato, thinly sliced	¼ cup commercial Italian dressing
2-4 ounces fresh or canned mushrooms, sliced	A very generous sprinkling of paprika

☐ Preheat oven to 325°.

☐ Place a large sheet of heavy-duty aluminum foil on a cookie sheet or shallow roasting pan. Place steak on top of foil, then layer with remaining ingredients in order given.

☐ Cover all with another sheet of foil, crimping the edges together to seal. Bake at least 2 hours, but no more than three.

☐ You may serve the goulash directly from its foil packet, and, if you'd like, accompany it with Sun Sands Salad and a good, crusty bread.

THE RUNWAY TAVERN's
FRIDAY NIGHT STEW

Serves: 6
Prepare: 15 minutes
Bake: 1½ hours

Years and years ago, The Runway Tavern served this oven stew on Friday nights...pay check night. It's a real man-pleaser to this day. Make it Thursday, if you'd like; it does nothing but get better!

2 large onions, chopped
2-3 tablespoons butter
2 pounds beef chuck, cut
    in ¾-inch cubes
2 cloves garlic, minced
3 tablespoons paprika (yes!)
¾ teaspoon dried
    marjoram

½ teaspoon caraway seed
1 teaspoon salt or to taste
¼ cup catsup
2-4 cups beef broth
6 medium potatoes, peeled
    and quartered

☐ Preheat oven to 350°.

☐ In a large Dutch oven, sauté onions in butter until lightly browned. Add remaining ingredients in order given (use only 2 cups beef broth to begin with). Cover and bake 1½ hours, or until meat is tender, adding more broth if necessary.

With this, you'll like a simple green vegetable, sliced tomatoes dressed with chopped herbs and a seasoned vinegar, and Johnny Cake.

Along came deer season. Hunters would stop for a bite to eat, then they'd become so interested in the beer and the fellowship that they'd stay and stay 'til it was too late to go hunting. Then they'd go back to the city and their wives and tell them of sitting on the trails and runway for hours, waiting for their prize buck to come along. So I suggested to Mr. Taylor that he'd name his place "Taylor's Runway" to keep the hunters honest...and he did.

ELGIE's BURGUNDY MEAT PIE

Serves: 4
Prepare: 30 minutes
Cook: 1 hour, 15 minutes
45 minutes
Bake: 25 minutes (optional)

Elgie claims that he has no special, cooking talents, but it is well-known that that's not so. Follow this recipe for a delicious meal. If you do not wish to finish it as a pie, you can serve it just as the hearty stew it is, topping it with Herb Dumplings.

3 slices bacon, cut in ½-inch strips
1-1½ pounds beef or venison stew meat, cut in 1-inch cubes
1 clove garlic, crushed
3 medium onions, quartered
2 cups beef broth
1-3 cups red burgundy wine (some for sipping, as you cook!)
1 cup stewed tomatoes or tomato sauce

1 tablespoon currant jelly
1 bay leaf
¼ teaspoon each marjoram and thyme
1 stalk celery, cut in chunks
2 stalks parsley
4 cloves
½ cup stew broth
1-2 parsnips, cubed to bite-size (optional)
6 small carrots, halved
1½ tablespoons flour
Salt and freshly ground pepper to taste

☐ Place bacon pieces in a Dutch oven or heavy kettle before setting over heat. Then, partially brown bacon over medium heat, and pour off all but 1-2 tablespoons fat.

☐ In same pot with bacon, brown meat quickly, in small batches, over medium-high to high heat. When finished, reduce heat, returning all of browned meat to pan; then add garlic, onions, and beef broth. Pour enough wine in to cover, then add tomatoes, currant jelly, and herbs. Tie up celery, parsley, and cloves in a piece of cheese cloth, and nestle into stew mixture.

☐ Simmer, covered, 1¼ hours. Discard cloth pouch. Remove a ½-cup broth from stew and set aside. Add parsnips and carrots to pot. Cover, and simmer 45 minutes.

☐ With a small whisk or fork, combine flour with cooled broth. Stir into finished stew, and simmer for a minute or so to thicken. Season with salt and freshly ground pepper to taste.

□ *To bake as a pie:* Stew should be cold to lukewarm before covering with pastry. Preheat oven to 425°. Turn cooled stew into a 2-quart casserole. Top with pastry for a 1-crust pie (see index). Flute edge and cut slits in top for steam vents. Bake 25 minutes.

HERB DUMPLINGS

Serve: 4
Prepare: 10 minutes
Cook/Bake: (see below)

These can be cooked with the stew in its pot, or baked on top of the stew in a casserole.

1 cup sifted cake flour	1 egg
2 teaspoons baking powder	Milk to measure ½ cup
½ teaspoon salt	(see below)
3 tablespoons chopped chives or parsley	Melted butter (optional)

□ Combine dry ingredients in a bowl with a whisk. Add chopped herbs. Place egg in a measuring cup, adding milk to measure a ½-cup. Beat egg and milk together, then stir into dry ingredients with a fork, blending well.

□ *For dumplings in the pot:* Dip a small serving spoon into cold water, then fill with batter and drop onto bubbling stew. Continue until you have enough dumplings that each is not quite touching another. Cover and simmer 2 minutes. Turn dumplings over, then cook another 2 minutes.

□ *For dumplings in a casserole:* Heat stew in a shallow casserole at 350°. Twenty minutes before serving, top with dumpling batter as above. Drizzle each dumpling with melted butter, if you wish. Bake until lightly browned.

GERTIE K.'s BEEF
with SAUERKRAUT

Serves: 4-6
Prepare: 30 minutes
Cook: 45 minutes
1-1½ hours

We had a Finnish friend, Gertie K., who lived on Sugar Island, where we used to cut timber. We loved to spend the night with her and watch the foreign boats go up the St. Mary's river from the Soo Locks.

She always served us this good stew, and, if there were some left over and we happened to stay two nights, everything was just that much better!

We no longer cut timber there and Gertie K. has passed away, but it's nice to remember.

2-3 pounds lean stew meat,
    cut in 1½-inch cubes
1 tablespoon oil
1 tablespoon butter
2 onions, thinly sliced
1 clove garlic, crushed
1 tablespoon sugar
1 teaspoon paprika

8 ounces tomato purée
¾ cup water
Salt and freshly ground
    pepper to taste
2 cups sauerkraut,
    well-drained
1 cup sour cream
Chopped parsley

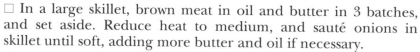

☐ In a large skillet, brown meat in oil and butter in 3 batches, and set aside. Reduce heat to medium, and sauté onions in skillet until soft, adding more butter and oil if necessary.

☐ Return meat to skillet, and stir in garlic, sugar, paprika, tomato purée, water, salt, and pepper. Cover tightly and simmer slowly for 45 minutes.

☐ Stir in sauerkraut and sour cream. Tightly cover and continue cooking *very gently*, until meat is quite tender; about 1 to 1½ hours. Check seasoning.

☐ Garnish with a goodly amount of chopped parsley, and serve with buttery noodles or mashed potatoes.

■ Note: This freezes nicely.

ISLANDER BEEF
SHORT RIBS

Serves: 6
Prepare: 15 minutes
Cook: 1½ - 2 hours

We like this for a September dinner when the evenings are a bit nippy but we can still use some good things from the garden.

4 pounds beef short ribs
1-2 tablespoons oil
1 16-ounce can pineapple
  bits, drained
½ cup chopped onions
3 tablespoons brown sugar
½ teaspoon dry mustard
2 teaspoons salt

½ cup catsup
¼ cup vinegar
¼ cup water
1-2 green peppers, cut in strips
1-2 tablespoons flour
½ cup water
2-3 tomatoes, cut in eighths

☐ In a large, deep skillet or Dutch oven over medium-high heat, brown the short ribs on all sides in several batches. Reduce heat to low, cover tightly, and cook slowly for 1 to 1½ hours, until meat is *just* beginning to fall off the bones. Drain off fat.

☐ Combine pineapple, onions, brown sugar, mustard, salt, catsup, vinegar, and ¼-cup water. Pour over meat. Cover and continue to cook slowly another 25 minutes, then add peppers. Simmer, covered, another 5 minutes.

☐ Remove meat and peppers to a warm platter. Combine 1-2 tablespoons flour (depending on thickness of sauce desired) with ½-cup water and stir into sauce. Cook, stirring constantly, until thickened. Pour over meat, then garnish platter with tomatoes.

Good with this are buttered rice, Yellow Squash and Sweet Corn, and Mile High Biscuits.

MARV's POT ROAST

Serves: 6
Prepare: 20 minutes
15 minutes
Bake: 2-3 hours

What makes this special is the puréeing of the vegetables to make a thick, rich gravy.

1 3-pound bottom round pot roast	1 10½-ounce can beef consommé
2-3 tablespoons butter	½ cup dry red wine
1 onion chopped	1 teaspoon salt
3 stalks celery (leaves and all), coarsely chopped	Freshly ground pepper to taste
3-4 carrots, coarsely chopped	½ teaspoon paprika
1 clove garlic, crushed	1 tablespoon capers
¼ pound mushrooms, coarsely chopped	1 cup sour cream

☐ Preheat oven to 350°.

☐ In a Dutch oven, over medium-high heat, brown meat in butter. Remove meat and reduce heat to medium. Add onion, celery, carrots, and garlic, and sauté until onion is soft. Add mushrooms, consommé, wine, salt, pepper, paprika, and capers.

☐ Return meat to pan. Cover and bake 2-3 hours, or until meat is tender. (Note: You can do this on top of stove instead. Simmer very gently, tightly covered.)

☐ Remove meat to a platter and cover with foil to keep warm. Skim any fat, then purée the vegetables in their broth in a food processor or blender. Return to pan and reheat on stove. (If you wish a thicker gravy, mix 3 tablespoons flour with 3 tablespoons water and stir in with a whisk. Cook until thickened.)

☐ Stir in sour cream but do not boil. Slice meat, then cover with gravy.

Good with this are homemade noodles and Collards (or kale) With Bacon Bits.

Swedish immigrants were among the earliest settlers of this part of the country. Brothers by the name of John and Charles Erickson came across the Atlantic in the early -1880s. Because of the confusion of so many Ericksons entering the country in the same period of time, they were asked to change their name. They chose that of their Swedish village, Hessel. They and their families were active in building their new community, so, when John became the first postmaster of his tiny town, it seemed logical to give it his name.

SWEDISH POT ROAST

Serves: 6-8
Prepare: 15 minutes
Cook: 2-3 hours

This produces an unusually rich, dark gravy, which makes it ideal for venison, and it is so easy to prepare.

2 tablespoons oil
2 tablespoons butter
1 5-pound boneless beef or
   venison roast (chuck,
   rump, or brisket)
1 large onion, chopped
4 tablespoons flour

4 cups beef broth
2 tablespoons vinegar
1 tablespoon dark corn syrup
1 bay leaf, broken in half
Salt and freshly ground
   pepper to taste

☐ Heat oil and butter in a large Dutch oven over medium to medium-high heat. Brown meat on all sides, then remove and set aside.

☐ In same pan, sauté onion until soft. Sprinkle with flour, then cook 1-2 minutes more, stirring. With a whisk, stir in remaining ingredients.

☐ Return meat to pot. Bring to a boil, then immediately reduce heat. Cover and simmer gently for 2-3 hours.

☐ Remove meat to warm platter, and cover with foil until serving time. Skim any fat from gravy. Boil briskly for 5 minutes or so, if it needs to thicken. Check seasoning then pour into a gravy boat to serve with the roast.

Good with this are mashed potatoes or Baked Hominy With Cheese, Fried Carrots, and Green Beans and Turnips.

MUSTARD STEAK

Serves: 6 or so
Prepare: 5 minutes
Marinate: 5 hours
Barbecue: 30-45 minutes

Only a man would think this one up! Our friend Bill Madigan gets all the credit.

1 2½ to 3-pound chuck roast, bone-in, 2 inches thick*	1 cup or more prepared yellow mustard

☐ Wipe meat dry with paper towels, and place on a plate. Thickly frost all over with mustard.

☐ Bill says that it is very important that you let the steak sit for 5 hours. It does not need to be refrigerated or covered.

☐ Get a *very hot* charcoal fire going. Grill the meat quite close to the fire, planning 15 minutes per side for medium-rare. The mustard will blacken and form a crust. When ready, give the grill a good whack. The crust will fall away. Thinly slice diagonally to the grain. Fantastic!

We don't know what Bill serves with this, but we like Country Tomato Pie and Warm Spinach Salad.

■ Note: *Bill likes to use a 7-bone chuck roast, but nowadays butchers find it easiest to remove the bone before packaging it for the store case. Thus, you may have to make a special request.

MEATLOAF PIE

Serves: 5-6
Prepare: 15 minutes
Bake: 25 minutes
10-15 minutes

When we feel like something different for an easy family supper.

1 pound lean ground beef
½ cup fresh bread crumbs
½ cup tomato sauce
¼ cup chopped onions
¼ cup chopped green
   pepper

¼ teaspoon oregano
1½ teaspoons salt
Freshly ground pepper
   to taste

☐ Preheat oven to 350°.

☐ Combine above ingredients, mixing gently but well. Pat into a 9-inch pie plate to form a shell with a 1-inch fluting around edge.

1⅓ cups instant rice
1 cup water
1½ cups tomato sauce

½ teaspoon salt
1 cup grated sharp
   cheddar cheese

☐ Combine rice, water, tomato sauce, salt, and ¼-cup of the cheese. Fill meat shell, and cover with foil. Bake 25 minutes.

☐ Uncover and sprinkle with remaining cheese. Continue to bake, uncovered, another 10-15 minutes.

SNOWS CHILI
(alias Cincinnati Chili)

Serves: 6-8
Prepare: 20 minutes
Cook: 1-3 hours

Early in this century, Big LaSalle Island began to draw summer people from Cincinnati. Over the years, it and the surrounding bays have become a haven for a number of southern Ohioans.

Cincinnati Chili is an institution in that town. Supposedly, it was the creation of a Greek immigrant who started a chain of restaurants there featuring solely this "chili."

It will always be debated as to whether or not it is truly a chili, but it is so good, who cares? As the recipe has moved north, and each cook has had to go by what is in his summer cabin's cupboards, it has taken on a different character. Thus, some feel free to call it "Snows Chili," the colloquial name for the Islands.

2 large onions, chopped
4 cloves garlic, minced
2 teaspoons butter
2 teaspoons oil
2 pounds lean ground beef
2 15-ounce cans whole or stewed tomatoes
2 10½-ounce cans tomato soup
2 15-ounce cans kidney or pinto beans, undrained (optional)
2-4 cups beef broth

½ ounce unsweetened chocolate
4 tablespoons chili powder
1 teaspoon each ground allspice, cinnamon, and cumin
½ teaspoon cayenne pepper
¼ teaspoon ground cloves
1 bay leaf
2 tablespoons cider vinegar
Salt to taste

☐ In a large Dutch oven or heavy pot, gently sauté onions and garlic in butter and oil until soft. Add meat and cook over medium-high heat, continually stirring, until no longer pink.

☐ Add remaining ingredients (beginning with 2 cups beef broth), and barely simmer, uncovered, for 1 to 3 hours. Add more beef broth and cover, if it begins to be too thick. You want it to have a soupy consistency.

1 pound spaghetti, cooked
2-3 cups shredded cheddar cheese
1-2 cups chopped onions
Oyster crackers

☐ To serve, place small amounts of spaghetti in warm, shallow, soup bowls; then add piping hot chili and garnish with cheese and onions. Pass the oyster crackers.

KIDS' NIGHT
SPAGHETTI SAUCE

Serves: 8
Prepare: 15 minutes
Cook: 2 hours, minimum

Lots of thought was given to whether or not this should be included in the book, but the younger generation insisted (and the rest of us cheered!).

2-2½ pounds lean
    ground beef
2 15½-ounce cans
    tomato sauce
2 10½-ounce cans
    tomato soup
1 cup water
2 tablespoons
    Worcestershire sauce

¼ teaspoon Tabasco sauce
4 bay leaves
12 peppercorns
3 cloves garlic, thinly sliced
½ teaspoon basil
¼ teaspoon thyme
¼ teaspoon marjoram
⅛ teaspoon cayenne
    pepper

☐ In a large, heavy skillet, brown meat just until no longer pink. Stir in remaining ingredients. Bring to a boil, then immediately reduce heat. *Barely* simmer at least 2 hours, stirring periodically. If the sauce becomes too thick, add a little water.

ROAST HAUNCH
of VENISON

Serves: 10-12
Prepare: 15 minutes
Marinate: 6 hours plus
Roast: 3½ - 4 hours
Stand: 30 minutes plus

There just isn't a better dinner to serve to good friends in the heart of winter. Along with a full-bodied red wine, offer Lida's Wild Rice, Carrots and Swiss Cheese Casserole, and broccoli; then Indian Pudding for dessert.

1 large onion, chopped
1 stalk celery, chopped
1 large carrot, chopped
2 cloves garlic, chopped
3 tablespoons butter
1 teaspoon each dried
   thyme, rosemary,
   and marjoram
1 teaspoon salt

Freshly ground pepper
6 cups claret or Burgundy
   wine
1 haunch of venison, 8-10
   pounds
4 whole cloves
4 juniper berries
1 bay leaf

☐ In a medium skillet, sauté onion, celery, carrot, and garlic in butter until tender. Add thyme, rosemary, marjoram, salt, a good grinding of pepper, and *2 cups* of the wine. Simmer 5 minutes, then purée in an electric blender.

☐ Wipe the meat with a damp towel. Place in a large earthenware, glass, or stainless steel bowl, along with the cloves, juniper berries, and bay leaf. Combine puréed mixture with remaining 4 cups of wine and pour over haunch. Cover and let marinate at room temperature for at least 6 hours, turning periodically.

2-3 cloves garlic, slivered
6 strips thickly sliced bacon
1 cup currant or plum jelly

Juice of 1 lemon
½ cup sour cream
2 ounces brandy (optional)

☐ Preheat oven to 450°.

☐ Drain marinade from haunch and reserve. With the tip of a sharp knife, cut slits in meat at intervals and insert garlic slivers. Place haunch in roasting pan, then lay bacon over top. Insert meat thermometer in thickest part.

☐ Roast 20 minutes at 450°, then reduce temperature to 325° and roast about 3¼ hours for medium-rare, or to desired doneness. Baste periodically with reserved marinade. (Remove from oven a little ahead of time to allow for internal cooking while roast sits.)

☐ Let stand on carving board, loosely covered with foil, for 30-45 minutes before carving. This will aid in tenderizing the meat.

☐ To prepare the sauce, combine pan drippings with remaining marinade, jelly, and lemon juice. Let simmer 10 minutes or so. Check for seasoning then remove from heat and whisk in sour cream and brandy. Pour into a sauceboat to serve.

VENISON

The proud hunter may swear that he brought home a young buck, but often it's hard to tell its age. Also, where the deer has grazed and how much exercise he has had can affect the quality of the meat.

For tough meat and cuts, grind to make meatloaf or mincemeat. Very lean cuts from the shoulder and leg are good for stews. Tender loin cuts grill well.

☐ Marinating venison is a matter of choice, but it definitely helps tough and too gamey meats. A mixture of equal parts vinegar and red wine, boiled for a minute with a tablespoon or two of crushed juniper berries is good; cool, then marinate the venison in it for 6 to 24 hours.

☐ Chops are good marinated for an hour or two in 1 part lemon juice to 6 parts orange juice with a couple healthy pinches of rosemary or thyme.

☐ Frozen venison will quickly lose its juices if thawed at room temperature. For best results, use a microwave oven, thawing according to the manufacturer's directions.

☐ Before cooking, always rinse venison well then pat dry.

SWISS VENISON STEAK

Serves: 3-4
Prepare: 15 minutes
Cook: 1½ - 2 hours

Hunters like their meat and potatoes when they come in at dark... their energy all spent. When Betty Smith cooks for the camp, she always makes her grandmother's recipe for bread pudding for their dessert, baking it in the wood stove oven. Often there aren't any spices on hand, yet it's still real good with just vanilla and maybe some warm applesauce.

After supper, they, the hunters, head for the bunk house to tell their tall tales of the day. Some are honest but a lot are stretched...I think.

An ideal way to prepare venison...and it will give you a wonderful gravy for the mashed potatoes you should serve with it...and don't forget Squaw Corn!

1¼ -1½ pounds venison steak, 1-1½ inches thick
Flour
Salt and freshly ground pepper
Chili powder (optional)

2-3 tablespoons butter
2 onions, sliced
1 16-ounce can tomatoes
½ teaspoon marjoram
½ teaspoon thyme
½ cup red wine

☐ Dredge steak in flour that's been well-seasoned with salt and freshly ground pepper, and pound into meat. (Add some chili powder to the flour for a different touch.)

☐ In a large, heavy skillet, brown meat quickly in butter, then set aside. Sauté onions in pan until soft. Return meat to pan, covering it with the onions and then tomatoes. Add herbs and wine.

☐ Cover and simmer slowly for 1½ to 2 hours, until tender. During that time, turn the meat once or twice. If the gravy becomes too thick, add a little more wine.

BUSH BAY MEATLOAF

Serves: 4-6
Prepare: 20 minutes
Bake: 1-1¼ hours

Are you adventuresome? The biggest complaint about meatloaf is that it can be boring. Well, this one certainly isn't!

We love it for venison because the different spices help if the meat tends to be gamey. If you have a food processor, it's a snap!

1½ pounds lean ground beef or venison
½ pound lean ground pork
1 cup finely chopped onion
½ cup grated carrot
½ cup finely chopped celery
¼ cup finely chopped green pepper
2 cloves garlic, minced

1 teaspoon salt
1 teaspoon freshly ground pepper
½ teaspoon cumin
½ teaspoon nutmeg
¼ teaspoon cayenne pepper
¾ cup dry bread crumbs
½ cup catsup
3 eggs, beaten
½ cup light cream

□ Preheat oven to 350°.

□ Combine all ingredients lightly but thoroughly. Place in a 9x5-inch loaf pan. Bake 1 to 1¼ hours, until done.

■ Note: Makes wonderful next-day sandwiches for die-hard fishermen!

Best story I ever heard was the one about the hunter who came up for almost the whole season, but never could find his wool socks that supposedly his wife had packed for him. He went back without a buck and furious about no socks. When he accused her of forgetting them, she opened his gun case and there they all were. Some bunch of hunting he had done!

Then the fellow from Detroit who had worked up until 11 p.m., then drove all night up here and went straight into the woods to hunt. He sat down against a tree just to rest for a minute but fell asleep. He woke up to see a deer right in front of him. In his panic, instead of pulling the trigger he racked every shell out on the ground. The buck shook his head then ambled off into the woods.

PASTOR KAISER's HASSENPFEFFER

Serves: 4-6
Prepare: 10 minutes
Marinate: 2 days
Prepare: 15 minutes
Cook: 1½ - 2 hours

Our snowshoe rabbits are a little bigger and sturdier than their southern cousins, the cottontails, so they need a touch more marinating and cooking.

When Pastor Kaiser was with the Bethel Lutheran Church in Cedarville, he gave his favorite recipe for stewed rabbit to the Ladies' Altar Guild for their wonderful cookbook, The Cedar Chest. *It's now the most popular rabbit dish in town!*

1½ cups dry red wine	2 bay leaves
1½ cups water	3 tablespoons sugar
¾ cup cider vinegar	2 teaspoons salt
15 whole cloves	1 teaspoon dry mustard
15 black peppercorns	2 snowshoe rabbits, dressed

☐ Combine all above ingredients (except rabbits) in a saucepan and boil for 2 minutes. Set aside to cool.

☐ Cut rabbits into serving-size pieces. Place in a glass or earthenware bowl, then cover with cooled marinade. Cover and refrigerate for 2 days, once in awhile turning the pieces in the marinade.

Flour	¾ cup sour cream
4 tablespoons butter	Chopped parsley
1 cup thinly sliced onions	
1½ cups reserved marinade	

☐ Remove rabbit pieces from marinade; pat dry with paper towels, then dust with flour. Strain and reserve marinade.

☐ Melt butter in a Dutch oven or heavy, deep skillet. Brown rabbit and onions. Pour off fat, then add 1½ cups strained marinade.

☐ Cover and simmer over low heat until rabbit is very tender; 1½ to 2 hours. Turn the pieces from time to time, adding more marinade if necessary.

☐ Arrange rabbit pieces on a warm platter. Sample broth to correct seasoning. If you wish a thicker gravy, mix a little flour with some of the reserved marinade, and stir into the sauce with a whisk. Simmer, stirring, for 2 minutes.

☐ Stir in sour cream and heat but *do not* boil. Pour over rabbit pieces, and sprinkle all with chopped parsley.

So-o-o good with buttered noodles, Apple-Filled Acorn Squash or Guess-Again Carrots, and green peas.

HUNTERS' STEW with APPLE CIDER

Serves: 4-6
Prepare: 25 minutes
Cook: 1½ hours

With a spiciness like sauerbraten, this has such good flavor that even those who don't relish game will enjoy it. If you wish to use beef instead, it will still give you a great dinner. It's best prepared a day ahead.

4 strips bacon, cut up
2½ pounds venison or beef stew meat, cut in 1½-inch cubes
1 large onion
4 whole cloves
1 cinnamon stick
1 bay leaf

1 teaspoon minced fresh ginger root (½ teaspoon powder)
2 cups apple cider
¾ cup red wine vinegar
Salt and freshly ground pepper to taste

☐ In a Dutch oven, fry bacon until crisp. Remove and drain on a paper towel. Pour off all but 2 tablespoons fat. Brown meat in several batches.

☐ Cut onion in half and stud each half with cloves. Add to pot with all of meat, plus bacon and remaining ingredients. Cover and gently simmer 1½ hours, or until meat is very tender, stirring occasionally.

☐ Remove onion halves, cinnamon stick, and bay leaf. If making ahead, refrigerate before removing fat.

1½-2 cups dry pumpernickel bread crumbs

Juice and grated rind of ½ lemon
¼ cup chopped parsley

☐ Near serving time, bring stew to a simmer. Add enough bread crumbs to thicken to desired consistency. Add lemon juice, then sprinkle with grated rind and chopped parsley.

With this we like to serve Country Baked Noodles, Tangerine Carrots, and just a simple tossed green salad.

In 1960, when Marv had an accident at the mill, I knew he wasn't able to go hunting and would miss all the fun and lingo. So, I invited about 20 or so of his hunting buddies for breakfast opening day. That meant awful early because hunters want to be in the woods "before daylight in the swamp," as they say.

WILD DUCK ROASTED
with PINEAPPLE

Serves: 4
Prepare: 15 minutes
Roast: 20 minutes
30-40 minutes

Our son, M.J., says he does his best cooking when he's at his hunting camp. He can make do with almost anything in the cupboard, and it always turns out just great. Here's the way he fixed duck last fall...his first endeavor, and everyone loved it!

We set up our dining table in the living room then added sawhorses with boards to extend it, covering everything with sheets. I made a full breakfast with all the trimmings... fried potatoes, bacon, milk gravy and biscuits, our own maple syrup and our own tomato juice and lots of hot coffee.

4 wild ducks, dressed*
Salt and freshly ground
   pepper
2 tablespoons butter,
   softened
2 lemons, quartered
1 10-ounce can pineapple
   spears, drained

4 strips bacon, halved
1 cup beer
1 cup apricot-pineapple
   preserves
2 tablespoons prepared
   mustard
Grated rind of 1 orange

☐ Preheat oven to 475°.

☐ Although ducks have been dressed, check carefully for imbedded shot and feathers. Wash and dry well. Sprinkle insides with salt and pepper, then rub softened butter over outsides.

☐ Tuck 2 quarters of lemon inside each duck, then pineapple spears, dividing equally. Place ducks, breast side up, in a shallow roasting pan. Place 2 halves of bacon lengthwise over each breast. Roast, uncovered, for 20 minutes.

☐ In the meantime, combine the remaining ingredients in a saucepan. Bring to a boil, stirring constantly, then remove from heat.

☐ Reduce oven temperature to 400°. Pour sauce over birds, and roast another 30-40 minutes for rare to medium, basting periodically.

☐ To serve, skim fat from gravy then pour through a sieve into sauce bowl. Accompany the ducks with Lida's Wild Rice or Winter Rice, and Squaw Corn.

■ Note: *If you are concerned that the ducks may be too gamey, soak 30 minutes to 3 hours in water to which you've added about 1 tablespoon each of baking soda and salt.

LIDA's GROUSE in SOUR CREAM with WILD RICE

Serves: 4-6
Prepare: 15 minutes
Roast: 1 hour
2 hours

Two dishes that our dear friend Lida can prepare better than anyone else we know are wild rice and roasted grouse or pheasant.

2-3 grouse or pheasants	3-4 tablespoons butter
Flour	¼ cup hot water
Freshly ground nutmeg	1 pint sour cream
Salt and freshly ground pepper	

☐ Preheat oven to 300°.

☐ Cut birds into quarters. Dredge lightly in flour seasoned with nutmeg, salt, and pepper to taste.

☐ In a large skillet, over medium to medium-high heat, brown the grouse in butter on all sides.

☐ Place in a shallow roasting pan. Add ¼-cup hot water to pan drippings, stirring with a flat whisk, then pour over birds. Bake, uncovered, 1 hour, basting twice. Spread sour cream over top, then bake another 2 hours.

☐ This yields a delicious gravy. Serve with WILD RICE, cooked Lida's way.

To serve 6, Lida soaks 1⅓ cups raw wild rice in cold water overnight, then rinses it well, and simmers it in 2 cups rich chicken broth, covered, for 30-45 minutes; until liquid's absorbed. She usually combines it with sautéed chopped onions and sliced mushrooms (and maybe a touch of garlic), and a good splash or 2 of sherry. And then, the secret...for about an hour before dinner, she steams it in the top of a double boiler. Gives it a wonderful texture!

Go-Betweens

potatoes, rice, hominy, and noodles

Dear Bonnie,

Well, Marvin put the sign up at the Hessel crossroad... we've opened the Stand. It looks so pretty. We have lots and lots of lettuce... leaf and red salad bowl, and that wonderful Hawaiian lettuce from the seeds that our summer friends, the Hefferans, sent us. We have kale and chard and broccoli, peas, baby carrots, spinach, and all sorts of herbs.

Those darling, little potatoes that our customers like so much will be ready soon. The beans have a little time to go, and it will be another couple of weeks for the beets.

FRESH
VEGETABLES
2½ NORTH
CHARD:RD

Of course, no tomatoes 'til the very end of this month. We think we're lucky if the corn is knee-high by the fourth of July. This year, it's waist-high! But the deer are becoming as bothersome as the coons.

What did we talk about at T-time today? The dance our neighbors, the Douds, had ever so long ago... when we were living between Trout Lake and Rudyard back in the early thirties. The music was homestyle... anyone who could play an instrument did... fiddle, drums, harmonica. We had the best bean sandwiches ever! Can't remember exactly how they were made except they were on homemade bread. They were Michigan northern white beans that had been cooked in ham or bacon, then mashed. We had such a good time!

The first beautiful hollyhocks are blooming. I took a picture of the robins taking their bath at the Stand yesterday. Maru saw the mourning dove with her two babes.

There will be raspberries like rain in a few days.

Love 'ya, Judy Chard

DARLING POTATOES
with FRESH DILL

Serves: 3-4
Prepare: 15 minutes

By mid-July, the little new potatoes that our customers call "darling," are beginning to grow up! They are still a treat just simply prepared as follows:

1 pound new potatoes, scrubbed
2-3 tablespoons sour cream
1 tablespoon chopped fresh dill

Salt and freshly ground pepper to taste
Dill flowers

□ Cut potatoes in half. Gently boil until tender; about 7-10 minutes. Drain well, then toss with remaining ingredients. Serve hot, garnished with dill flowers.

LEMON CHIVE BUTTER for NEW POTATOES

Yield: ⅓ cup
Prepare: 5 minutes

We try not to hide the wonderfully subtle, earthy taste of new potatoes...this simple sauce is all that's wanted.

¼ cup melted butter
Grated rind of 1 lemon
2 tablespoons lemon juice
1 tablespoon chopped
    chives

Pinch of nutmeg
Salt and pepper to taste

□ Combine and pour over hot, boiled potatoes...there's plenty for at least 3 pounds.

GARLIC ROASTED NEW POTATOES

Serves: 6
Prepare: 10 minutes
Roast: 1 hour

So simple and good.

2 pounds small new
    potatoes, unpeeled
2 tablespoons olive oil
½ teaspoon salt
Generous grinding of black
    pepper

3-4 garlic cloves, thinly
    sliced
3 tablespoons chopped
    parsley

□ Preheat oven to 350°.

□ Depending on size of potatoes, halve or quarter to bite-size.

□ In a shallow roasting pan, toss potatoes with oil, salt, pepper, and garlic. Roast 1 hour, or until tender and golden, tossing 2 or 3 times.

□ Toss with parsley to serve.

HOT POTATOES

Serves: 3-4
Prepare: 15 minutes

Perfect for barbecue suppers.

1 pound new potatoes
5 tablespoons olive oil
1½ tablespoons red
   wine vinegar
2 teaspoons Dijon
   mustard

¼ cup finely chopped
   sweet onion
Salt and freshly ground
   pepper to taste
Chopped parsley

☐ Thickly slice potatoes or cut into chunks. Cook in boiling, salted water until just tender; about 7-10 minutes. Drain.

☐ Combine oil, vinegar, and mustard, beating well with a whisk. Pour over hot potatoes. Add onion, season with salt and pepper to taste, and gently toss. Place in warm serving dish and garnish with chopped parsley.

SIMPLY-POTATO CASSEROLE

Serves: 6
Prepare: 10 minutes
Bake: 30-40 minutes

We like this because it's painless to fix and isn't all gussied up with fattening things like sour cream and cheeses. You can make it ahead and just let it sit until baking time.

1½ cups milk
6 tablespoons butter
2 pounds frozen, shredded
   potatoes
2 tablespoons dried minced
   onion

Salt and freshly ground
   pepper to taste
Freshly grated Parmesan
   cheese

☐ Preheat oven to 375°.

☐ In a large saucepan, bring milk and butter just to a boil, then stir in potatoes, onion, and salt and pepper to taste. Put in a buttered, 2-quart casserole, and sprinkle top with cheese.

☐ Bake, uncovered, until top is browned; about 30-40 minutes.

MEG's SCALLOPED POTATOES

Serves: 8
Prepare: 20 minutes
Bake: 1½ hours

It's hard to come up with a better scalloped potato recipe...again the gift of a summer visitor.

8 medium potatoes, unpeeled
1 small onion, thinly sliced
3 tablespoons butter
12 ounces sharp cheddar cheese, grated
¾ cup milk
½ cup chicken broth
2 tablespoons soy sauce
2 tablespoons chopped parsley
1 teaspoon garlic powder
1 teaspoon oregano
½ teaspoon thyme
½ teaspoon salt
½ teaspoon pepper
½ cup fine bread crumbs
1-2 tablespoons butter

☐ Preheat oven to 350°.

☐ Butter a 2½ to 3-quart, deep baking dish. Scrub, then thinly slice potatoes into baking dish. Layer with onion, then dot with 3 tablespoons butter, and cover with cheese.

☐ Combine remaining ingredients, except bread crumbs and butter, and pour over all. Top with bread crumbs and dot with butter. Bake, uncovered, 1½ hours.

CAMP HASH BROWNS

Serves: 6
Prepare: 15 minutes
Cook: 15 minutes

Before you start, there are several secrets to Omar Sanderson's legendary hash browns. One is that the potatoes are best if they've been boiled the day before and refrigerated overnight; and he says they have to be finely chopped...by hand...not by any fancy machine. Secondly, they must be fried in a well-seasoned, cast iron skillet. Third is the addition of bread. It's fabulous...you'll see!

Enjoy them topped with poached or fried eggs and crisp strips of bacon. It's the next best thing to a real hunting camp breakfast with the old, blue-enameled pot of coffee steaming away on the back of the wood stove.

8 cold, boiled potatoes
1 large onion
3 tablespoons bacon fat
2 slices bread, broken into
   small pieces

Salt and freshly ground
   pepper to taste

☐ Finely chop potatoes and onion. Heat bacon fat in a large, iron skillet. Add potatoes, onion, and bread pieces. Salt and pepper to taste.

☐ Cook slowly, turning often as potatoes brown.

SWEET POTATO
SPOON BREAD

Serves: 8
Prepare: 15 minutes
Bake: 1 hour

Not really a bread...more like a heavy soufflé with a delightful crunchiness...it adds a lot to a pork or ham dinner.

4-5 sweet potatoes (about
   2½ pounds)
1 orange
1 lemon
½ teaspoon each ground
   cloves, cinnamon,
   and nutmeg

½ teaspoon salt
4 eggs
½ cup milk
1 cup honey
½ cup light vegetable oil

I always leave a few lumps in my mashed potatoes. Lets persons know they're real honest-to-goodness potatoes ...not some tasteless mess from a box.

☐ Preheat oven to 325°.

☐ Scrub sweet potatoes and remove any eyes, but do not peel. Grate or finely shred (a food processor will save time and knuckles!). Place in a large mixing bowl.

☐ Grate the rinds and squeeze the juices of the orange and lemon. Add to the shredded potatoes, along with the spices and salt. Stir with a fork to blend.

☐ In a separate bowl, beat eggs, then whisk in remaining ingredients. Stir into sweet potato mixture.

☐ Pour into an oiled, shallow, 1½ to 2-quart baking dish. Bake, uncovered, 1 hour. Serve hot, warm, or cold...it's good any way!

At our camp, Windswept, on the hearth of the log cabin's fireplace, sits a three-legged, iron skillet filled with prized fossils and eye-catching stones...beachcombers' treasures gathered over the years.

The skillet had belonged to my grandmother, and maybe her grandmother before her, but only recently did I learn its purpose...for baking bread in the fireplace. It has 3-inch legs, which were to keep the pan above the coals; and once had a lid (sadly, ours is long gone), so that coals could be placed on top to aid the baking.

Thus, the name SPIDER BREAD from the pan's odd appearance. I found a recipe for it in one of my grandmother's books, and have adapted it to today's kitchen...we think it's quite delicious.

SPIDER BREAD

Serves: 6
Prepare: 10 minutes
Bake: 25 minutes

A very moist bread, it forms a custard-like base so it should be eaten with a fork. It's a wonderful substitute for rice or noodles or mashed potatoes; so try it with fricasseed or creamed chicken, or Polish Veal Cutlets, or for brunch with creamed chipped beef. It's best served right from the oven.

4 tablespoons butter	2 teaspoons baking powder
1⅔ cups yellow or white cornmeal	1 teaspoon salt
⅓ cup flour	2 eggs
1½ tablespoons sugar	2 cups milk
	1 cup milk

☐ Preheat oven to 400°.

☐ While preparing the batter, slowly melt the butter in a heavy, 11 to 12-inch skillet with an oven-proof handle. Tip the pan to coat well before adding batter.

☐ In a medium-size bowl, thoroughly combine the dry ingredients with a whisk. Beat the eggs in a larger bowl, then whisk in 2 cups of milk. Stir in the dry ingredients *just* to moisten.

☐ Immediately pour into prepared skillet, then drizzle remaining cup of milk evenly over top.

☐ Pop into oven, uncovered, and bake until firm; about 25 minutes. Serve immediately, cutting into wedges.

BAKED HOMINY
with CHEESE

Serves: 4-6
Prepare: 10 minutes
Bake: 1 hour, 20 minutes

Those of you who are tired of peeling potatoes, try this...it will become a regular in your menus. Everyone loves it!

4 tablespoons butter	2 15-ounce cans white
4 tablespoons flour	hominy, drained
2 cups light cream	⅓ cup freshly grated
2 teaspoons horseradish	Parmesan cheese
Salt and white pepper	
to taste	

☐ Preheat oven to 300°.

☐ In a medium saucepan, melt butter, then stir in flour with a whisk. Cook 1 minute, stirring, then gradually add cream. Cook until thickened, stirring constantly. Blend in horseradish, salt, and white pepper; then add hominy.

☐ Place in a buttered, 2-quart, deep casserole, and sprinkle with cheese. Bake, covered, 1 hour and 20 minutes.

BRAISED RICE and ONIONS

Serves: 4
Prepare: 10 minutes
Bake: 1 hour

Any time of the year, this goes nicely with fish or meat courses and will win lots of compliments.

2 cups water
¼ teaspoon salt
½ cup uncooked rice
4 tablespoons butter
4 cups thinly sliced onions
  (about 2 large)

½ teaspoon salt
⅛ teaspoon white pepper
¼ cup heavy cream
½ cup grated Swiss or
  Jarlsberg cheese
Chopped parsley

☐ Preheat oven to 300°. In a medium saucepan, bring 2 cups water and ¼ teaspoon salt to a boil. Stir in rice, cover, and simmer *exactly* 5 minutes. Drain immediately.

☐ Melt butter in a 2½ to 3-quart, deep casserole. Add onions and coat well. Stir in rice, salt, and white pepper. Cover and bake 1 hour, stirring once or twice.

☐ Up to this point, the dish may be made ahead of time. When ready to serve, reheat and stir in cream and cheese...and a touch more butter, if no one is looking! Check seasoning, sprinkle with parsley, and serve.

GREEN RICE

Serves: 4-6
Prepare: 10 minutes
(except rice)

We have so many nice herbs in our garden...they can turn the plainest food into something exotic.

1½ cups uncooked rice
6 green onions, finely
  chopped
4 tablespoons butter

¼ cup chopped parsley
¼ cup chopped dill
¼ cup chopped tarragon
  or chervil

☐ Cook rice according to package directions. In a medium skillet, sauté the onions in butter until soft; about 5 minutes. Stir in herbs, let cook for only a few seconds, then add rice. Serve hot.

WINTER RICE

Serves: 6
Prepare: 10 minutes
Bake: 1 hour

For wild duck and game dinners, this is a nice stand-in for wild rice. In any season, it can become a beautiful vegetable dish when surrounded with baby carrots and/or peas or green beans.

4 cups cooked rice	3 tablespoons butter
½ medium onion, finely chopped	Salt
½ pound mushrooms, coarsely chopped	

□ Preheat oven to 350°. In a medium skillet, sauté onion and mushrooms in butter until tender and liquid has been absorbed; about 7-8 minutes. Combine with rice, then salt to taste. Pack into an ungreased, 4-cup mold. Place, uncovered, in shallow pan filled with ½-inch warm water. Bake 1 hour. Unmold to serve.

■ Note: This may be made ahead. To reheat, cover mold with foil and set in hot water in 350° oven for a few minutes.

EASY SAVANNAH RED RICE

Serves: 4
Prepare: 10 minutes

I know it seems funny to put a southern recipe in a book about northern Michigan, but one of our really good summer friends, a professor from the University of Cincinnati who visits on Beavertail, gave it to me. Marv and I love it with Lake Huron Salmon Loaf and Best-Ever-Broccoli.

1½ cups instant rice	1 garlic clove, pressed
1 onion, chopped	1 6-ounce can tomato paste
1 stalk celery, chopped	Salt and freshly ground
¼ cup chopped green pepper	pepper to taste
2 tablespoons butter	4 strips bacon, fried crisp and crumbled (optional)

□ Prepare instant rice according to directions on box. In a 10-inch skillet, sauté onion, celery, and green pepper in butter until tender. Add rice and remaining ingredients. Stir and serve.

Did you know that we made the Big-Time? A writer for the Princeton, New Jersey, newspaper was visiting the Sheppards over on Marquette Island. Pat and Carl brought him by the Stand one day. His name was Michael Dorn.

He was so excited about the Les Cheneaux that when he got home, he wrote all sorts of nice things about everyone and everything, and also about all the good food we grow and eat here. He even told about making pâté out of whitefish livers. (Boy! Are they ever good!) Pat said the story got reprinted in the New York Times!

COUNTRY BAKED NOODLES

Serves: 6
Prepare: 15 minutes
Bake: 25-30 minutes

This is great with stews, pot roasts, or sauced meats like Polish Veal Cutlets, and it can be made ahead except for baking. Use only fine noodles, though; medium or wide will not work. You may question the amount of noodles, but it is correct.

4 ounces *fine* noodles
1 cup small-curd cottage cheese
1 cup sour cream
1 small onion, finely chopped
1 clove garlic, minced

1 tablespoon Worcestershire sauce
Dash or 2 of cayenne pepper
½ teaspoon salt
Freshly ground pepper to taste
Paprika

☐ Cook noodles in boiling, salted water according to package directions, until just tender. Drain. Combine with remaining ingredients except paprika.

☐ Place in a buttered, 1 to 1½-quart, deep casserole. At this point, the dish may be set aside or refrigerated until baking time.

☐ Preheat oven to 350°. Bake, uncovered, 25-30 minutes, or until thoroughly heated. Sprinkle generously with paprika and serve.

▪ Note: This recipe is easy to prepare in large quantities to feed a crowd.

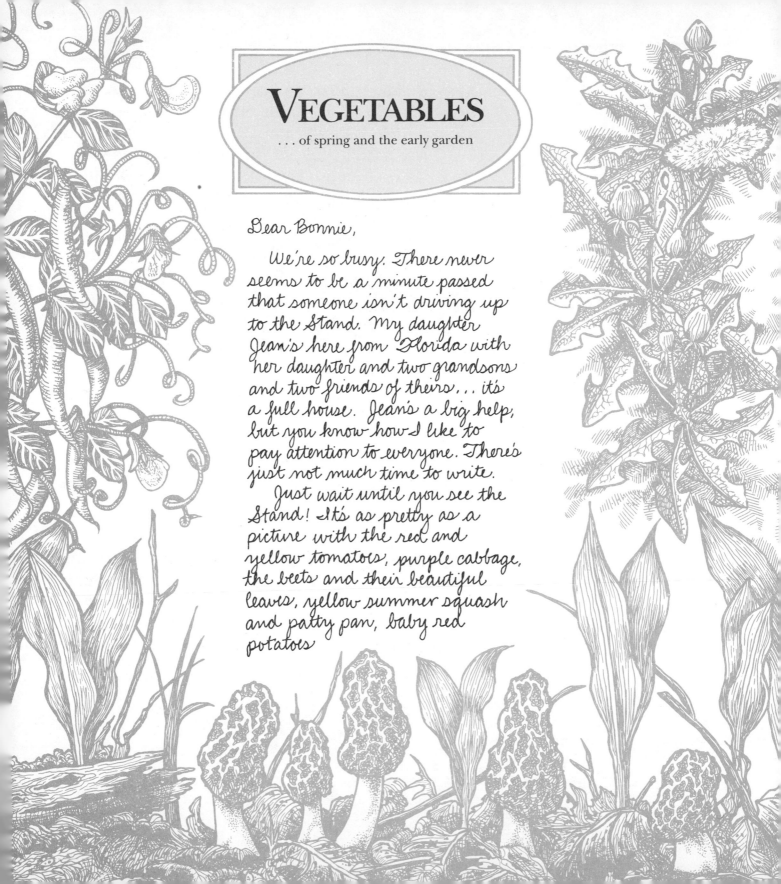

VEGETABLES

... of spring and the early garden

Dear Bonnie,

We're so busy. There never seems to be a minute passed that someone isn't driving up to the Stand. My daughter Jean's here from Florida with her daughter and two grandsons and two friends of theirs... it's a full house. Jean's a big help, but you know how I like to pay attention to everyone. There's just not much time to write.

Just wait until you see the Stand! It's as pretty as a picture with the red and yellow tomatoes, purple cabbage, the beets and their beautiful leaves, yellow summer squash and patty pan, baby red potatoes tiny zucchinis, green onions, red and green sweet peppers, cucumbers, bush beans and sugar snaps, perfect little Brussels sprouts.

Marv has his special sprinkling system set up so that it drips, ever so gently, down on the vegetables... they look as if the morning's dew is still upon them.

A new customer stopped by the other day, and she couldn't keep from talking about it... the Stand. She said that with its wishing well look and the robins nesting in the eaves, she expected little elves to come tumbling out from under. That made us feel so good.

I'm sending you a whole bunch of recipes from all of our thoughtful customers who are so generous about sharing. One of the nicest things about the Stand is the many new friends it brings to us.

Love 'ya,

Judy Chard

P.S. The blueberries are luscious this year. Jean made two out-of-this-world pies. Makes me think of the time we went berry picking at Gilcrest. You couldn't move without stepping on blueberries, let alone sit!

FIDDLEHEADS

You may see these baby ferns in markets, but they won't compare to the ones you'll find in spring woods. Pick them while they are still furled and rusty looking, and no higher than 4 inches, breaking them off with your fingers as close to the ground as possible.

Rub them between your hands to remove their rusty-brown coats. Then prepare as you would asparagus, cooking them in lightly salted water until just fork-tender.

Drain well and dress with burnt-brown butter and freshly grated Parmesan cheese, or Hollandaise.

WILD LEEKS

Also known as ramp, to many the wild leek is respected as a true delicacy, but it must bear the brunt of acerbic comment even more than its garlic cousin. The story persists that at the local grammar school in earlier years, the Indian children, who enjoyed leeks as part of their daily fare, sometimes had to be dismissed early because of the pervasive aroma.

The true leek lover will even sacrifice friendship to devour a leek. He will tell you that there is nothing more exquisite than a butter sandwich filled with raw leeks.

To cook this springtime treat, simply discard leaves and split the leeks in half lengthwise. Place in a skillet in a minimal amount of salted water. Cover tightly and cook until tender; about 15 minutes. Serve with butter and a touch of lemon juice.

DANDELION GREENS

Serves 6
Prepare: 15 minutes

Always use only the tenderest of leaves...young dandelions that have yet to blossom. If you think the greens may be too bitter, either soak them in salt water, then rinse, or drain off first cooking water and proceed with recipe.

3 quarts water
1 tablespoon salt
½ teaspoon baking soda

2 quarts dandelions (leaves, crowns, unopened buds)
Butter and vinegar

☐ Bring water to boil in a large kettle. Add salt and baking soda, then dandelions. Boil 10 minutes, then drain well. Serve hot, topped with pats of butter, and pass a cruet of vinegar.

SWEET and SOUR DANDELIONS

Serves: 6
Prepare: 15 minutes

As children, we were told we had to eat our dandelion greens because they "clear your blood" in the spring. We had no trouble eating them when they were fixed like this.

Boiled dandelion greens
   (see recipe above)*
4-6 slices bacon, slivered
1 medium onion, chopped

1 egg, slightly beaten
¼ cup brown sugar
¼ cup vinegar
¼ cup water

☐ In a skillet, fry bacon until crisp. Remove and drain on paper toweling.

☐ Sauté onion in pan drippings until tender. Combine remaining ingredients and pour over onion. Stir with a flat whisk until slightly thickened. Stir in greens. Serve topped with bacon bits.

■ Note: *If you'd like to treat this as a salad, do not pre-cook greens. Clean 1 quart of young, tender leaves, and chop. Toss in hot sauce in skillet just until wilted, then toss again with bacon bits and serve garnished with hard-cooked egg slices.

Years ago, before refrigeration, there was no more welcome sign of spring than dandelion greens. After a long winter, they would be our first fresh vegetable...cooked or in salads.

We still relish them, although we have to laugh when we see them sold in the big-city markets as a delicacy!

MORELS in a CASSEROLE

Serves: 4-6
Prepare: 10 minutes
Bake: 20 minutes

We've served this with simply prepared steaks and roasts, but we particularly like it for lunch with just a nice salad. If, sadly, you have no morels on hand, the common mushroom will certainly do.

1 pound mushrooms, halved
¼ cup butter, melted
1 tablespoon chopped chives
½ teaspoon marjoram

¼ teaspoon salt
Freshly ground pepper to taste
¼ cup dry sherry
½ cup chicken broth
Thin slices buttered toast

□ Preheat oven to 350°. Combine all but the toast in an ungreased, 1½-quart casserole. Cover and bake 20 minutes.

□ Halve or quarter enough thinly sliced, buttered toast to accommodate 4 for lunch or 6 as side servings. Place in individual ramekins or shallow bowls. To serve, ladle hot mushrooms and broth over toast points.

When is the first day of spring for the gardener? If he grows asparagus, it's probably when he spots a lavender tip poking its way through the desolate soil of winter's end.

During its season, we harvest daily, cutting only those that measure the width of one's first finger.

PARMESAN ASPARAGUS

Serves: 4
Prepare: 10 minutes

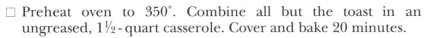

Asparagus is special just cooked tender-crisp then dressed with browned or lemony butter. Here's my cooking method plus a nice finishing touch.

1½ pounds fresh asparagus
Salt to taste

Butter
3-4 tablespoons freshly grated Parmesan cheese

□ Snap off stems of asparagus where *they* want to snap, to leave you the tenderest part. Bring 1 inch of water to boil in a 10 to 12-inch skillet. Add asparagus and salt to taste. Partially cover to return to a boil, then uncover and cook until *just* fork-tender; about 2-3 minutes. Drain immediately, and toss with butter.

□ If preparing ahead, layer asparagus in a baking dish; top with cheese and dots of butter. When ready to serve, run under broiler just until cheese begins to melt.

PEAS with MINT

Serves: 3-4
Prepare: 5 minutes

The simpler the better.

1½ cups peas or Sugar
   Snaps
2 tablespoons butter
1-2 tablespoons chopped
   mint leaves

1 teaspoon lemon or
   lime juice
Pinch or 2 of sugar
Salt and pepper to taste

☐ Cook peas in a small amount of lightly salted water until barely tender; about 3-4 minutes (1-2 minutes for Sugar Snaps). Drain, then toss with remaining ingredients.

NEW PEAS and TINY POTATOES

Serves: 4
Prepare: 20 minutes

We think this is such a pretty way to show off spring vegetables. You are wondering about the canned milk? You'll be pleasantly surprised by how you'll still have a tasty dish without the richness of cream.

4 strips bacon, diced
1¼ pounds tiny, new
   potatoes
2 young carrots, diced
   (just enough for a
   touch of color)

1¼ cups shelled peas*
1 5-ounce can evaporated
   milk
2 teaspoons cornstarch
Salt and freshly ground
   pepper to taste

☐ Fry bacon until crisp. Drain on paper towels. Boil potatoes in their jackets in salted water, until just fork-tender. Drain and keep warm.

☐ Place carrots in a saucepan with ¼-cup water (see note), then top with peas and lightly salt. Cover tightly and steam until peas are barely tender, about 3-4 minutes. Do not drain.

☐ Stir in canned milk and cornstarch. Heat just until milk is thickened, gently stirring. Pour over hot potatoes. Salt and pepper to taste, then top with crisp bacon bits.

■ Note: *If substituting frozen peas, cook diced carrots first, for 2 minutes, then add peas, milk, and cornstarch. Cover and bring to a simmer. Uncover, and stir until sauce is smooth.

PURÉE of PEAS

Serves: 8
Prepare: 15 minutes

The color and flavor are glorious, and it's so pretty paired with other vegetables.

3 10-ounce packages frozen peas (3 pounds fresh)	½ teaspoon dried thyme
	Salt and freshly ground pepper to taste
1 small carrot, quartered	4 tablespoons butter
2 green onions, chopped	¼ cup heavy cream
½ cup water	

☐ Place peas, carrot, green onions, water, and seasonings in a large saucepan. Cover and cook until tender. Drain, discarding carrot.

☐ Purée in several batches in an electric blender or food processor (a blender will give you a smoother purée). Add butter (cut up) and cream. Process again. Check seasoning.

☐ Reheat in a microwave, or place in a buttered baking dish set in a pan of warm water and bake, uncovered, at 300° for 20-30 minutes.

☐ *To pair with other vegetables:* Cut steamed crookneck or patty pan squashes in half, scoop out pulp, and fill with purée, garnishing with chopped chives or herbs...

...*or,* pour a little of the purée into a warmed, shallow serving bowl, set a head of steamed cauliflower in bowl, then pour rest of purée over, leaving portions of cauliflower peeking through...

...*or,* pour purée over chopped, canned salsify in a buttered baking dish, set in a pan of warm water and bake, uncovered, at 300° for 20-30 minutes.

SWISS CHARD ITALIAN-STYLE

Serves: 4
Prepare: 15 minutes
Cook: 20-25 minutes

The perfect vegetable dish to go with fish or grilled steaks.

2 cloves garlic, split	¼ cup freshly grated Parmesan cheese
2 tablespoons olive oil	Salt to taste
4 pear tomatoes, peeled and quartered	
1 bunch (1 pound) Swiss chard	

☐ In a large saucepan, sauté garlic in oil over medium heat for a minute or so, but do not allow to brown. Add tomatoes, lower heat, and simmer 15 minutes, uncovered, stirring periodically.

☐ Wash chard but do not dry. Cut stems into 1-inch pieces, and the leaves into 2 to 3-inch sections.

☐ After the tomato mixture has cooked 15 minutes, add chard stems. Cover and cook 5 more minutes, then add leaves. Cover and simmer 15-20 minutes. Salt to taste.

SESAME SPINACH

Serves: 4
Prepare: 10 minutes

When you want a different accent for a fish or chicken menu.

2 pounds fresh spinach	1 tablespoon soy sauce
3 tablespoons sesame seeds	Salt and freshly ground pepper to taste
3 tablespoons butter	

☐ Wash and remove tough stems from spinach. Tear leaves into bite-size pieces. Cook, covered, in only the water that clings to its leaves, for 2-3 minutes; *just* until soft. Drain well.

☐ In a small skillet over low heat, lightly brown sesame seeds in butter. Stir in soy sauce. Add to spinach with salt and pepper to taste. Turn into serving dish.

Spinach straight from the garden makes it well-worth the drudgery of washing each leaf. To keep in the refrigerator, wrap in paper or cloth towels after washing and store in a plastic bag. It will stay nice for several days. Then give it a quick rinse and cook it in only the water that clings to its leaves...so briefly that it barely knows it's been in the pot!

FRESH SPINACH
with RED ONIONS

Serves: 6
Prepare: 15 minutes

Great color, great combination.

2 pounds fresh spinach
2 red onions, thinly sliced
2 tablespoons olive oil

2 teaspoons fresh lemon juice
Salt and freshly ground
   pepper to taste

☐ Wash and dry spinach, removing stems.

☐ In a large skillet, sauté onions in oil over medium heat just until limp. Add spinach and cook, stirring, until just wilted. Remove from heat.

☐ Add lemon juice, and salt and pepper to taste. Toss and serve immediately.

I've got a surprise for you! Did you know that cooking nettles removes the sting and they become a delicacy? Pick only the new, young shoots (wearing gloves, of course!), and cook them in chicken broth with a little chopped bacon for about 10-15 minutes...puts spinach to shame.

COLLARDS with
BACON BITS

Serves: 4
Prepare: 15 minutes

A delicious way to prepare this under-appreciated vegetable...and you can use the same method for kale.*

2 bunches collards (about
   1½ pounds)
6 slices bacon, slivered
1 tablespoon bacon fat

1-2 tablespoons butter
Salt (optional)
Sour cream

☐ Wash collards and remove tough portion of stems. Finely shred with a knife.

☐ In a large skillet, sauté bacon until crisp. Drain on paper toweling. Reserve 1 tablespoon bacon fat in pan and add butter. Melt over low heat, then stir in greens. Gently sauté, stirring periodically, for 10 minutes or until tender but still bright green.

☐ Salt to taste, if necessary. Toss with bacon, and serve with sour cream as a garnish.

▪ Note: *When preparing kale, use only the leaves.

KALE in a CASSEROLE

Serves: 6
Prepare: 10 minutes
Bake: 30 minutes

We can have two feet of snow mounding the garden, and still see the bright-green, curly leaves of kale peeking through. That's actually when it's at its best...after Jack Frost has come.

Not only does kale make one of the greatest soups you can eat (see index), but it is wonderful just chopped and sautéed for 2 to 3 minutes in a little oil and butter with a touch of minced garlic.

Here's a recipe that can be made ahead, except for baking, and is perfect with hearty meat or game dishes.

1½ pounds kale, chopped or shredded
1 onion, finely chopped
3 tablespoons butter
⅓ cup soft bread crumbs
1 cup light cream

½ cup chopped pecans
½ teaspoon nutmeg
Salt to taste
2 tablespoons butter
¼ cup soft bread crumbs

☐ Wash kale and trim completely free of stems. In a large pot of boiling, salted water, cook kale for 4 to 5 minutes, or until barely tender. Drain well, then shred with a large knife or chop in a food processor.

☐ In a small skillet, sauté onion in 3 tablespoons butter until soft. Combine with kale, ⅓-cup bread crumbs, cream, pecans, nutmeg, and salt. Turn into a buttered, 1½-quart, deep baking dish.

☐ In same skillet, melt remaining 2 tablespoons butter and stir in ¼-cup bread crumbs. Sprinkle over top of kale mixture. At this point, the dish may be covered and set aside.

☐ Bake, uncovered, at 350° for 30 minutes.

VEGETABLES

. . . from mid-summer's garden

Dear Bonnie,

The sweet corn is in now...
our best seller. We have both
yellow and white. If Marv isn't
on his tractor, hauling crates of
it to the Stand, he's out in the
field picking it. Word sure got
around fast that it's sweeter than
ever.

Been busy making thimbleberry
jam. It's the prettiest red one can
imagine, and tastes that good,
too. Like morels, everyone here
has her secret spot for picking.

We still have time for T-time,
though. Today we talked about
the beautiful drive we made
along the northern shore of Lake
Superior to Wawa, Ontario, in

PLEASE
BLOW YOUR
HORN
OR COME TO
THE DOOR
THANKS.

1951 with Great-Great-Grandpa Chard and our teenage great-grandsons! Yes... a five generation span! Did you know that Wawa means "wild goose" in Ojibway? Thousands of geese rest there on Lake Wawa during migration.

Then about Marv Jr. graduating from high school the same time as his sister Ruth's daughter! How proud we were of him... he got a scholarship to Lake Superior State College (now a university).

It's getting close to Labor Day... Did you ever do that annual hike across the Mackinac Bridge? Well, I did! My granddaughter, Linda, went with me. It was great fun. Which makes me think... we have enough zucchini to stretch across the Bridge and back again, and then some.

Last night we took time out to go to Search Bay with Ruth and her husband, Roy, in their camper. The Indian pipes were up in the woods, and the daisies, Indian paintbrush, and fringed gentians were all along the beach... made me think of you. Your mother told me that she calls your birthday "Gentian Day", since that's when one first sees them... so, Happy Gentian Day!

Your friend,

Julia Chard

FRIED CARROTS

Serves: 4
Prepare: 10 minutes

Garlic lovers will now eat their carrots!

¼ cup butter
8 medium carrots, sliced

2-3 cloves garlic, crushed

☐ Over medium-high heat, melt butter in a heavy skillet, then add carrots and garlic. Stir constantly for 3 minutes. Reduce heat to medium, and sauté carrots, stirring occasionally, until tender and browned but not burnt. Pour off excess butter.

Must check the garden to see what's been left in the ground all winter. Carrots are so sweet and crisp when they've been forgotten in the fall.

HONEYED CARROTS

Serves: 3-4
Prepare: 15 minutes

These work well in a menu that needs a sweet touch.

½ to ¾-pound carrots, sliced
2 tablespoons butter
2 tablespoons honey
2 teaspoons finely chopped mint (¼ teaspoon dried)

1 teaspoon Dijon mustard
Grating of nutmeg
Salt to taste
2 tablespoons coarsely chopped toasted almonds (optional)

☐ Cook carrots in boiling, salted water until just tender; about 7 to 10 minutes. Drain.

☐ Combine remaining ingredients, except almonds, and heat. Stir into carrots along with chopped almonds.

TANGERINE CARROTS

Serves: 3-4
Prepare: 20 minutes

Tangerines give a special flavor to this for Thanksgiving and Christmas dinners. But when they are not in season, oranges will certainly do. This can be made ahead, and freezes nicely.

1 pound carrots	1 cup tangerine juice
4 teaspoons sugar	Grated rind of 1 tangerine
2 teaspoons cornstarch	Salt and white pepper to taste

☐ Peel and slice carrots, in any pretty way you wish, from ⅛ to ¼-inch thick. Cook, covered, in boiling salted water until just tender; about 7-10 minutes. Drain.

☐ Meanwhile, combine sugar, cornstarch, juice, and rind in a small saucepan. Over medium heat, cook, stirring with a whisk, until mixture thickens and bubbles. Add to carrots. Salt and pepper to taste.

GUESS-AGAIN CARROTS

Serves: 4-6
Prepare: 15 minutes
Bake: 40 minutes

One sure way to please everyone and to keep them guessing as to why this is so good!

1½-2 pounds carrots, cooked	6-8 ounces sharp cheddar cheese
2 tablespoons butter	½ teaspoon salt
1 small onion, grated	Freshly ground pepper to taste
½ green pepper, finely chopped (optional)	Buttered fresh bread crumbs (see index)

☐ Preheat oven to 350°.

☐ Mash carrots with butter, then combine with remaining ingredients except bread crumbs. Place in a buttered, deep, 1-quart casserole and top with crumbs. Bake 40 minutes, or until bubbling.

SWISS CARROT CASSEROLE

Serves: 6-8
Prepare: 20 minutes
Bake: 25 minutes

A really good, make-ahead dish...perfect for potlucks and buffets.

12 carrots
¼ cup butter
2 tablespoons minced onion
¼ cup flour
1 teaspoon salt
¼ teaspoon celery salt
½ teaspoon dry mustard (or 2 tablespoons yellow)
Freshly ground pepper to taste
2 cups milk
½ pound thinly sliced or shredded Swiss or Jarlsberg cheese
Buttered fresh bread crumbs*

☐ Preheat oven to 350˚.

☐ Slice and cook carrots in lightly salted water until just tender. Drain.

☐ In a medium saucepan, melt butter and sauté onion until soft. Stir in flour with a whisk. Cook 1 minute. Whisk in seasonings and milk, cooking until thickened.

☐ In a buttered, shallow, casserole, place half of carrots, all of cheese, then rest of carrots. Pour sauce over all and sprinkle with crumbs. Bake 25 minutes.

*(See index, under Bread Crumbs, for a helpful hint.)

ROMAINE and BROCCOLI

Serves: 4
Prepare: 15 minutes

Nowadays, broccoli is a winner in vegetable popularity. No longer does one have to disguise it with rich sauces or whatever. Here's a dish that's crisp and green and very up-front!

1 small head romaine
   lettuce
1 large head broccoli
2 slices bacon, slivered

¼ cup hot water
½ teaspoon sugar
½ teaspoon salt

☐ Wash and dry romaine. Tear into bite-size pieces. Cut florets from broccoli; discard stem (or save for a good soup).

☐ In a 12-inch skillet, over medium-high heat, fry bacon until crisp. Add broccoli, stirring and tossing it in the hot bacon drippings until it turns a bright green. Add ¼-cup hot water. Cover and simmer over medium to medium-low heat for 4 minutes.

☐ Add romaine, sugar, and salt. Cook, stirring constantly, 2-3 more minutes, or until romaine is tender-crisp. It must not lose its color. Serve immediately.

BEST-EVER BROCCOLI

Serves: (per person)
Prepare: 10 minutes
Broil: 2 minutes

As with asparagus, the simplest ways are the best, and this is one. Also, it may be prepared in advance except for broiling.

Fresh broccoli, cut up
1-2 teaspoons butter
Dash of garlic powder
   or salt

2 teaspoons freshly grated
   Parmesan cheese

☐ Steam desired amount of broccoli until just tender, then drain well. Place in a shallow baking dish. Dot generously with butter and sprinkle with garlic powder or salt, then cheese.

☐ You may set aside until just before serving time, then run under pre-heated broiler for a minute or two, about 6 inches from element.

BROCCOLI
with TOMATOES

Serves: 4
Prepare: 15 minutes

A nice combination, and the colors are great!

1½ pounds broccoli
2-3 tablespoons butter
1 large tomato, coarsely chopped
2 tablespoons chopped chives

Salt to taste
3 tablespoons freshly grated Parmesan cheese

☐ Cut florets from broccoli (see note regarding stems), and steam in ¼-cup salted water until just tender-crisp. Drain.

☐ Melt butter in a 10-inch skillet. Add tomato, stir for a minute, then broccoli and chives. Stir and toss for another minute or so to heat through. Salt to taste, sprinkle with cheese, and serve.

■ Note: Broccoli stems make a nice dish when thinly sliced, steamed until tender, and served with lemon and butter.

Just wait until you see the stand! It's as pretty as a picture with the red and yellow tomatoes, purple cabbage, the beets and their beautiful leaves, yellow summer squash and patty pan, baby red potatoes, tiny zucchinis, green onions, red and green sweet peppers, cucumbers, bush beans and Sugar Snaps, perfect little Brussels sprouts...

BROCCOLI FLORETS
and CHERRY TOMATOES

Serves: 4
Prepare: 10 minutes
Cook: 1-2 minutes

Another painless way to serve this beautiful pair of vegetables. Cook the broccoli ahead, if you wish.

1½ pounds broccoli
1-2 tablespoons butter
12 cherry tomatoes, cut in half
Juice of ½ lemon

1 fresh basil leaf, chopped (¼ teaspoon dried)
Salt and freshly ground pepper to taste

☐ Cut florets from broccoli to bite-size (reserve stalks for Buttermilk Broccoli Soup!). Cook in ¼-cup water until tender-crisp. Immediately rinse under cold water to maintain color; drain.

☐ Just before serving, melt butter in a 10-inch skillet over medium-high heat. When bubbling, add florets and cherry tomatoes. Toss only until heated through. Sprinkle with lemon juice, basil, salt and pepper. Gently toss once more; serve immediately.

BARBECUE-FLAVORED
BAKED ONIONS

Serves: 4
Prepare: 15 minutes
Bake: 30 minutes

A make-a-header that you'll love to serve with grilled steaks or hamburgers.

12 small, white onions
  (1½-inch)
¼ cup catsup
1 tablespoon brown sugar
2 tablespoons water
1 teaspoon cider vinegar

¼ teaspoon salt
Freshly ground pepper
  to taste
4 slices bacon, chopped
  and fried crisp

☐ Preheat oven to 375°.

☐ Boil onions in lightly salted water to cover for 4-5 minutes. Drain, and place in a buttered, shallow, 1½-quart baking dish. Combine remaining ingredients and pour over onions. At this point, the dish may be set aside.

☐ Bake, uncovered, until onions are tender; about 30 minutes.

SCALLOPED ONIONS

Serves: 6
Prepare: 30 minutes
Bake: 30 minutes

This is kind of a first cousin to cheese fondue. You can treat it as a supper dish or as a vegetable casserole to serve with meats.

6 large onions, sliced
¼ cup butter
¼ cup flour
½ teaspoon salt
¼ teaspoon pepper
2 cups milk
1 teaspoon Worcestershire
  sauce

1½ cups shredded Swiss
  cheese (6 ounces)
6 slices day-old French
  bread
Butter, softened
Paprika

☐ Preheat oven to 350°. Butter a shallow, 1½ to 2-quart baking dish.

☐ Place sliced onions in a large skillet with a cup or so of water, plus salt to taste. Tightly cover. Bring to a boil, reduce heat, and simmer until just tender; about 10-12 minutes. Drain well.

☐ Melt butter in a medium-size saucepan. With a whisk, blend in flour, salt, and pepper. Cook 1 minute, stirring constantly. Whisk in milk and Worcestershire sauce. Continuing to stir, simmer until sauce thickens and bubbles. Stir in cheese until melted. Remove from heat.

☐ Generously butter both sides of bread slices, then cut into large cubes.

☐ Combine well-drained onions and cheese sauce, and place in buttered baking dish. Sprinkle with paprika for color. Arrange bread cubes around edge of casserole. Bake 30 minutes, or until bread cubes are golden.

GRILLED RED ONIONS

Serves: 6 as side dish
12 as garnish
Prepare: 5 minutes
Marinate: 1 hour
Grill/Broil: 10-15 minutes

The men in the family love these with grilled steaks or fish. The onions stay nicely tender-crisp but become sweeter, and the slightly burnt edges add something.

6 medium red onions	1½ tablespoons chopped
¾ cup vegetable oil	fresh thyme
	(2 teaspoons dried)

☐ Peel, then cut onions in half *lengthwise*...yes, for they will hold together better.

☐ In a shallow dish, marinate onions in oil and thyme for at least 1 hour, turning once or twice to coat.

☐ Place directly on grill, cut-side down, over medium coals. Grill 10 minutes. Or broil in an oven, cut-side up on a sheet of foil, 4-6 inches from element, for 10-15 minutes.

FANTASTIC FRIED ONION RINGS

Serves: 4-6
Stand: 2-3 hours
Prepare: 10 minutes

They really are fantastic...the batter stays on the onion and is as light as light can be. They can be made even a day ahead, then reheated in a 400° oven for 4 to 5 minutes.

1½ cups flour
1½ cups beer (flat or
    freshly opened)

3 large onions
4 cups light cooking oil
Salt

☐ Place flour in a large bowl, then gradually blend in beer with a wooden spoon. Cover and let stand at room temperature for 2-3 hours.

☐ Slice onions ¼-inch thick, then separate into rings. Heat oil in a deep-fryer or large skillet until hot.

☐ Use a fork to coat onion rings in batter and place in hot oil. If using a skillet, be sure to loosen rings from bottom of pan as they cook. Fry until golden brown and crisp, then drain on paper towels. Salt to taste just before serving.

▪ Note: To keep warm until serving, place on heavy brown paper in a 200° oven.

TOMATO and CARROT CASSEROLE

Serves: 6
Prepare: 15 minutes
Bake: 30 minutes

Naturally, garden tomatoes are the best for this pretty dish. Make it ahead of time, if you wish.

2 onions, thinly sliced
½ cup chopped celery
   (optional)
3 tablespoons butter
1 cup very thinly sliced
   carrots (or shredded)
1 teaspoon salt
Freshly ground pepper
   to taste

3-4 large tomatoes,
   peeled*
2 cups shredded Cheddar
   cheese
½ cup buttered fresh
   bread crumbs

☐ Preheat oven to 350°. Butter a 1½-quart casserole.

☐ In a large skillet, gently sauté onions and celery in butter just until soft. Add carrots, sliced paper-thin, and salt and pepper. Cover and steam 2 to 3 minutes. Spoon into casserole.

☐ Slice tomatoes and place over carrot/onion mixture. Sprinkle with cheese, then buttered crumbs. Bake 30 minutes.

■ Note: *To skin tomatoes easily, place in boiling water for 10-15 seconds.

BAKED TOMATOES in CREAM

Serves: 6-8
Prepare: 10 minutes
Bake: 20 minutes

One may groan about having to fool with sauce dishes, but the sauce is what makes this one of the nicest and most delicious ways I know to serve garden-ripe tomatoes.

6-8 good-size tomatoes	2 cups heavy cream
Sugar	2-3 tablespoons chopped
6-8 pats of butter	chives
Salt	1-1½ teaspoons salt

□ Peel tomatoes by immersing in boiling water for 10 seconds or so to loosen skins. Cut out a cone-shaped piece, about 1-inch long, from each stem-end. Place the tomatoes in a shallow, glass baking dish.

□ Fill their hollows with sugar. Top each with a pat of butter, then sprinkle with salt. Fill baking dish with ¼-inch warm water.

□ Bake at 350° for 20 minutes, or until tomatoes are tender. Do not bake too long, or they will lose their shape.

□ In the meantime, combine the cream, chives, and salt in a saucepan. Heat but do not allow to boil.

□ To serve, place the tomatoes in individual sauce dishes. Spoon equal amounts of tomato broth and hot cream mixture over tomatoes. Taste sauce for balance of flavors before serving; sometimes you may wish to add more of the sweet broth or more of the salty cream.

■ Note: This recipe may be made ahead except for baking the tomatoes and warming the sauce.

FANCY TOMATO PIE

Serves: 4-6
Prepare: 30 minutes
Bake: 35 minutes
Cool: 15 minutes

When the ladies come for lunch.

1 9-inch pie crust,
   unbaked (see index)
1 cup finely chopped onion
2 tablespoons butter
2 medium tomatoes,
   peeled and chopped
⅛ teaspoon thyme
Dash of salt
3 eggs, beaten

1 cup milk
½ teaspoon salt
½ cup freshly grated
   Parmesan cheese
1 cup grated Swiss or
   Jarlsberg cheese
2 medium tomatoes, peeled
   and sliced

☐ Partially bake pie crust at 400° for 7 minutes. Cool.

☐ In a medium saucepan, sauté onion in butter until soft. Add tomatoes, thyme, and a dash of salt. Cover and simmer 5 minutes.

☐ Uncover pan and mash tomatoes. Cook briskly, uncovered, over medium heat until all liquid has evaporated. Depending on the tomatoes, this will take from 10-20 minutes. Cool.

☐ Reduce oven temperature to 350°.

☐ Whisk together eggs, milk, and ½ teaspoon salt. Stir in grated cheeses and cooled tomato mixture. Pour into prepared pie crust. Bake 35 minutes or until center of pie is firm to touch. Cool on a rack for 15 minutes, then garnish top with sliced tomatoes.

☐ Serve with a pretty, mixed-greens salad, lightly dressed.

COUNTRY TOMATO PIE

Serves 4-6
Prepare: 15 minutes
Bake: 30 minutes

This is very good served with sausages for a brunch or as a simple supper dish with a pretty green salad.

2-3 large tomatoes	Salt and freshly ground
1 9-inch, deep-dish pie shell, baked (see index)	pepper to taste
	¾ -1 cup mayonnaise
3 green onions, thinly sliced	1 cup grated sharp cheddar cheese
1 tablespoon chopped fresh basil (1 teaspoon dried)	

☐ Preheat oven to 350°. Peel tomatoes by dipping in boiling water for 10 seconds or so, to split skins.

☐ Thickly slice tomatoes, then layer in baked and cooled pie shell, sprinkling each layer with green onions, basil, and salt and pepper to taste. Combine mayonnaise and cheese, and spread over tomatoes. Bake 30 minutes.

SCALLOPED TOMATOES

Serves: 6
Prepare: 5 minutes
Bake: 15-20 minutes

Popular for lots of good reasons...easy, full of flavor, can be made ahead, and adds great color to a menu.

4 cups canned tomatoes, undrained	¼ cup sugar
	1 teaspoon salt
4 tablespoons butter	Freshly ground pepper to taste
4 cups medium-coarse, fresh bread crumbs	Ground allspice

☐ Preheat oven to 400°. Butter a 1½ quart, shallow baking dish.

☐ Place undrained tomatoes in a medium saucepan, breaking up or mashing if necessary. Add butter. Heat only until butter is melted. Stir in bread crumbs, sugar, salt and pepper. Spoon into baking dish, and sprinkle lightly with allspice. Bake, uncovered, 15-20 minutes, or until just set and lightly browned.

VEGETABLES

... at the peak of the garden

Dear Bonnie,

The Stand will soon be closed. That means all our summer friends will be gone... I'll miss them a lot. They are such interesting, intelligent, and friendly people. Many stay in touch through the winter. Did I tell you about the time I was in the hospital in Florida and received over 150 get-well cards? A table was brought into my room to put the flowers on. Friends, friends, friends,... how fortunate we are.

There's still lots and lots of corn, in spite of the raccoons. Genevieve Taylor just bought

20 dozen ears for the big corn roast they're giving for their neighbors and friends. She said they're having nothing but hot dogs and "Mrs. Chard's corn"... all you can eat!

The winter squashes seem earlier this year. There's acorn, butternut, spaghetti, and, of course, the pumpkins in the corn field.

We have turnips, parsnips, and rutabagas... good winter keepers. The grape arbor is loaded, and Marv just brought in a peck of plums. Guess it's time to make some pies. I'll send two over to Elaine and Marv Jr. across the road... he says he lives for grape pie.

Mrs. Patrick's son-in-law brought us 1½ bushels of apples from Ohio. I'll have to do those up. He gave me the best recipe for apple butter. I'm sending it along to you.

It's a beautiful day today.

> Love ya all,
> Judy Chard

CRISP GREEN BEANS

More and more cooks are preparing green beans so that they seem to have just been plucked from the vine. We love them this way...not just because they are so fresh to the taste, but, properly chilled, they can be made ahead for beautiful salads and casseroles.

Try this method for Green Bean and Tomato Casserole and Smoked Whitefish Salad, or create a green bean salad, using Pesto as its dressing. The Chards' good friend and customer, Jack Daugherty, writes it up this way:

"Here's a different way to cook this vegetable...it renders a barely cooked bean that virtually squeaks when bitten into.

"Bring lightly salted water to a rapid boil in a large pan. Snap off ends of beans (unless stringless), but leave whole, and drop into water.

"After 5 minutes, test a bean by first running under cold water then biting into it. It should be crunchy-tender and still a bright green. If it's necessary to cook longer, do so for only a minute or two.

"When done, *immediately* drain and run under very cold water, or place in an ice cube bath, until completely chilled through."

■ Notes: Store the processed beans in plastic bags in the refrigerator.

To serve as a hot dish, toss with butter and a touch of herbs in a skillet over medium-high heat until just heated through. Season to taste.

GREEN BEAN and
TOMATO CASSEROLE

Serves: 6-8
Prepare: 15 minutes
Bake: 15-20 minutes

A make-ahead casserole of good things from the garden, and it stays fresh in looks and flavor.

3 slices bacon, slivered
6 green onions, chopped
3-4 cups fresh green and/
    or wax beans, cooked
    (see index)
½ cup grated sharp
    cheddar cheese

¼ cup sour cream
¼ cup mayonnaise
Salt and freshly ground
    pepper to taste
2 fresh, unpeeled tomatoes,
    quartered

□ Sauté bacon until barely crisp. Pour off all but 1 tablespoon fat, then add green onions. Sauté until onions are soft; about 2 minutes.

□ Combine with remaining ingredients except tomatoes. Place in a lightly buttered, 2½-quart casserole. Cover with quartered tomatoes.

□ Casserole should be at room temperature before baking. Fifteen to 20 minutes before serving time, bake, covered, at 325° until heated through.

GREEN BEANS and TURNIPS

Serves: 3-4
Prepare: 15 minutes

Green beans can work their way into almost any menu, but they can also tend to get boring. Surprise yourself and your fussy eaters with this unusual duo (and it can be made ahead).

1 medium turnip
¾ pound fresh green
    beans
1 tablespoon butter

Grating of nutmeg
Salt and freshly ground
    pepper to taste

□ Peel and cut up turnip to resemble matchsticks. Cook, covered, in lightly salted, boiling water to cover until crisp-tender; about 8-10 minutes. Drain immediately.

☐ Trim and cut beans into ½-inch lengths. Drop into boiling, salted water, and cook until *just* tender; about 7-8 minutes. Immediately drain and run under cold water to stop cooking process.

☐ When ready to serve, melt butter in a pan or skillet. Toss vegetables in butter until heated through. Season with a good grating of nutmeg, and salt and pepper.

FARMERS' MARKET CASEROLE

Serves: 6
Prepare: 15 minutes
Bake: 1¼ hours

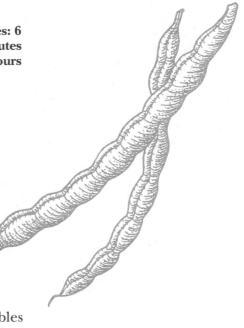

A wonderful way to take advantage of the garden.

2 large potatoes, thinly sliced
1 large onion, thinly sliced
2 medium zucchini, cut in small chunks
4 tomatoes, cut in small chunks
2 carrots, thinly sliced
Thyme and marjoram to taste

Salt and freshly ground pepper to taste
¾ cup dry white wine
2-3 tablespoons butter
1 cup small, fresh bread cubes.
2 cups grated sharp cheddar cheese

☐ Preheat oven to 375°.

☐ In an ungreased, shallow, 8x11-inch casserole, layer vegetables in order given, seasoning each layer with sprinklings of thyme and marjoram and salt and pepper to taste.

☐ Pour wine over all. Cover and bake 1 hour.

☐ Melt butter in a small skillet, then stir in bread cubes until they've absorbed butter. Sprinkle cheese over casserole, then buttered bread cubes. Bake, uncovered, another 15-20 minutes.

■ Note: The casserole may be prepared a couple hours ahead, except for last 15 to 20 minutes of baking, keeping at room temperature in the interim.

FRESH VEGETABLE POT

Serves: 4
Prepare: 10 minutes
Cook: 15 minutes

Vegetables should always look like this...as if they've barely left the garden. This method can be used to serve a crowd...just find a bigger pot and give it a little more time, yet be sure not to overcook.

3-4 young carrots, cut in thirds
1 yellow turnip (rutabaga), cut in large cubes (optional)
½ small head cauliflower, cut into florets
¼ small head of cabbage, cut in wedges

6 small, white onions (not pearl), cut in half
3 cloves garlic, split
1 cup green peas*
Salt and freshly ground pepper

☐ In a large, heavy saucepan, layer vegetables (except peas, if they have been frozen) in order given, seasoning each layer with salt and freshly ground pepper to taste.

☐ Add 1-inch of water, cover tightly, bring to a boil, and simmer over medium to medium-low heat until vegetables are just tender; about 15 minutes.

☐ *If using frozen peas, thaw and sprinkle over top of vegetables a minute or so before cooking is finished, just to heat through.

■ Note: New red-skinned potatoes and florets of broccoli can be substituted for the yellow turnip and peas.

SUMMER SQUASH CASSEROLE

Serves: 6
Prepare: 15 minutes
Bake: 30 minutes

One of our nice customers gave this recipe to us, along with a can of green chilies...since that's just about the only thing we don't grow in our garden!

We're crazy about it...even the chilies! It makes a good, main supper dish served with Cherry Tomato Salad.

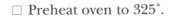

2 pounds yellow summer squash (or zucchini)
Salt to taste
4 eggs
½ cup milk
½ cup chopped parsley
3 tablespoons flour
2 teaspoons baking powder
1 teaspoon salt

1 4-ounce can diced green chilies
8 ounces ricotta or small-curd cottage cheese
8 ounces sharp cheddar cheese, grated
3 cups small, fresh bread cubes
3-4 tablespoons butter

☐ Preheat oven to 325°.

☐ Cube or slice squash. Place in a medium-size saucepan or skillet with no more than a ½-cup water and salt to taste. Cover and cook until barely tender; about 3 minutes. Drain well, then set aside to cool.

☐ Beat eggs in a medium-size bowl. Mix in remaining ingredients, except bread and cheese, in order given. Add cooked squash.

☐ Butter an 8x11-inch, shallow baking dish. Sprinkle bottom with ½ of bread cubes. Pour in squash mixture. Top with rest of bread then dot with 3-4 tablespoons butter. Bake, uncovered, for 30 minutes.

ZUCCHINI PUFF

Serves: 4-6
Prepare: 15 minutes
Bake: 45 minutes

This can make zucchini almost elegant!

6 tablespoons butter
1 clove garlic, split
2 pounds zucchini
   (4 medium)
2 eggs, beaten

Salt and freshly ground
   pepper to taste
2 tablespoons grated
   Parmesan cheese

☐ Preheat oven to 375°.

☐ Slowly melt butter, adding split garlic. Let stand while preparing zucchini, in order to develop flavor.

☐ Cube unpeeled zucchini. Cook until tender in just enough lightly salted water to cover. Thoroughly drain in a colander.

☐ Mash zucchini. Beat eggs and add to zucchini. Remove garlic halves from butter, discarding; then mix butter into zucchini along with salt and pepper to taste. Pour into a buttered, 1½-quart, deep casserole. Sprinkle with cheese. Bake 45 minutes.

This summer, we have enough zucchini to stretch across the Mackinac Bridge and back again...makes me think of the times I did the Labor Day hike across it. When I was 60, I went with my granddaughter, Linda Nye, who was 12...broke my own record... 5 miles in 65 minutes! They gave me a beautiful certificate.

That's a real privilege to walk the most beautiful bridge in the whole world, high above the Straits; the great blue waters of Lake Michigan on one side of you and Lake Huron on the other.

ZUCCHINI in DILL CREAM

Serves: 3-4
Prepare: 10 minutes

Every cook seems to try to find another way to deal with the prolific zucchini, thus often there can be 101 versions of one dish. This may be the 102nd, but you'll like its simplicity and balance.

1 small onion, minced
2 tablespoons butter
3 medium zucchini, cut in
   thick strips
Juice of ½ lemon
½ cup sour cream

2 teaspoons flour
1 teaspoon sugar
1 tablespoon chopped fresh
   dill (1½ teaspoons
   dried)

☐ In a 10-inch skillet, sauté onion in butter until soft. Add zucchini strips, then tightly cover. Simmer until tender-crisp; about 3-4 minutes. Add lemon juice.

☐ Combine remaining ingredients and stir into pan. Cook, stirring, until bubbly and slightly thickened.

EFFORTLESS ZUCCHINI

Serves: 3-4
Prepare: 10 minutes
Broil

We don't know what else to call this. It's a breeze to make, can be done ahead except for broiling, and you can double, triple, or whatever.

3 medium zucchini, cubed (enough to yield 3½-4 cups)	1 tablespoon lemon juice
½ cup sour cream	Freshly ground pepper to taste
2 tablespoons mayonnaise	Buttered fresh bread crumbs*

☐ Place zucchini in a skillet with ¼ to ½-cup lightly salted water. Cook, covered, until barely tender; about 2 minutes. Drain well.

☐ Place zucchini in a small, shallow, unbuttered baking dish. Combine remaining ingredients except bread crumbs. Spread over top. Sprinkle with crumbs. Broil until bubbly.

■ Note: *Whenever there is 2-day-old bread for which I have no other use, I butter it and crumble it in my food processor; storing in plastic bags in the freezer to be handy for toppings such as this.

ZUCCHINI CANOES

Serves: 6
Prepare: 20 minutes
Bake: 15 minutes

Wonderful for summer menus...without losing their garden-fresh appearance, they can be held several hours before baking, or reheated in the microwave.

3 medium zucchini
½ cup finely chopped
  raw spinach
2 tablespoons minced
  onion
2 tablespoons freshly grated
  Parmesan cheese

2 tablespoons melted butter
½ cup fresh bread crumbs
½ teaspoon salt
Freshly ground pepper
  to taste
Crisply cooked bacon,
  crumbled (optional)

☐ Preheat oven to 350°.

☐ Cut zucchini in half lengthwise. Place in a large skillet with just enough lightly salted water to cover. Cover and boil until *just* tender; about 7 minutes. Drain immediately.

☐ In a bowl, combine remaining ingredients except bacon. When zucchini has cooled enough to handle, scrape out centers with a spoon and add to spinach mixture.

☐ Fill zucchini shells with mixture. Place in an ungreased, shallow baking dish. Bake 15 minutes. Sprinkle with crumbled bacon and serve. (You may wish to cut canoes in half for easier serving.)

BAKED ZUCCHINI and BROWN RICE

Serves: 6
Prepare: 20 minutes
Bake: 45 minutes
Cool: 10 minutes

A great make-ahead casserole for barbecues or potlucks or to please vegetarians.

2 pounds zucchini
1 large onion, finely chopped
3 tablespoons oil
3 cloves garlic, minced
2 tablespoons whole-wheat flour
½ cups zucchini liquid and milk
1½ cups cooked brown rice

¾ cup freshly grated Parmesan cheese
½ teaspoon thyme
Salt and freshly ground pepper to taste
1 tablespoon oil
2 tablespoons freshly grated Parmesan cheese

☐ Coarsely grate zucchini. Place in a large sieve over a bowl, then press as much liquid from squash as possible and reserve.

☐ In a 10-inch skillet, sauté onion in 3 tablespoons oil until soft; about 5 minutes. Add zucchini and garlic and toss a minute or two. Stir in flour and cook another 2 minutes.

☐ Measure reserved zucchini liquid, then add enough milk to it to make 1½ cups. Blend into zucchini mixture. Add cooked rice, ¾-cup Parmesan cheese, thyme, salt and pepper.

☐ Pour into a buttered, shallow, 8x12-inch baking dish. Drizzle top with 1 tablespoon oil and sprinkle with remaining 2 tablespoons Parmesan cheese.

☐ At this point, the dish may be covered and refrigerated until baking time.

☐ Preheat oven to 425°. Bake 45 minutes or until browned and bubbly, but most of liquid has absorbed. Let cool 10 minutes before cutting into squares to serve.

GARDEN SPAGHETTI SAUCE

Yield: 4 cups
Prepare: 20 minutes

What better way to use the garden than this?! Become adventuresome, and include cubes of purple eggplant, baby green beans, slivers of yellow pepper, broccoli florets...and on and on.

Serve over your favorite pasta or steamed spaghetti squash (see index), garnishing with bouquets of fresh herbs. Have lots of freshly grated Parmesan cheese on hand.

1 medium onion, chopped	1 6-ounce can tomato paste
2 cloves garlic, crushed	1 teaspoon Italian seasoning
1 tablespoon butter	½ teaspoon salt
1 tablespoon oil	Freshly ground pepper
½ green pepper, chopped	to taste
1 cup sliced mushrooms	Cooked spaghetti
1 medium zucchini, sliced	Freshly grated Parmesan
to bite-size	cheese
1 28-ounce can whole,	
peeled tomatoes,	
undrained	

☐ In a 12-inch skillet, sauté onion and garlic in butter and oil for 1-2 minutes. Add green pepper and sauté another 2 minutes. Add mushrooms and zucchini and cook only until mushrooms start to soften.

☐ Add remaining ingredients (except spaghetti and cheese), breaking up tomatoes. Simmer, uncovered, 20 minutes or until thickened, stirring occasionally. Serve over hot spaghetti, and top with Parmesan cheese.

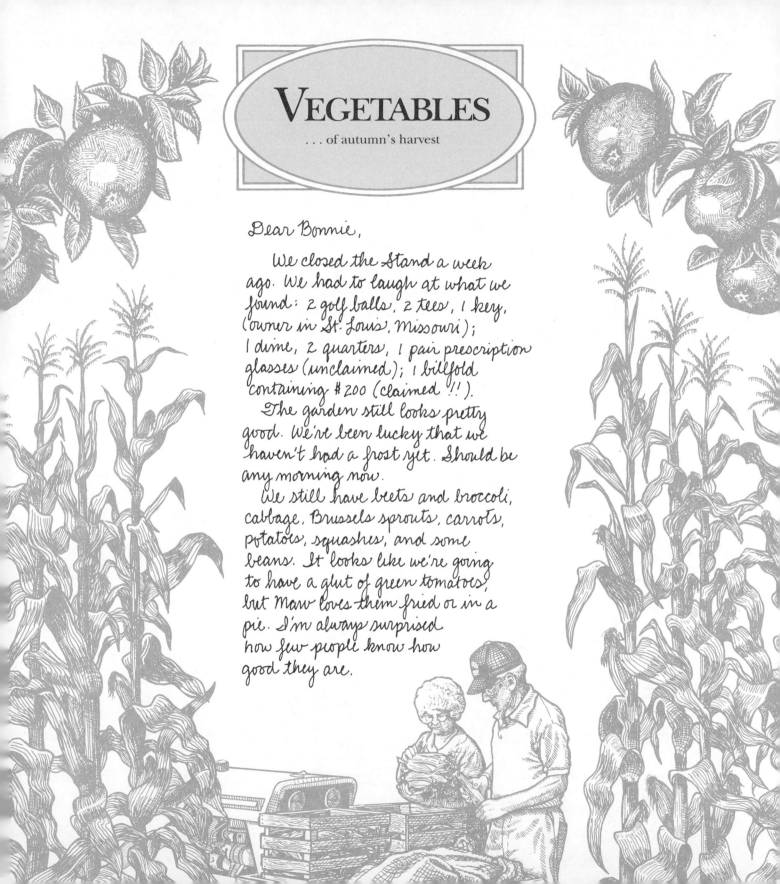

VEGETABLES

. . . of autumn's harvest

Dear Bonnie,

We closed the Stand a week ago. We had to laugh at what we found: 2 golf balls, 2 tees, 1 key (owner in St. Louis, Missouri); 1 dime, 2 quarters, 1 pair prescription glasses (unclaimed); 1 billfold containing $200 (claimed !!).

The garden still looks pretty good. We've been lucky that we haven't had a frost yet. Should be any morning now.

We still have beets and broccoli, cabbage, Brussels sprouts, carrots, potatoes, squashes, and some beans. It looks like we're going to have a glut of green tomatoes, but Maw loves them fried or in a pie. I'm always surprised how few people know how good they are.

The sunflowers are standing in a row, so tall, with their heads nodding away. The birds are going to have a ball.

I've been pickling and canning my heart out. Today it's cucumbers and crab apples. Ruth and M. J's wife, Elaine, help whenever they have some time to spare.

I love seeing the rows and rows of the "fruits" of our efforts lined up on our cellar shelves. No fancy store display can ever match these beautiful, sparkling jars with jewel-like colors. Harry Harris took a picture of them for me to send to you.

The loons are calling to each other in the bays, and Maw just saw a V of Canada geese fly honking overhead... you know what that means.

Love you as always,
Judy Chard

BAKED SHOE PEG CORN

Serves: 6-8
Prepare: 5 minutes
Bake: 25 minutes

Keep a few cans of white corn on your shelf and some hot pepper cheese in the fridge or freezer...a great dish for impromptu occasions, and boating or camping. We love it with game.

3 eggs
3 12-ounce cans Shoe Peg
   corn, drained

9 ounces hot pepper cheese,
   shredded

☐ Preheat oven to 350°. Beat eggs in a medium-size bowl. Stir in corn and cheese. Place in a buttered, shallow, 2-quart casserole. Bake, uncovered, 25 minutes.

YELLOW SQUASH and SWEET CORN

Serves: 4
Prepare: 15 minutes, if that

This will certainly beat succotash in a beauty contest, and it's a delicious combo.

2 or 3 small, yellow
   crookneck squash
2-3 tablespoons water
2 or 3 ears sweet corn
Butter

Salt and white pepper
   to taste
Pinch or 2 of fines herbs
   or thyme

☐ Slice squash about ⅓-inch thick. Place in a heavy 10 to 12-inch skillet with 2-3 tablespoons water and a sprinkling of salt. Cover tightly and simmer until barely tender, about 2 to 3 minutes. Drain any liquid from pan.

☐ Cook corn in boiling water for 3 to 4 minutes. Drain. When cool enough to handle, use a sharp knife to cut off kernels, then scrape cobs to get all the sweet milk. Add corn to skillet and gently reheat with butter, salt and white pepper to taste, and a pinch or so of herbs.

☐ If you wish to make this ahead, you can reheat it in a covered casserole in the oven, but do not overcook. The freshness of the vegetables gives the dish its character.

CORN MUSH

Years back, Country Gentleman was the sweetest corn that one could grow...small, pale kernels that were the most succulent imaginable.

Today's sophisticated agriculturists have retired the old gentleman to the back forty. Now there are such enticing varieties as Kandy Korn, Silver Queen, Summer Sweet Butterfruit, Platinum Lady, Golden Beauty. Our choice, though, due to our climate and short growing season, is Early Sunglow, and it is truly wonderful.

When we freeze corn to enjoy in the winter, we put up a very special treat for very special days. We call it "Corn Mush," but it's not what you think.

We blanch our cobs of corn by dropping just a few at a time in a kettle of boiling water. The moment the water returns to a boil, we remove the ears with tongs and run them under cold water to stop the cooking process.

After cutting and freezer-packing the kernels from the blanched ears, we scrape the cobs with the back of a knife to obtain the "mush." This can make a huge mess of your kitchen, so line your counter with wax paper or paper towels, and scrape the corn on a platter.

It will take at least 8 to 12 ears to fill a pint, but that pint will become the caviar of corn lovers.

It freezes beautifully. Just thaw and heat in the top of a double boiler or a microwave, adding butter and salt to taste. You'll think summer has returned.

CORN in a CASSEROLE

Serves: 10-12
Prepare: 15 minutes
Bake: 1 hour

This version is lighter, more delicate than most, and it includes a method for freezing the dish that will make any cook happy!

6 cups cut raw corn (from about 18 cobs)	1 teaspoon salt
1 tablespoon flour	1 cup milk
1 tablespoon sugar	5 eggs, beaten
	Butter

☐ When you cut the corn from the cobs, be sure to scrape them with the back of your knife to get all those good juices.

☐ Combine the dry ingredients and sprinkle over corn. Combine milk and eggs, and stir into corn.

☐ At this point, the mixture may be frozen in desired baking dishes. Thaw before baking.

☐ To bake, preheat oven to 350°. Dot with butter and bake, uncovered, for 1 hour, or until center is firm to the gentle touch. Let sit for 5 minutes or so before serving, so that center may fully set.

■ Note: If you are making several times the recipe, be sure to refrigerate or freeze each batch as soon as it is mixed.

BACON-FRIED CORN

Serves: 4
Prepare: 15 minutes

For barbecues and shore dinners, this is a very pretty and tasty dish that can be prepared in an iron skillet over the open fire, or made ahead to be reheated without losing its freshness.

4 strips bacon, diced
2 tablespoons bacon fat
1 small onion, chopped
2 cups fresh corn
    (about 4 ears)*
½ red bell pepper,
    chopped

2 tablespoons minced
    parsley
2 tablespoons milk
Salt and freshly ground
    pepper to taste

☐ In a heavy skillet, sauté bacon until crisp. Remove with a slotted spoon and reserve. Pour off all but 2 tablespoons fat.

☐ Over medium heat, sauté onion in bacon fat until barely soft. Stir in corn and red pepper. Stirring frequently, cook until just tender, about 3-4 minutes.

☐ Stir in remaining ingredients and garnish with reserved bacon. (If made far ahead of serving time, do not include the parsley and bacon until after gently reheating the dish.)

■ Note: *You'll be spared the mess from cutting raw corn, if you blanch the ears first for a minute or two.

The Taylors are having their annual corn roast...Genevieve just bought 20 dozen ears! Some folks husk their corn then butter and wrap it in foil to grill, but we just pull the husks back, brush away the silk, then rewrap the husks around the corn and soak the ears in cold water for 10 minutes or so. Then we grill them for 15-20 minutes, turning once in awhile, or bake them on the racks in the oven at 375° for 20 minutes.

FEATHER-LIGHT CORN FRITTERS

Yield: 12
Serves: 3-4
Prepare: 15 minutes

Fritters are much easier to make than one may think. Except for the addition of the egg whites, this recipe can be prepared an hour or more ahead of time, refrigerating until ready.

We love them for breakfast with maple syrup, or at a ham or chicken dinner with butter and dollops of honey.

3 tablespoons flour
¾ teaspoon baking powder
½ teaspoon salt
2 eggs, separated

¼ cup milk
¾ -1 cup corn
Light vegetable oil

Here's another favorite way we have to charcoal-roast corn. We husk it, then wrap it in bacon and grill it until the bacon is crisp and the corn that's showing is toasty brown.

☐ In a medium-size mixing bowl, combine flour, baking powder, and salt.

☐ Beat 2 egg yolks with milk. Stir into flour mixture with a fork, then add corn. If making ahead, refrigerate at this point.

☐ When ready to fry fritters, beat the 2 egg whites until they form soft peaks, and fold into corn mixture.

☐ Pour a ½-inch or so of oil into a large skillet over medium-high heat. When oil is hot and rippling, drop a few tablespoonfuls of batter at a time into oil. Fry until golden brown, turning with a slotted spoon, then drain on paper toweling. Keep warm in oven if necessary.

SQUAW CORN

Serves: 4
Prepare: 10 minutes
Bake: 50 minutes

The perfect dish to serve with game for a winter meal. It is reminiscent of dried corn...a unique flavor that recalls years gone by.

6 slices bacon, chopped
1 tablespoon bacon fat
1 medium onion, diced
3 eggs
1 17-ounce can cream-style corn
½ teaspoon salt
Freshly ground pepper to taste

☐ Preheat oven to 350°.

☐ In a small skillet, fry bacon until crisp. Remove to a paper towel to drain. Pour off all but 1 tablespoon bacon fat. Add onion and sauté until soft.

☐ In a medium bowl, lightly beat eggs. Mix in corn, bacon, onion, salt, and pepper.

☐ Pour into a greased, 1-quart casserole. Bake, uncovered, 50 minutes.

KAY's JULIENNE BEETS

Serves: 4
Prepare: 10 minutes

You're only a few minutes away from a delicious way to enjoy beets...the taste secret is the browned onions.

1 medium onion, chopped
2 tablespoons butter
1 15-ounce can julienne beets

2-3 tablespoons beet juice
2 tablespoons cider vinegar
Salt and freshly ground pepper to taste

☐ Sauté onions in butter until nicely browned. Drain beets, reserving 2-3 tablespoons of juice. Add beets and juice to onions, along with vinegar. Season to taste with salt and pepper. Heat and serve.

BEETS with RAISINS

Serves: 4-6
Prepare: 15 minutes

Maybe this is for grown-up tastes, but we love it.

1   16-ounce can sliced or
       julienne beets
¾ cup beet juice
1   tablespoon cornstarch
¼ cup orange juice
1   tablespoon grated
       orange rind

½ cup sugar
¼ cup cider vinegar
1   cup raisins
Pinch of salt

☐ Drain liquid from beets to measure ¾-cup, adding water if necessary. Set beets aside. Place beet juice in a medium saucepan, along with remaining ingredients.

☐ Over medium heat, stir with a whisk until thickened. Reduce heat to very low, and let simmer gently for 10 minutes. Add beets to heat through, and serve.

APPLES and BEETS

Serves: 4
Prepare: 15 minutes

Wonderful! Special in color and flavors, this is an ideal side dish for pork, sausage, turkey, or ham, and it can be made ahead.

¾ cup chopped onions
¾ cup chopped, unpared
       apples
2   tablespoons butter

1½ cups finely chopped,
       cooked beets
Salt to taste
Sour cream (optional)

☐ In a medium-size skillet, sauté onions and apples in butter until onion is transparent. Stir in beets to heat through. Salt to taste.

☐ Serve as is or garnish with sour cream.

FRIED GREEN TOMATOES
in CREAM

Serves: 4
Prepare: 10 minutes

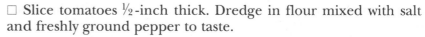

We try never to let a tomato get away from us. When the days shorten, so that our bounty of tomatoes can no longer catch enough sun to turn them a rich red, we bring them in to store in our fruit cellar or paper bags. The window sill is not the answer. They'll look awful pretty there but they'll taste awful poorly. In the total dark, they will ripen nicely after about 2 to 3 weeks.

If we can't wait that long, we make good things like India Relish or Green Tomato Apple Pie or, for dinner, fried tomatoes in cream....a favorite taste treat.

4 green tomatoes, unpeeled	2-3 tablespoons butter
Flour	2 teaspoons brown sugar
Salt and freshly ground pepper	½ cup heavy cream

☐ Slice tomatoes ½-inch thick. Dredge in flour mixed with salt and freshly ground pepper to taste.

☐ In a large, heavy skillet, melt butter over medium heat. When it begins to sizzle, add tomato slices, sprinkling each with a pinch or so of brown sugar. When lightly browned, turn. Sprinkle each again with brown sugar.

☐ When the slices have browned and are just beginning to soften, turn off heat and immediately pour in cream. Gently turn tomatoes in the thickening cream, then serve immediately.

BESS's BUTTER BEANS

Serves: 8
Prepare: 5 minutes
Bake: 60-70 minutes

This recipe gets passed around as much as a baby at a baptism! It's ideal for picnics, barbecues, potlucks, and so on; and the secret taste-touch is the molasses, so don't leave it out!

¼ cup melted butter
½ cup sour cream
½ cup brown sugar
2 tablespoons molasses

1½ teaspoons dry mustard
Dash of salt
4 15-ounce cans butter or
    lima beans, drained

☐ Preheat oven to 350°.

☐ Mix together butter, sour cream, brown sugar, molasses, dry mustard, and salt. Combine with beans and turn into a buttered, 3-quart casserole.

☐ Cover and bake 30 minutes. Uncover and bake another 30 to 50 minutes; until liquid begins to cook away but not until dry.

■ Note: The dish can be made a day or so ahead, then reheated. Also, if need be, you can bake it at different temperatures for different lengths of time. For example, for 2 to 2 ½ hours at 300° (at this lower temperature, it will not need to be covered in the early stage).

SPAGHETTI SQUASH

Why has it taken so long for this wonderful vegetable to be discovered and appreciated? Of all the winter squashes, it's the most versatile and appealing. It's mild in flavor and fascinating in texture, and has practically zero calories. It should never bear the name "squash"!

Spaghetti squash can be cooked hours ahead of time, so it's great for potluck casseroles. It's quite glamorous at a buffet when its own shell is used as the serving dish, and intriguing to children when presented with spaghetti sauce.

There are three ways to cook it. We prefer the top-of-the-stove method, but if the squash is particularly large, then you will probably have to bake it.

☐ For either stove or oven, cut squash in half, lengthwise, then scrape out seeds and fibre with a large spoon.

☐ *Top of stove:* Fill a pot or deep roasting pan (with a tight-fitting lid) with 1 inch warm water. Place squash halves, cut sides down, in pan. Cover and boil slowly but steadily on top of stove for 20 minutes.

☐ *Oven:* Place squash, cut sides down, in a shallow roasting pan or baking dish in ½-inch warm water. Bake, uncovered, at 350° for 1 hour.

☐ *Microwave:* Keep squash whole; prick in several places with a fork. Cook at full power until tender, about 10-20 minutes, turning once or twice. When done, the squash will give a little when you gently press it.

☐ To serve as is, scrape out the flesh with a butter curler or large spoon, using long strokes so as not to break the strands. Season with salt, pepper, and a touch of nutmeg, and top with butter.

■ Note: If you plan to serve a squash recipe in its own shell, the steaming method on top of the stove or microwaving will give you a prettier "dish."

Spaghetti squash is harvested when it turns a creamy yellow. It will keep at least a month in a cool, dark place, if it has a stem of at least 2 inches.

SPAGHETTI SQUASH
with CHEESE

Serves: 6-8
Steam: 20 minutes
Prepare: 10 minutes
Bake: 30 minutes

Just as good made the day before, this creates a delicious supper that vegetarians will applaud when it is completed with sliced tomatoes and a beautiful green salad.

1 spaghetti squash
1 onion, finely chopped
¼ cup butter
½ cup sour cream

Salt and white pepper
  to taste
2 cups shredded Monterey
  jack or Jarlsberg cheese

☐ Steam the squash for 20 minutes (see opposite page). As soon as it is cool enough to handle, scrape out all of the flesh with a butter curler or large spoon, using long strokes so as not to break the strands.

☐ In a small skillet, sauté the onion in the butter until soft. Add to the squash with the sour cream, salt and white pepper to taste, and 1½ cups of the cheese.

☐ Place in a buttered, 1½-quart, deep casserole or return to a squash shell. Sprinkle top with remaining ½-cup of cheese.

☐ Bake, uncovered, at 325° for 30 minutes. (If baking in the shell, place in a shallow roasting pan with a ½-inch of water.)

■ Note: If you wish to add a touch of color at serving time, sprinkle with chopped chives or slivered red bell pepper.

BUTTERNUT SQUASH BAKED
with TOMATOES and CHEESE

Serves: 6
Prepare: 20 minutes
Bake: 35-40 minutes

Warm colors and appealing flavors...wonderful on its own for vegetarians, or with almost any simple meat or poultry dishes from autumn through early spring. It can be made hours ahead of time except for baking.

2 pounds butternut squash
2 tablespoons butter
2 tablespoons oil
Salt and freshly ground
   pepper to taste
8-10 green onions, sliced
   (include light-green
   portion)

4 tomatoes, peeled, seeded,
   and chopped
½ teaspoon thyme
4 ounces sharp cheddar
   cheese, grated (1 cup)

☐ Preheat oven to 325°.*

☐ Peel squash (a sturdy potato peeler works well). Cut in half and remove seeds and pith. Slice into bite-size pieces, about ¼-inch thick.

☐ In a heavy skillet, over medium to medium-high heat, sauté squash slices in butter and oil until lightly browned. Salt and pepper to taste, then transfer to a buttered, shallow baking dish (about 8x10-inch).

☐ In same skillet, over reduced heat, gently sauté onions until soft, adding a little more butter and oil if necessary. Add a dash more of salt and pepper, and spoon over squash.

☐ Peel tomatoes by immersing in boiling water for 10 seconds or so to loosen skins. Seed and chop. Place in same skillet, seasoning with ½-teaspoon thyme and salt and pepper to taste. Cook briskly over medium-high heat, stirring from time to time, until soft and thickened, with no excess liquid; about 10 minutes.

☐ Spoon tomatoes over onions and squash. Top with cheese. Bake, uncovered, 30 minutes. Increase heat to 425°, and bake another 5 to 10 minutes; until cheese just begins to brown.

■ Note: *The baking temperatures and times can be easily adjusted as to your menu needs. You may bake it, uncovered, for 15 minutes at 425°; or, covered for 30 minutes at 350°, then uncover and brown quickly under broiler.

APPLE-FILLED
ACORN SQUASH

Serves: 6
Prepare: 15 minutes
Bake: 35 minutes
25 minutes

Apples and squash do such good things together.

3 acorn squash, halved
   lengthwise and seeded
4 tart apples, peeled and
   sliced
2 teaspoons lemon juice

¾ cup brown sugar
¼ teaspoon ground ginger
Salt and freshly ground
   pepper to taste
6 tablespoons butter

☐ Preheat oven to 350°. Place squash halves, cut-sides down, in a buttered baking dish. Bake 35 minutes.

☐ Combine apples, lemon juice, brown sugar, and ginger.

☐ Turn baked squash over and sprinkle with salt and pepper to taste. Fill with apple mixture, then dot with butter. Return to oven for another 25 minutes.

SWEET POTATO-APPLE CASSEROLE

Prepare: 15 minutes
Bake: 50-60 minutes

A winter holiday dinner seems incomplete without sweet potatoes. Combined with apples, this becomes a delicious dish to share the groaning board with a roast of goose, turkey, pork, or ham.

3-4 large, cooked sweet
    potatoes (or 2 18-
    ounce cans)
3 large, tart apples
¼ cup melted butter
¼ cup brown sugar

¼ cup honey
½ teaspoon ground allspice
1 tablespoon lemon juice
1 tablespoon bourbon or rum
Garnish: chopped mint leaves
    or toasted pecans

☐ Preheat oven to 375°.

☐ Slice sweet potatoes ¼-inch thick, then peel and slice apples ¼ to ½-inch thick. In a small bowl, combine remaining ingredients except garnish.

☐ In a buttered, 2½-quart casserole, layer ⅓ of the potatoes then ⅓ of apples. Using a rubber spatula, spread apple layer with ⅓ of brown sugar/honey mixture. Repeat twice more.

☐ Bake, uncovered, 50-60 minutes. Serve garnished with chopped mint or toasted pecans.

■ Note: This dish may be prepared ahead, then baked when necessary. It is also quite good reheated.

RED CABBAGE and APPLES

Serves: 6-8
Prepare: 10 minutes
Cook: 2 hours

Our hands-down favorite way to enjoy red cabbage. Great with pork or game.

2 tablespoons butter
2 tablespoons sugar
½ cup red wine vinegar
1 cup water
4 whole cloves
2 onions, quartered

2 unpeeled cooking apples,
   cored and cut in eighths
1 head red cabbage,
   quartered
Salt to taste

☐ Melt butter in a heavy pot or Dutch oven. Add sugar, vinegar, water, and cloves. Add remaining ingredients, gently combining.

☐ Cover and simmer 2 hours. If necessary, drain before serving.

CABBAGE and NOODLES

Serves: 4
Prepare: 10 minutes
Cook: 10 minutes

Not only is this a good way to use left-over noodles, but the tender-crispness of the cabbage keeps them from being boring! It's a Sunday supper favorite with bratwurst.

½ cup coarsely chopped
   onion
2 tablespoons butter
2 cups shredded cabbage
   (packed)

2 cups cooked, medium
   noodles
Salt and freshly ground
   pepper

☐ In a 10-inch skillet, sauté onion in butter until golden. Stir in cabbage. Cover and cook gently until cabbage is barely tender; about 10 minutes. Add noodles, and salt and pepper to taste. (If noodles have been chilled, douse with hot water to separate, draining well before adding to cabbage mixture).

■ Note: For variety's sake, try adding diced ham or bacon when browning the onions...or seasoning the dish with a couple teaspoons of poppy or caraway seeds.

179

BAKED TURNIPS in CREAM

Serves: 6
Prepare: 10 minutes
Bake: 45 minutes

The right dish for winter holiday dinners, and particularly with wild duck or grouse.

2 pounds turnips
2 tablespoons butter
Pinches of thyme
Salt and freshly ground
    pepper

1 cup heavy cream
¼ cup freshly grated
    Parmesan cheese

☐ Preheat oven to 350°. Peel and thinly slice turnips. Layer in a buttered, shallow, 2-quart, earthenware casserole or glass baking dish. Dot each layer with butter and sprinkle with a few pinches of thyme, then salt and pepper to taste. Pour cream over all. Bake, uncovered, for 30 minutes. Top with Parmesan cheese and bake another 15 minutes.

APPLE SCALLOP

Serves: 6-8
Prepare: 15 minutes
Bake: 50 minutes

Really, really good with pork dishes.

6 baking apples, peeled
    and cored
¾ cup sugar
Grated rind of 1 orange
¼ cup melted butter
½ teaspoon salt

Ground ginger
Nutmeg
Cloves
3-4 drops almond extract
⅓ cup orange juice

☐ Preheat oven to 350°.

☐ Slice apples cross-wise. Combine sugar, orange rind, butter, salt, and a generous dash each of ginger, nutmeg, and cloves.

☐ Layer half of the apples in a well-buttered, 9x12-inch baking dish, then half of the sugar mixture. Repeat. Add a few drops of almond extract to orange juice and pour over all. Cover and bake 30 minutes. Uncover, then bake another 20 minutes. Run under broiler if you wish an even browner top.

LIGHT TOUCHES

salads, dressings, and sauces

Dear Bonnie,

Now comes fall, and this year the leaves on the maple trees were so pretty... a mix of red, gold, and green. The last to fall is the gold, and the air is full of them today. Such fun to walk in the woods on a day like this and kick the clean dry leaves.

Our friend, Mrs. Ruth Patrick, is still here in the trailer nearby, but I think she will be going back to Ohio next week. She says she likes to stay until the snow flies. You know she is 80 years old like your mother. Too bad they haven't met. Maybe next year.

She loves our Indian summer, and wrote such a nice little piece about October's bright-blue weather here in God's country. I know your mother has always thought it to be our most beautiful month, so maybe you would like to send this along to her.

"This autumn, Nature first gave us lovely plumes of red here and there, then the oranges came, and last the maples' gold that makes the woods look like sunshine even on a cloudy day. Then She spread a beautiful Paisley shawl over our big hill and we were treated to Heaven's finest colors."

"We here at the home-place are especially favored when the winds come to bring the golden leaves whirling down like a dance of fairies. We have witnessed one of Nature's most beautiful miracles, the grand finale of a bountiful season and the promise of a new one to come. This is October in Michigan."

It's duck and partridge season, and deer season for bow and arrow hunters. M.J. shot two ducks, the first in his life! He took them into camp, cleaned them, then stuffed them with pineapple and baked them. Said they were wonderful.

It's time to check that everything is put away before it is covered by snow to be forgotten until spring. We haven't yet had snow to stay on, but it can happen any day.

There's one, lone, beautiful hollyhock left among the fallen leaves in front of the kitchen window. We've heard the raven's call... winter's coming.

I miss you,

Judy Chard.

WILTED LETTUCE

Serves: 6
Prepare: 10 minutes

This recipe goes so far back that I swear my grandmother's grandmother made it. Maybe in those times, though, fat-back was called for instead of bacon; and green onions have replaced plain ones. Whatever, it's just good home-cooking that goes with almost anything.

5-6 slices bacon, chopped	¼ cup cider vinegar
2 tablespoons bacon fat	2 tablespoons water
1 pound leaf lettuce (or see note)	1 tablespoon sugar
	½ teaspoon salt
3-4 green onions, chopped	Freshly ground pepper to taste
2 hard-cooked eggs, chopped	

☐ In a small skillet, fry bacon until crisp. Remove with a slotted spoon to drain on paper toweling. Reserve 2 tablespoons bacon fat in skillet.

☐ Tear lettuce into salad bowl in bite-size pieces. Add chopped onions and eggs.

☐ Add remaining ingredients to reserved bacon fat in skillet. Heat just until boiling. Pour over lettuce, tossing lightly. Garnish with bacon pieces and serve immediately.

■ Notes: Everything can be prepared ahead. Just reheat the dressing, then toss all together to serve.

Also, this dressing is good over dandelion greens, spinach, or just plain head lettuce, torn into pieces. For variety's sake, you might like to add ¼-teaspoon dry mustard to it and/or some chopped fresh herbs; or try crumbled blue cheese and a couple splashes of cream tossed in with the lettuce.

LEAF LETTUCE SALAD

Serves: 4
Prepare: 10 minutes

Usually the very first treat from our garden is leaf lettuce...so young and tender. Unfortunately, the deer and the rabbits love it as much as we!

We are having dandelion greens for dinner...spring tonic, you know! Will write down how I cook them...same with lamb's-quarters.

2 nice bunches leaf lettuce
1 bunch green onions, finely chopped
3 hard-cooked eggs, sliced
⅓ cup heavy cream
2 tablespoons white wine or tarragon vinegar

2-3 teaspoons sugar
¼ teaspoon dry mustard
½ teaspoon salt
⅛ teaspoon white pepper
Chopped chives (optional)

☐ Gently wash and dry lettuce. Place in salad bowl or on individual plates, then top with onions and eggs. Combine remaining ingredients with a whisk, adjusting sugar to tartness of vinegar. Whip until quite foamy then pour over salad. Sprinkle with chives.

MARINATED DANDELION CROWNS

Serves: 2-3
Prepare: 10 minutes
Chill

Treat as a side dish, or serve in lettuce cups as a salad.

2 quarts water
2 cups young dandelions (leaves, crowns, unopened buds)
¼ cup salad oil
¼ cup vinegar

1-2 tablespoons honey or sugar
¼ teaspoon garlic salt
¼ teaspoon onion salt
2 hard-cooked eggs (optional)

☐ In a medium saucepan, bring water to boil and add greens. Boil 5 minutes.

☐ Drain well, then place greens in a bowl. Combine remaining ingredients, then pour over and toss. Chill before serving.

☐ Garnish with sliced hard-cooked eggs.

SUN SANDS SALAD

Serves: 6-8
Prepare: 20 minutes

The social life among the summer camps on the Islands is spontaneous, relaxed, and always fun-filled. Many of the families are related or have grown up so closely-knit, that they might as well be.

There are no telephones available, and if there is such a thing as a written invitation, it is done on birch bark and delivered via boat.

Since it is respected by all that as little time be spent in the kitchen as possible, most everyone shares in a supper menu. The Sun Sands camp is often asked to bring their renowned salad. What makes it so good? It's simple, the croutons are large and freshly made, and the dressing is great.

1 head iceberg lettuce
1 head Bibb lettuce
1 large red onion, thinly sliced
2 avocados, diced
6 hard-cooked eggs, diced

4 thick slices white bread (½ to ¾-inch)
4 tablespoons butter
1 cup shredded cheddar or jack cheese (4 ounces)

☐ Tear lettuces into salad bowl in bite-size pieces. Add onion, avocados, and hard-cooked eggs. Cut bread slices into ¾-inch cubes, and sauté in butter until lightly browned and crisp. Add to salad bowl along with cheese.

1 egg, coddled*
2 tablespoons olive oil
2 tablespoons red wine vinegar
1 tablespoon Dijon mustard

Pinch of sugar
Pinch or 2 of oregano, basil, or tarragon
Salt and freshly ground pepper to taste

☐ Combine above ingredients in an electric blender. Just before serving, add to salad and toss.

■ Note: *To coddle egg, place egg (in its shell) in a pan of very hot (but not boiling) water, and let stand as it cools for 15 minutes.

SPINACH SALAD
with SLICED APPLES

Serves: 4-6
Prepare: 15 minutes

Looks and tastes as good as it sounds.

1 bunch spinach
1 apple, unpeeled
4 strips bacon, slivered
    and fried crisp

1 bunch green onions,
    chopped
2 ounces Amish or jack
    cheese, cubed

☐ Wash and dry spinach. Remove stems, then tear leaves into bite-size pieces.

☐ Cut apple in half lengthwise, then crosswise. Removing core, thinly slice.

☐ Place spinach and apple slices in salad bowl, along with bacon, chopped onions, and cheese.

¼ cup olive oil
3 tablespoons white wine
    vinegar with tarragon
1 teaspoon sugar

½ teaspoon dry mustard
Garlic salt to taste
Freshly ground pepper

☐ Whisk together above ingredients and pour over salad. Lightly toss.

WARM SPINACH SALAD

Serves: 4-5
Prepare: 15 minutes

A very pretty salad that doesn't try to overly impress you.

1¼ pounds fresh spinach
1 cup sliced fresh
    mushrooms
¾ cup finely chopped
    red onion
Salt and freshly ground
    pepper to taste

½ cup olive oil
¼ cup red wine vinegar
1 clove garlic, minced
1 teaspoon dried basil
2 eggs, hard-cooked and
    finely chopped

☐ Wash and dry spinach. Trim, then tear into bite-size pieces. Place in salad bowl or heat-proof dish, and top with the mushrooms and onion. Salt and pepper to taste. (This may be done in the morning, covered with plastic wrap, and refrigerated.)

☐ In a small saucepan, heat oil over medium heat. Whisk in vinegar, garlic, and basil. Simmer ever so gently for 5 minutes.

☐ Pour hot dressing over spinach and toss. Dress with finely chopped eggs and serve immediately.

HAWAIIAN LETTUCE, ARCTIC TOMATOES, and SUGAR SNAPS

Lettuce and celery will crisp up real fast when placed in a pan of cold water with a few slices of raw potato.

Every March, while the ice and snow are still on the ground, we look forward to the lettuce seeds that our summer friends, the Hefferans, send us from the Hawaiian Islands. The packets are a promise that we'll have another beautiful crop by July.

The Arctic tomatoes are our favorite variety to grow because of the too-short summers here. One way I like to display the lettuce and tomatoes is on a relish tray, along with Sugar Snap peas, baby carrots, and finger-size zucchinis...all fresh from the garden...and a bowl of Mother's Mayonnaise, sprinkled with curry powder.

Our Sugar Snaps seldom make it to the pot! They are so crisp and sweet eaten as they are plucked from the vine, pods and all. Some people string them, but ours don't seem to need it.

To cook them, put them in a skillet with a small amount of boiling salted water, and blanch for only a minute. Serve immediately, tossed in butter. Or, run under cold water to stop the cooking process, and chill; then serve in summer soups or salads.

SLICED ARCTIC TOMATOES with CHEESE and FRESH BASIL

Our tomatoes never ever see the refrigerator. Chilling would stop their ripening dead in its tracks, as well as their heavenly flavor.

So, straight from the garden or the window sill, here's another beautiful salad.

Ripe tomatoes	Olive oil
Jarlsberg, jack, or	Freshly ground pepper
mozzarella cheese	Fresh basil leaves or sprigs

☐ Slice tomatoes and cheese. Arrange alternately, in overlapping rows, on salad plate. Drizzle with olive oil, then add a generous grinding of black pepper. Garnish with basil leaves.

CHERRY or YELLOW TOMATO SALAD

Serves: 4
Prepare: 5 minutes

So simple...but, of course, that's what makes it good!

1 pound cherry or baby
   yellow tomatoes
   (2 pint-baskets)
2 tablespoons chopped
   chives
1 tablespoon finely
   chopped mint

1 teaspoon sugar
Salt and freshly ground
   pepper to taste
2 tablespoons white wine
   vinegar

☐ Slice tomatoes onto a pretty serving dish. Sprinkle with remaining ingredients.

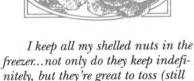

I keep all my shelled nuts in the freezer...not only do they keep indefinitely, but they're great to toss (still frozen) into salads or desserts at the last minute for added crunchiness.

GREEN GODDESS PEA SALAD

Serves: 4-8
Prepare: 10 minutes
Chill: optional

Someone is always asking me for a pea salad recipe. There are lots of versions in lots of cookbooks, but here's ours.

2 10-ounce packages
   frozen green peas,
   thawed (4 cups)
1 bunch green onions,
   chopped
½ pound bacon, chopped
   and fried crisp

½ recipe Green Goddess
   Dip, omitting anchovies
   (see index)
Lettuce cups
½ cup chopped, dry-
   roasted peanuts (optional)

☐ Toss together peas, green onions, bacon, and Green Goddess Dip. If making ahead, chill up to 24 hours.

☐ Serve in lettuce cups, garnished with chopped peanuts if you wish, as a main dish salad for 4 or a side dish for 8.

NEW POTATO SALAD

Serves: 12
Prepare: 15 minutes
Marinate: 30 minutes, minimum
Prepare: 15 minutes
Chill: 3-24 hours

They say the mark of a good cook is his or her potato salad.

10-12 medium red-skinned potatoes (to make 6 cups cubed)
2 tablespoons French or Russian dressing
1½ cups chopped celery with leaves
8-10 green onions, chopped
½ red onion, chopped
¼ green bell pepper, finely chopped
¼ red bell pepper, finely chopped
¼ cup finely chopped sweet pickles
¼ cup finely chopped parsley
3 tablespoons finely chopped chives
7 eggs, hard-cooked
2-3 teaspoons salt
Freshly ground pepper to taste
⅔ cup Mother's Mayonnaise (see index)
Paprika and chopped parsley

☐ Leaving the pretty skins on, scrub and dice potatoes into cubes no larger than ¾-inch. Boil in salted water until *just* tender; about 5 minutes. Drain and rinse briefly in cold water to stop cooking process. Toss in French or Russian dressing and chill at least 30 minutes.

☐ Combine celery, onions, peppers, pickles, parsley, and chives with the marinated potatoes. Chop 5 of the eggs, reserving the other 2 for garnish. Add to salad, along with salt, pepper, and mayonnaise. Check seasoning. Refrigerate at least 3 hours...better overnight.

☐ Check seasoning again. (Potatoes like a lot of salt when they've been sitting awhile.) Place in serving bowl. Slice remaining 2 eggs and decorate top, sprinkling with paprika and chopped parsley.

SUNSHINE PASTA SALAD

Serves: 8-12
Prepare: 15 minutes
Chill

Pretty, pretty picnic fare, and a hit at potlucks any time of the year...it's a snap to make if you have a food processor.

1 12-ounce package twisted noodles (or 6 cups cooked)*
1 20-ounce can chunk-style pineapple
2 cups broccoli florets
1 cup chopped celery
½ cup coarsely chopped parsley
⅓ cup chopped green onion
⅓ cup diced sweet red pepper or pimento
¾ cup olive oil
⅓ cup cider vinegar
2 tablespoons Dijon mustard
2 tablespoons pineapple juice
2 tablespoons lemon juice
2 teaspoons dried basil
1 clove garlic, crushed
Salt to taste

☐ Prepare noodles according to package directions. Drain pineapple, reserving 2 tablespoons juice for the dressing, then finely chop. Place in a large bowl along with the cooked noodles, broccoli florets, chopped celery, parsley, green onion, and sweet pepper.

☐ To prepare dressing, blend together remaining ingredients with a whisk. Pour over salad and toss. Salt to taste, then chill at least 1 hour or overnight.

■ Note: *If you can find the packaged combination of spinach, tomato, and plain twisted noodles, they make an unusually colorful salad.

TWELVE-HOUR, TWELVE-LAYER SALAD

Serves: 8
Prepare: 30 minutes
Chill: 6-12 hours

Layered salads, prepared in deep, glass bowls, are popular these days because they can be made ahead and yet still look pretty. This one is a rainbow of colors. As you make it, be sure that you work each layer to reach the side of the bowl so that it's visible.

Right now the Stand looks like a giant salad bowl...just gorgeous! In the early mornings, when the dew is heavy and the robin is singing her heart out and I have the garden all to myself, I don't know of anything more pleasant than setting up the Stand for the first bunch of customers. Each time it's different...each time I think prettier.

1 head iceberg lettuce, shredded
1 bunch parsley, chopped (about ¾-cup)
4 hard-cooked eggs, chopped
1 red bell pepper, thinly sliced
4 carrots, shredded
1 cup black olives, sliced
12 ounces peas or green beans, crisply cooked (see index)

2 tablespoons chopped fresh dill (1½ teaspoons dried)
1 cup sliced radishes
12 ounces Swiss or cheddar cheese, shredded
½ pound chopped, crisply cooked bacon
1 red onion, thinly sliced

☐ Place lettuce in bottom of 3-quart, straight-sided glass bowl. Layer with rest of above ingredients in order given.

2 cups mayonnaise
½ cup sour cream
½ cup chopped parsley
¼ cup chopped chives
2 tablespoons sugar
1 tablespoon tarragon vinegar

Salt and freshly ground pepper to taste
Garnish: 2 tablespoons chopped parsley

☐ Whisk together above ingredients, except parsley garnish. Spread *half* of dressing over salad evenly, reserving rest for serving time. Sprinkle with the 2 tablespoons chopped parsley.

☐ Cover tightly with plastic wrap and refrigerate 6-12 hours.

☐ When serving, urge your diners to "dig in," so that all layers are reached. Keep a bowl of the extra dressing at hand.

CONFETTI SPINACH SALAD MOLDS

Serves: 12-14
Prepare: 15 minutes
Chill: 2-3 hours

I've seen this served at the fanciest of buffets, because it adds so much color and complements all kinds of menus. It's particularly attractive when prepared in individual round molds, then unmolded onto lettuce cups and garnished with pimento strips and sprigs of watercress.

1 6-ounce package lemon-flavored gelatin
2 cups boiling water
Juice of 2 lemons
3 tablespoons cider or tarragon vinegar
2 teaspoons salt
1 bunch spinach, finely chopped (about 2-2½ cups)

4 pimentos, finely chopped
¾ cup finely chopped onion
2 cups creamed, small curd cottage cheese

☐ Dissolve gelatin in boiling water. Stir in lemon juice, vinegar, and salt. Chill until partially set.

☐ Combine remaining ingredients. Fold into gelatin mixture, then pour into oiled, 4 to 6-ounce molds or a 2-quart mold. Chill until firmly set; at least 2 hours.

SOUR CREAM CUCUMBER MOLD

Serves: 4
Prepare: 10-15 minutes
Chill

Everyday I think how wonderful it is to have good friends, and how many of them have come to be that because of our garden stand. The recipe for this pretty-as-can-be salad is a nice reminder of their generosity in sharing thoughts about good food.

1 3-ounce package lemon-flavored gelatin	1 teaspoon dried dill weed
½ cup hot water	¾ teaspoon salt
1 cup sour cream	1 large cucumber (to yield 1 cup finely chopped)
2-3 tablespoons lemon juice	1 avocado, diced
1 teaspoon Beau Monde seasoning	2 tablespoons minced onion

☐ Dissolve gelatin in ½-cup hot water. With an egg beater or whisk, beat in sour cream, then lemon juice, seasoning, dill weed, and salt.

☐ Peel cucumber, then seed if chopping by hand. Finely chop to yield 1 cup. Fold into gelatin mixture along with avocado and onion. Pour into a lightly oiled, 4-cup mold. Chill until well set.

Makes a very nice luncheon dish when served with shrimp or crabmeat or a simple chicken salad.

FROSTY FRUIT
SALAD RING

Serves: 8-10
Prepare: 15 minutes
Freeze
Thaw: 2 hours

Thanks to the wonders of this modern world, fresh strawberries usually can be found in the market, even in the dead of winter. So think of this as a year-around dish...so pretty for buffets or even as a light dessert.

3 cups sour cream
¾ cup sugar
3 tablespoons lemon juice
⅛ teaspoon salt
1 heaping cup diced
   strawberries*

1 8-ounce can crushed
   pineapple, drained
2 bananas, mashed
Garnish: strawberries,
   seasonal fruits, watercress
   or mint

☐ In a bowl, combine sour cream, sugar, lemon juice, and salt. Stir in remaining ingredients except garnish. Pour into a lightly oiled, 6 to 7-cup (9-inch), ring mold. Cover and freeze.

☐ To give it its refreshingly frosty consistency, set in refrigerator 2 hours before serving to partially thaw. Unmold onto a large platter and garnish with watercress or mint, and as many pretty fruits as you can find...strawberries, grapes, peaches, orange segments or mandarin oranges, blueberries, raspberries.

■ Note: *Diced mandarin oranges can be substituted.

SPICED PEACH SALAD

Serves: 8
Prepare: 15 minutes
Chill

Sometimes we call this our "Easter Salad" because it's so good with ham. The recipe came to me from one of our special customers who summers at her camp, Lakanwood, on Marquette Island. It's one of her favorites for her ever-popular summer parties.

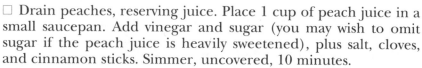

1 29-ounce can peach halves
1 cup peach juice
¼ cup cider vinegar
¼ cup sugar (or to taste)
Pinch of salt
24 whole cloves
4 cinnamon sticks

1 3-ounce package cream cheese
¼ cup chopped pecans or chives
1 3-ounce package orange-flavored gelatin
2 cups cold water/peach juice

☐ Drain peaches, reserving juice. Place 1 cup of peach juice in a small saucepan. Add vinegar and sugar (you may wish to omit sugar if the peach juice is heavily sweetened), plus salt, cloves, and cinnamon sticks. Simmer, uncovered, 10 minutes.

☐ In the meantime, form the cream cheese into 8 balls, and roll in chopped nuts or chives. Place in peach halves (there should be 8 halves to the can). Arrange peaches in a lightly oiled, 6-cup ring mold (or individual molds), stuffed-side down.

☐ When peach juice mixture has simmered 10 minutes, remove from heat and immediately stir in gelatin to dissolve. Add cold water plus any remaining peach juice, totaling 2 cups. Strain through a sieve and pour over peaches. Chill until well set.

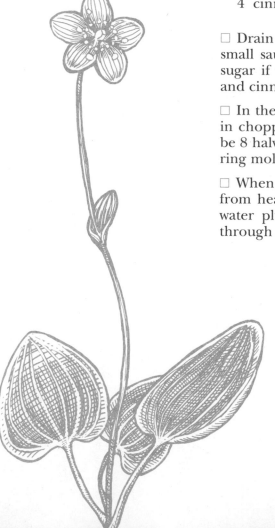

PRETTY EGG SALAD RING

Serves: 10-12
Prepare: 20 minutes
Chill: 3 hours, minimum

There are many ways to work this pretty salad into special occasion menus. Such as treating it as the main dish for a summer luncheon, surrounding it with crisply cooked green beans (see index), cherry tomatoes, and clusters of watercress.

Or, using it to complete a buffet of sliced ham and smoked turkey, hot buttered biscuits, Scalloped Tomatoes, and a luxurious green salad.

Or, for individual salads, chilling in small custard cups, then inverting onto meaty slices of tomato, and garnishing with dill flowers or sprigs of watercress.

2 tablespoons gelatin
¼ cup cold water
½ cup hot water
12 hard-cooked eggs
1½ cups mayonnaise
Juice of 1 lemon
½ cup finely chopped
   green pepper
½ cup chopped parsley
½ teaspoon salt
¼ teaspoon dry mustard
¼ teaspoon onion salt
⅛ teaspoon garlic salt
2-3 drops Tabasco sauce
Garnish: chives with
   blossoms (optional)

☐ Stir gelatin into cold water, then add hot water to dissolve. Set aside to cool.

☐ Place eggs in a large bowl, and finely chop with a pastry blender.

☐ Combine remaining ingredients (except chives) with chopped eggs, then stir in cooled gelatin. Pour into an oiled, 6-cup, ring or melon mold (or 10-12 individual molds). Chill at least 3 hours.

☐ To serve, unmold and sprinkle generously with chopped chives. For fun, crown with a bouquet of lovely, purple chive blossoms.

GREAT AUNT LYLA's MOLDED BEET SALAD

Serves: 8-10
Prepare: 15 minutes
Chill: 2-3 hours

One of our favorite salads for winter holiday dinners...particularly with roast pork, goose, or venison. Aunt Lyla's Sauce is a must with it.

Thanks to our customers, the world is very small and wonderful. We didn't know Great Aunt Lyla Baker...she belonged to a friend of a friend way out west who gave us some of Aunt Lyla's famous recipes. It turned out, though, that Aunt Lyla, who was born in 1887, grew up on a farm in Ontario...right where Marv's family came from. Guess you could say this recipe has gone full circle.

By the way, Aunt Lyla was supposed to be so much fun that even though she didn't imbibe, she could get high on tea at any good party.

- 1 16-ounce can julienne beets
- 2½ cups beet juice plus water
- ½ cup tarragon or white vinegar
- ¼ cup sugar
- 2 whole cloves
- Dash each of ginger, cinnamon, and salt
- 1 6-ounce package lemon-flavored gelatin

☐ Drain juice from beets into a quart measuring cup. Place beets in an oiled, 5 to 6-cup mold.

☐ Add water to beet juice to measure 2½ cups. Place in a saucepan with vinegar, sugar, spices, and salt. Boil 3-4 minutes. Remove from heat, and discard cloves. Stir in gelatin to dissolve. Pour over beets in mold. Chill until firm.

☐ When ready to serve, unmold on pretty lettuce leaves or surround with bouquets of parsley, and provide a bowl of Aunt Lyla's wonderful sauce.

AUNT LYLA's SAUCE

Yield: ¾ cup
Prepare: 10 minutes
Chill: 2-3 hours

Although this goes with Aunt Lyla's Molded Beet Salad, I always double it to have on hand to serve with fish...it beats any tartare sauce. It will keep a good week in the fridge.

- ½ cup mayonnaise
- 1 tablespoon tarragon or white vinegar
- 1 tablespoon chopped parsley or chives
- 1 clove garlic, minced
- 1 hard-cooked egg, chopped

☐ Combine and refrigerate.

MOTHER's MAYONNAISE

Yield: 2 ½ cups
Prepare: 5 minutes

This is what real mayonnaise is really about! Use in your potato salad, and you'll find that no one else's can compare!

Or, for fun, instead of cider vinegar, substitute blueberry or raspberry vinegar (see index) for fish or chicken salads; or, for cold meats, Dijon mustard in place of yellow mustard.

2 egg yolks	3-4 tablespoons cider
1 egg white	vinegar
1 pint light vegetable oil	1 teaspoon salt
2 heaping teaspoons yellow prepared mustard	

☐ With an electric mixer, beat the egg yolks and white for 2 minutes. Add ⅔ of the oil in a steady, fine stream. Add mustard, vinegar, and salt, and beat 2 more minutes. Beat in rest of oil gradually.*

☐ Because this is a dressing prepared with fresh eggs, it must be kept refrigerated, and no longer than 1 week.

■ Note: *The preparation time is much faster with an electric blender, but the oil must still be added fairly slowly

GREEN MAYONNAISE

Yield: 2 cups
Prepare: 5 minutes

This can be served as a salad dressing, a colorful vegie dip, or a tasty and pretty sauce for fish.

2 cups mayonnaise	1 tablespoon chopped chives
¼ cup finely chopped spinach	1 tablespoon lemon juice (optional)
1 tablespoon chopped parsley	

☐ Combine and refrigerate.

PESTO

Yield: 1½ cups
Prepare: 5 minutes

This is the recipe I give my customers when they ask how to make a great pesto. Have you ever tried it over hot or cold green beans?

2¼ cups lightly packed
    basil leaves, washed
1 cup freshly grated
    Parmesan cheese
2-3 cloves garlic
¼ cup pine nuts
    (or walnuts)

½ cup olive oil
2 tablespoons butter,
    softened
Pinch of salt

☐ Make sure the basil is free of stems and flowers. Combine all ingredients in a food processor until smooth.

■ Note: To store, pour a film of olive oil over pesto's surface and keep, air-tight, in refrigerator for a week or so; or freeze.

CREAMY BASIL DRESSING

Yield: 3 cups
Prepare: 10 minutes

Serve over sliced tomatoes or crisp vegies, or as a dressing for a sumptuous, tossed green salad.

½ cup lightly packed
    fresh basil leaves
1 cup mayonnaise
½ cup sour cream
3-4 green onions, chopped
    (tops, too)
2 tablespoons chopped
    chives

1 clove garlic
3 tablespoons tarragon
    vinegar
1 teaspoon Worcestershire
    sauce
½ teaspoon dry mustard
Freshly ground black
    pepper to taste

☐ Combine all ingredients in a blender until smooth.

SWEET and SOUR MUSTARD

Yield: 2½ cups
Prepare: 5 minutes

Just the thing for dressing up turkey sandwiches and ham loaves; and it takes only a minute to make.

1 cup sugar	1 cup cream
1 tablespoon cornstarch	½ cup vinegar
4 tablespoons dry mustard*	1 egg yolk

☐ In a 1-quart saucepan, combine all ingredients with a whisk. Bring just to a boil, stirring constantly. Immediately remove from heat and cool.

☐ This will keep a week or more in fridge.

■ Note: *If the mustard is a little bit too hefty for you, you can cut it back a tablespoon or so.)

DILL MUSTARD SAUCE

Yield: 1½ cups
Prepare: 5 minutes

A sauce of just the right consistency and flavor to serve with Gravlax or slices of yesterday's roasted lamb or beef.

4 tablespoons Dijon mustard	1 clove garlic, crushed
4-5 teaspoons sugar	⅛ teaspoon salt
4 tablespoons white wine vinegar	Freshly ground pepper to taste
¼ cup chopped dill weed (3 teaspoons dried)	1 cup olive oil

☐ Prepare the above ingredients in a blender, or with a whisk in a medium-size bowl, slowly adding oil at the last. This keeps nicely, chilled.

HONEY DRESSING with MUSTARD SEED

Yield: 2 cups
Prepare: 5 minutes

Besides being delicious over lamb's-quarters, it is wonderful with watercress and citrus fruits, or mixed fruit salads, or chilled cooked vegetables and endive or escarole.

½ cup honey (or ¼ cup honey, ¼ cup maple syrup)	1 teaspoon mustard seed
	1 teaspoon celery seed (optional)
½ cup sugar	1 teaspoon dry mustard
¼ cup cider vinegar	1 teaspoon salt
½ small onion, chopped	1 cup light salad oil

☐ Combine honey, sugar, vinegar, onion, and seasonings in an electric blender. While blending at high speed, slowly pour in oil.

■ Note: The dressing will keep nicely in the refrigerator for several weeks.

SWEET FRUIT DRESSING

Yield: 3 cups
Prepare: 10 minutes
Chill

When you want an extra touch for fresh or molded fruit salads.

½ cup sugar (or to taste)	1 cup apricot, pineapple, peach, or cranberry juice
1½ tablespoons cornstarch	1 cup heavy cream
2 eggs, slightly beaten	

☐ In a medium-size saucepan, combine sugar and cornstarch with a whisk. Blend in eggs and fruit juice, and heat until mixture reaches a low boil, stirring constantly. Cool, then chill in refrigerator in an air-tight container.

☐ When ready to serve, whip cream into soft mounds then blend into chilled mixture.

Lamb's-quarters grows almost anywhere in North America, but is often forgotten as a springtime delicacy...except here in God's country! Old-timers will tell you where to quickly find a patch.

It is cabbage-like in flavor, thus, fresh or cooked, it substitutes nicely in most cabbage recipes. We love using its young leaves for a salad, drizzled with Honey Dressing, but I often use maple syrup in place of half the honey.

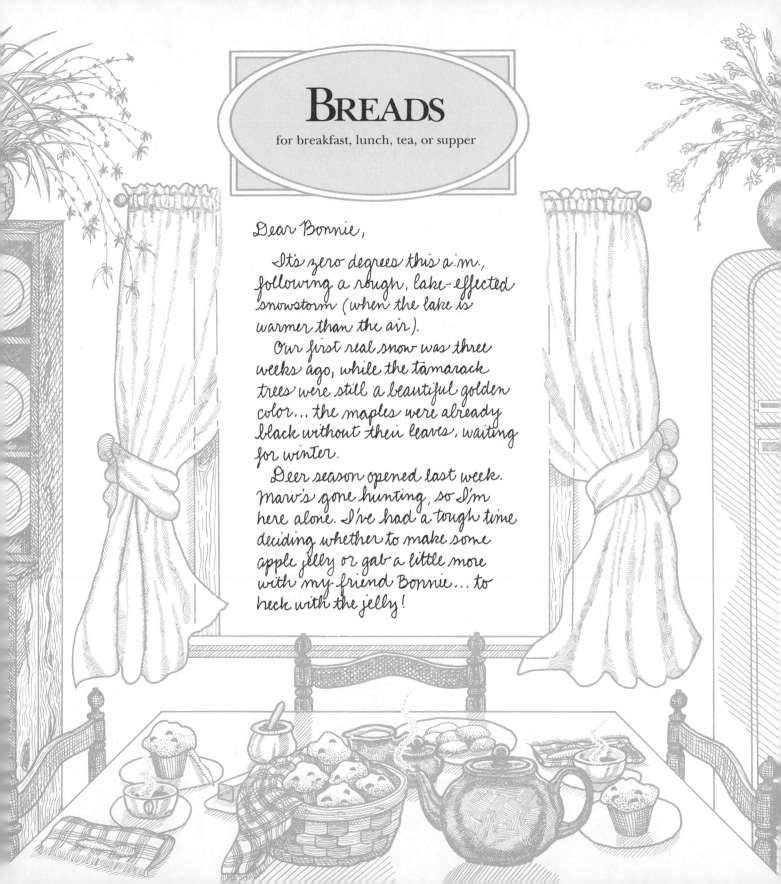

BREADS

for breakfast, lunch, tea, or supper

Dear Bonnie,

It's zero degrees this a.m., following a rough, lake-effected snowstorm (when the lake is warmer than the air).

Our first real snow was three weeks ago, while the tamarack trees were still a beautiful golden color... the maples were already black without their leaves, waiting for winter.

Deer season opened last week. Marv's gone hunting, so I'm here alone. I've had a tough time deciding whether to make some apple jelly or gab a little more with my friend Bonnie... to heck with the jelly!

Elda Nye and our Ruth were up for a visit Sunday. Ruth was on her way back to the hunting camp in the woods to take supper for Betty Smith's crew of deer hunters because it's Betty's birthday. She's the owner of the Country Curl Beauty Shop in Cedarville, you know.

I've been quite busy washing windows and cleaning house. I never get a chance to in the summer. I want to have everything ready for Thanksgiving. We're expecting twenty for dinner... family... some we haven't seen for some time. Ruth's going to do a lot of the cooking. I'm fixing the potatoes and baking 2 to 3 pies and pumpkin cake. Ruth's stuffing the turkey, I'm roasting it; then we'll stuff ourselves.

Did I tell you I cooked the spaghetti squash? It was a surprise... so sweet I just put a dash of salt, a dab of butter, and a bit of nutmeg on it. Everyone liked it. Now to try it with spaghetti sauce.

Someone brought us venison this a.m., so we'll have steak tonight. Marv wants fried potatoes with it... he's really not suppose to but he deserves a treat. We haven't had a pie in a coon's age... maybe I'll really do it up brown and make him a coconut pie... his favorite. Now there's a story!

Have a happy Thanksgiving and a good family gathering. There is so much to be thankful for.

Our love,
Judy Chard

WAFFLED FRENCH TOAST

Yield: 8-10 slices
Prepare: 5 minutes
Bake: 2-3 minutes

The kids love these...everyone does; and any leftovers can be reheated in the toaster.

½ cup milk
4 eggs
1 tablespoon sugar

½ teaspoon salt
2 tablespoons butter, melted
8-10 slices bread

☐ Preheat waffle iron. If the iron is well-seasoned (in other words, had its share of waffles baked in it without being abused by soap!), there should be no need to oil it.

☐ In a shallow bowl, with a flat whisk, combine milk, eggs, sugar, and salt, then melted butter.

☐ Dip bread slices, one at a time, in egg mixture, and drain. Bake in waffle iron 2 to 3 minutes, until brown.

☐ Serve with bacon or sausage and maple syrup or Strawberry Butter.

STRAWBERRY BUTTER

Yield: 2 ½ cups
Prepare: 5 minutes

Just wonderful over pancakes, waffles, and French toast.

½ pound butter, softened
10 ounces frozen
    strawberries, thawed
    and drained

½ cup powdered sugar

☐ Combine all in a mixer or food processor until smooth and creamy. It's best served at room temperature, but can be stored in fridge for several weeks.

CRISP WAFFLES

Serves: 4
Prepare: 10 minutes

Throw out all those other recipes...this one's wonderful! I found it in a great little cookbook a summer customer sent me from Lake Oswego, Oregon, called Rave Revues. *The group who wrote it deserves lots of credit.*

You can make a big batch, store them in the bread box or freezer, then just pop into the toaster for a speedy breakfast or after-school treat.

2 cups Bisquick
1 egg
½ cup vegetable oil

1⅓ cups club soda
    (1 10-ounce bottle)

☐ Preheat waffle iron (no oiling will be necessary if iron is seasoned).

☐ Combine ingredients with a wire whisk. Pour as needed onto hot iron, and bake until golden brown. Serve with your favorite toppings.

▪ Note: Try for supper, topped with creamed chipped beef.

APPLE OVEN PANCAKE

Serves: 4
Prepare: 15 minutes
Bake: 10 minutes

A celebration breakfast with crisp bacon or sausage links and creamy, scrambled eggs.

4 cooking apples	Pinch of salt
3 tablespoons butter	3 tablespoons milk
3 tablespoons sugar	2 egg yolks, lightly beaten
1 teaspoon cinnamon	2 egg whites
3 tablespoons flour	3 tablespoons sugar
¼ teaspoon baking powder	Sour cream (optional)

☐ Preheat oven to 400°.

☐ Peel, core, and slice apples ¼-inch thick. Melt butter in a heavy, 10-inch skillet. Combine sugar and cinnamon and stir into butter. Place sliced apples in skillet in an even layer. Cook over medium heat for 5 minutes.

☐ In a medium-size bowl, combine flour, baking powder, and salt. With a whisk, beat in milk and egg yolks. In a separate bowl, beat egg whites with 3 tablespoons sugar until they form soft peaks. Fold into flour mixture, then pour over apples.

☐ If skillet handle is not oven-proof, wrap with foil for protection. Place skillet in oven and bake 10 minutes.

☐ Serve directly from skillet or invert onto a warm serving platter. Offer sour cream as a garnish, if you'd like.

APPLESAUCE PANCAKES

Serves: 4
Prepare: 10 minutes

Even though these are substantial in character, they are still quite delicate in texture. Serve with warm Apple Cider Syrup for a special breakfast on a brisk, autumn morning.

1 cup sifted flour	¼ teaspoon grated orange rind
1 tablespoon sugar	
1½ teaspoons baking powder	¼ teaspoon vanilla
½ teaspoon salt	2 egg yolks, beaten
¼ teaspoon cinnamon	1 tablespoon melted butter
1 cup applesauce	2 egg whites

☐ Sift together dry ingredients into a large mixing bowl. Blend in applesauce, orange rind, vanilla, egg yolks, and melted butter. Beat egg whites until stiff but not dry, then fold into batter.

☐ Ladle batter onto hot griddle (lightly oiled, if necessary) to size of pancakes desired. Cook until small bubbles form throughout, then turn to nicely brown other side.

■ Note: Don't give in to the temptation to add liquid to the batter!

APPLE CIDER SYRUP

Yield: 1¾ cups
Prepare: 5 minutes
Cook: 20-25 minutes

2 cups apple cider	1 1-inch piece of cinnamon stick
1½ cups brown sugar	
	1½ teaspoons whole cloves

☐ Combine ingredients in a saucepan. Bring to a boil, lower heat to medium, and cook until liquid is reduced to about half, forming a syrup. Remove spices, then serve warm.

BUTTERMILK
BUCKWHEAT CAKES

Serves: 4
Prepare: 10 minutes

You couldn't ask for more flavor in a pancake, and, though buckwheat flour is coarser than others, these cakes are light and tender.

3 eggs
2¼ cups buttermilk*
3 tablespoons melted
    butter
1 cup buckwheat flour

½ cup unbleached flour
1 teaspoon baking soda
1 teaspoon baking powder
1 tablespoon sugar
½ teaspoon salt

☐ In a large mixing bowl, beat eggs until frothy, then add buttermilk and melted butter. In a separate bowl, combine dry ingredients with a whisk. Blend into egg mixture lightly but thoroughly. (If you wish thinner pancakes, add a splash or two of regular milk.)

☐ Ladle onto hot griddle (no greasing will be necessary, if griddle has been properly seasoned). Turn when bubbly and the undersides are toasty brown.

▨ Notes: This batter will keep well in the fridge for a day or two; just stir before using.

*Also, as a substitute for buttermilk, combine 2 tablespoons vinegar with 2¼ cups regular milk and let stand for several minutes.

CORN-APPLE HOTCAKES

Serves: 4
Prepare: 10 minutes

For lumberjacks and Sunday mornings...serve with gobs of butter and warm maple syrup.

⅔ cup yellow cornmeal
1⅓ cups unbleached
    flour
¼ cup sugar
2 teaspoons baking soda
1 teaspoon baking powder

1 teaspoon salt
⅛ teaspoon allspice
2 large apples, unpeeled
3 eggs
1½ cups buttermilk
4 tablespoons butter, melted

☐ Sift together dry ingredients into a large bowl. Core unpeeled apples and shred or grate, then stir into dry ingredients.

☐ In a separate bowl, beat the eggs until frothy then whisk in the buttermilk and melted butter. Add to apple mixture and combine. Let rest while heating griddle.

☐ Ladle batter on to hot, unoiled griddle to form 5-inch pancakes. Cook until small bubbles form before turning to brown other side...should yield 12 to 14 delicious hotcakes.

OLD-TIME DOUGHNUTS

Yield: 24 doughnuts
24 holes
Prepare: 15 minutes

In 1925, the Ladies Aid of the First Union Church in Cedarville put out a little cookbook. This was Mary Gagnon Hudson's recipe for a cake-type doughnut, and it's just as good today as it was then.

If you'd like, make the dough the night before.

Butter, the size of a walnut
   (2½ tablespoons,
   softened)
1 large cup sugar (1 stand-
   ard cup measure)
2 eggs
1 teaspoon vanilla
3½ cups flour, plus

1 teaspoon cream of tartar
1 teaspoon baking soda
1 teaspoon baking powder
½ teaspoon salt
½ teaspoon nutmeg
   (optional)
1 cup rich milk
4 cups oil

This morning, the men came in for coffee to get warm. They are grading lumber out in the yard. I made some old-time doughnuts...did I send you that recipe? I got it out of an old church cookbook hereabouts.

☐ With a wooden spoon, cream together butter and sugar, then beat in eggs and vanilla. Sift together dry ingredients. Lightly stir into egg mixture, alternating with milk. Add more flour if necessary for easier handling.

☐ On a lightly floured board or pastry cloth, roll dough out to ½-inch thickness. Cut out doughnuts and "holes," dipping cutter in flour each time.

☐ Heat oil in a skillet until rippling, then use a scrap of dough to test. When ready, fry a few doughnuts and holes at a time, turning with tongs as they brown. Drain on paper towels then serve immediately.

FRESH RASPBERRY BREAKFAST CAKE

Serves: 8-12
Prepare: 15 minutes
Bake: 30-40 minutes

It's July and there are raspberries like rain...just a quick step outside our backdoor and we can enjoy the best dessert of all in our minds.

Raspberries are so wonderful just being raspberries, that all they might need is a good splash of cream. This year, though, they were like rain...so many. So, we tried them in a breakfast cake. It couldn't have been better.

2 eggs, separated
¾ cup sugar
½ cup soft vegetable
    shortening
1½ cups sifted flour

1 teaspoon baking powder
½ teaspoon salt
⅓ cup milk
1 teaspoon vanilla
2 cups fresh raspberries*

☐ Preheat oven to 375°. Oil a 9-inch cake or tube pan.

☐ In a mixing bowl, beat together egg yolks, sugar, and shortening. Sift together flour, baking powder, and salt. With a wooden spoon, stir the dry ingredients into egg mixture along with the unbeaten egg whites just until well mixed. Stir in milk and vanilla. Fold in raspberries.

☐ Pour into prepared pan and bake until the center springs back to the light touch; about 30-40 minutes. Serve warm.

■ Notes: This makes a lovely, old-fashioned dessert when served in bowls with a sauce of Boiled Custard (see index).

*Fresh blueberries may be substituted, but lightly flour them before adding to batter so that they will not sink to bottom.

RHUBARB BUNDT CAKE

Serves: 12 or more
Prepare: 20 minutes
Bake: 1 hour

Wonderful with coffee, even if you don't like rhubarb!

1½ cups finely chopped rhubarb (about 3 stalks)
2 tablespoons sugar
2 teaspoons cinnamon
½ cup butter, softened
2 cups sugar
4 large eggs
½ cup light vegetable oil
3 tablespoons lemon juice

2 teaspoons vanilla
3 cups sifted unbleached flour*
1 tablespoon baking powder
½ teaspoon salt
½ cup milk
1 cup chopped pecans or walnuts

☐ Preheat oven to 350˚. Generously oil a 3-quart Bundt pan.

☐ Combine rhubarb with 2 tablespoons sugar and 2 teaspoons cinnamon, and set aside.

☐ In a large mixing bowl, cream together butter and remaining 2 cups sugar. Beat in eggs, 1 at time, then oil, lemon juice, and vanilla.

☐ Sift together flour, baking powder, and salt. With a wooden spoon or rubber spatula, stir flour mixture into mixing bowl in 3 batches, alternating with milk. Fold in nuts.

☐ Spoon ⅓ of batter into prepared pan. Top with ½ of the rhubarb mixture. Repeat, then cover with remaining ⅓ of batter.

☐ Bake 60-65 minutes, or until an inserted skewer comes out clean. Set cake on cooling rack. When cool enough to handle, invert onto serving plate. Before serving, you may wish to dust top with powdered sugar and a sprinkling of cinnamon.

☐ By the way, this cake freezes beautifully.

■ Note: *There really is no difference in baking quality between bleached and unbleached flour...we just think unbleached is more healthful.

ROZALIA's ZUCCHINI BREAD

Yield: 2 loaves
Prepare: 15 minutes
Bake: 40 minutes

I know...who needs another zucchini bread recipe?! But this is Rozalia's... please give it a try. There's less sugar than most, and the sesame seeds are a nice touch.

Rozalia Lofdahl was the Latin teacher at Cedarville High for years and years. In 1950, when we chaperoned the senior class for their trip to Chicago, Rozalia went too, as she was the class advisor. Marv drove the bus. You should have seen us going through The Loop...oh, we had such a good time! That's when we danced to the music of Guy Lombardo at the Aragon Ballroom.

3 eggs
1½ cups sugar
1 cup salad oil
1 tablespoon vanilla
2 cups grated, unpeeled zucchini (loosely packed)
2 cups flour

2 teaspoons baking soda
½ teaspoon baking powder
1 teaspoon salt
1 tablespoon cinnamon (yes, 1 tablespoon!)
1 cup chopped walnuts
½ cup sesame seeds

☐ Preheat oven to 350°. Oil 2 9-inch loaf pans.

☐ In a large bowl, beat eggs until frothy. Beat in sugar, oil, and vanilla until thick and lemon-colored. Stir in zucchini.

☐ Sift together flour, baking soda, baking powder, salt, and cinnamon. Stir into zucchini batter. Fold in nuts. Pour mixture into prepared pans. Sprinkle with sesame seeds.

☐ Bake 40 minutes, or until center springs back when lightly touched. Let cool 10 minutes before turning out on rack.

☐ These freeze so nicely.

FRESH APPLE-NUT BREAD

Yield: 1 loaf
Prepare: 20 minutes
Bake: 1 hour

Good for breakfast, lunch, or supper...spread with cream cheese for little tea-time sandwiches. The topping and a goodly amount of nuts give it its character.

1 cup sugar
½ cup butter, softened
2 eggs
1½ tablespoons buttermilk or sour cream
½ teaspoon vanilla
2 cups sifted flour
1 teaspoon baking soda

½ teaspoon salt
1 cup chopped pecans or walnuts
1 tablespoon flour
1 cup grated, peeled apples
1½ tablespoons sugar
½ teaspoon cinnamon

We love our morning T-time... sitting at the table by the kitchen window. There's always something to see and talk about...hummingbirds and hollyhocks, nice neighbors and special memories, and how the world should be at peace.

☐ Preheat oven to 350°. Oil a 9x5x3-inch loaf pan.

☐ In a mixing bowl, combine sugar, butter, and eggs, beating well. Beat in buttermilk and vanilla. Sift together flour, baking soda, and salt. Add to bowl, stirring in completely.

☐ Combine nuts with 1 tablespoon flour. Stir into batter along with grated apples. Pour into prepared loaf pan. Combine remaining sugar and cinnamon, and sprinkle over top.

☐ Bake 1 hour, or until an inserted toothpick comes clean. Cool on a wire rack before removing from pan.

◾ Note: This recipe may be divided into smaller loaf pans, but reduce the baking time accordingly.

PUMPKIN TEA BREAD

Serves: 12-14
Prepare: 20 minutes
Bake: 1 hour

We don't have tea time the way the rest of the world might. Most mornings, I stop at 10:00 to have a few minutes to relax and think and talk with Dad. That's our "T-time"...valuable time. We never mind though, when friends and neighbors drop in to join us.

⅔ cup soft vegetable
   shortening
2⅔ cups sugar
4 eggs
2 cups pumpkin
⅔ cup water
2½ cups flour
1 cup whole wheat flour
2 teaspoons baking soda

½ teaspoon baking powder
1½ teaspoons salt
1 teaspoon cinnamon
1 teaspoon cloves
½ teaspoon cardamon
   (optional)
1 cup chopped pecans or
   walnuts
1 cup raisins (optional)

☐ Preheat oven to 350°. Grease and flour a Bundt pan or 2 5x9-inch loaf pans.

☐ In a mixing bowl, cream together shortening and sugar. Beat in eggs. Add pumpkin and water, stirring until blended.

☐ Sift together dry ingredients and spices. Stir into pumpkin mixture with a wooden spoon just until blended. Fold in nuts and raisins.

☐ Pour into prepared pan(s). Bake 1 hour or until a toothpick tests clean.

☐ Let cool 10 minutes in pan, then turn out on rack to cool completely.

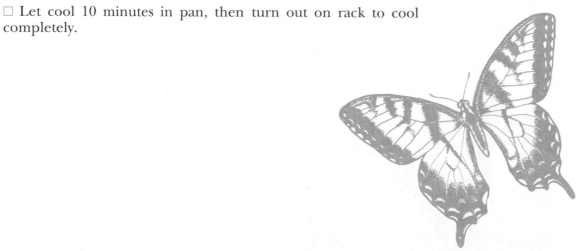

SIMPLY THE BEST BLUEBERRY MUFFINS

Yield: 12
Prepare: 15 minutes
Bake: 20-25 minutes

These stir sweet memories of gathering blueberries at Beavertail, in the company of darting dragonflies and lazy swallowtails and the gentle breezes from the lake.

1¾ cups sifted flour
2½ teaspoons baking powder
½ teaspoon salt
1 egg

Milk, to measure 1 cup
¼ cup butter, softened
½ cup sugar*
1 cup fresh blueberries**

☐ Preheat oven to 400°. Oil muffin tins.

☐ Sift together dry ingredients. Break egg into a glass measuring cup, then add enough milk to measure 1 cup.

☐ In a large mixing bowl, cream together butter and sugar. Beat in egg/milk mixture. Stir in dry ingredients *only* until blended. Do *not* beat. Gently stir in blueberries.

☐ Fill prepared muffin tins about ⅔-full. Bake 20-25 minutes.

☐ These keep nicely if you wish to make them a day ahead or freeze. Just wrap in foil, then warm before serving.

■ Notes: *If the blueberries are not nearly so sweet as Beavertail's, you may wish to add another couple tablespoons of sugar.

**Also, frozen berries (without syrup) may be used, but do not thaw before putting into batter.

CORN PATCH MUFFINS

Yield: 12-18
Prepare: 15 minutes
Bake: 20-25 minutes

My mother's recipe...Estella Ratliff of Lucasville, Ohio. Even though 75 years have passed, I love it still; tender muffins to suit tender corn.

2 cups sifted flour	1 egg, slightly beaten
2 tablespoons sugar	1 cup milk
3 teaspoons baking powder (1 tablespoon)	1 cup drained kernel corn (fresh is even better!)
¾ teaspoon salt	3 tablespoons melted butter

☐ Preheat oven to 400°. Oil muffin pans to accommodate 12 large or 18 medium-size muffins.

☐ Sift together dry ingredients into a large mixing bowl. Combine remaining ingredients in a smaller bowl; then stir them quickly into flour mixture, just enough to blend.

☐ Fill muffin tins ⅔-full. Bake 20-25 minutes. Let cool a few minutes before removing from pans. Serve warm with gobs of sweet butter.

▧ Note: These keep nicely. Just wrap in foil to warm.

THE IROQUOIS's CORNSTICKS

Yield: 14
Prepare: 10 minutes
Bake: 15-20 minutes

Sweet and crisp, without being dry...you'll love this version of a classic.

1¼ cups yellow corn meal
½ cup flour
3 tablespoons sugar
1½ teaspoons baking powder
½ teaspoon baking soda
½ teaspoon salt
1 cup buttermilk
1 egg, lightly beaten
⅓ cup peanut oil

□ Preheat oven to 425°.

□ Brush 2 cornstick molds generously with a light vegetable oil. Place on middle rack of oven to heat for at least 10 minutes.

□ Meanwhile, sift together dry ingredients into a mixing bowl. With a wooden spoon, vigorously beat in buttermilk and egg, then peanut oil.

□ With a large spoon, quickly ladle batter into smoking-hot molds. If you wish plumper cornsticks, fill only 12 of the 14 insets. Bake 12-15 minutes, until lightly puffed and brown.

Had to tell you that I baked the cornsticks just the way they were suppose to have been done years ago at the Iroquois Hotel on Mackinac... very good. They were all gone by lunch time. The men from the mill liked them a lot. I'm going to bake them with crisp bacon bits next time.

JOHNNY CAKE

Serves: 6
Prepare:10 minutes
Bake: 20 minutes

More American than apple pie! Here's a corn bread, flavored with bits of bacon, that is crisp on the outside and tender within, but won't fall apart into a mountain of crumbs. For ever so many years, it has been our family-favorite with hearty soups and stews.

6 slices bacon, chopped	2 teaspoons baking powder
2 tablespoons bacon fat	1 teaspoon salt
1 cup yellow corn meal	1 large egg (2 small)
1 cup flour	1 cup milk
⅓ cup sugar*	

☐ Preheat oven to 425°.

☐ Fry chopped bacon, then drain on paper towels. Brush the bottom and sides of a shallow, 8x8-inch baking dish with bacon fat. Reserve 2 tablespoons bacon fat for batter.

☐ Combine corn meal, flour, sugar, baking powder, and salt in a mixing bowl with a whisk.

☐ Set baking dish in preheated oven.

☐ Beat egg in a small mixing bowl. Whisk in milk and reserved bacon fat. Add bacon bits, and stir into dry ingredients just until well-blended.

☐ Pour into hot baking dish; bake 20 minutes. Serve immediately.

■ Note: *For those who like a sweeter bread, increase sugar to ½-cup.

MILE-HIGH BISCUITS

Yield: 12
Prepare: 10 minutes
Bake: 10-12 minutes

Maybe not a biscuit in the true sense...maybe even better! You can make them ahead, except for baking, refrigerating them on the baking sheet until ready.

2 cups flour	½ cup vegetable
4 teaspoons baking powder	shortening
1 tablespoon sugar	1 egg, beaten
½ teaspoon salt	⅔ cup milk

☐ Preheat oven to 450°.

☐ Sift together dry ingredients into a large bowl. Cut in shortening with a pastry cutter until mixture resembles coarse crumbs. Combine egg and milk with a whisk, then add all at once to flour mixture. Stir with a fork only until dough follows it around bowl.

☐ Turn dough out onto a lightly floured board. Knead very gently with the heels of your hands about 5 to 7 times. Do not be concerned about the moistness of the dough.

☐ Pat or roll out dough to ¾-inch thickness. Cut in 2-inch squares or use a 2-inch biscuit cutter dipped in flour. Place on an ungreased baking sheet, 1 inch apart. (At this point, you may refrigerate until baking time.)

☐ Bake at 450° for 10 to 12 minutes or until golden brown.

Because of being the oldest of the girls in the family and having so many brothers, I knew what work was about from an early age. When I was about 8, my father cut part of the legs off a table so that I could help my mother with the ironing and making biscuits. Well do I remember when my mother would tap my fingers with a wooden spoon if I let the dough go up over my second knuckle when I was kneading.

POTATO BREAD

Yield: 2 loaves
Prepare: 20 minutes
Rise: 1½ hours
Chill: overnight
Rise: 3 hours
1 hour
Bake: 35-40 minutes

Potato breads are particularly popular in this neck of the woods. Here's our favorite, one reason being that you can go off to town for several hours and not worry about the rising time...whatever will be will be, and it still comes out perfect!

For hamburger buns, after the first rising outside of refrigerator just shape into smooth, round balls about half the size of the bun to be; place on a greased baking sheet and let rise until double. Bake at 400° for 10-15 minutes.

1 large potato, peeled and diced	½ cup dry milk powder
1 cup water	3 eggs
1 teaspoon salt	2 packets dry yeast
½ cup butter	¼ cup warm water
½ cup sugar	6 cups flour

☐ Place the potato, water, and salt in a large saucepan. Boil, covered, until potato is tender. Remove from heat, but do not drain. Add butter and sugar, and beat with an electric mixer until smooth. Beat in dry milk powder and eggs.

☐ Dissolve yeast in ¼-cup warm water and add to mixture. With a wooden spoon, beat in enough flour to make a soft dough (about 4 cups). Work in remaining flour until smooth, turning out onto a floured board, if necessary.

☐ Place dough in a generously buttered, large bowl, turning it over so top is greased. Cover with a damp towel and set in a warm place. Let rise until double; about 1½ hours. Punch down, cover, and refrigerate overnight. ·

☐ The next day, let rise at room temperature for several hours.

☐ Divide dough into 2 9x5-inch, buttered loaf pans. Cover and let rise again until double...1 hour or so.

☐ Bake at 375° for 35-40 minutes. Set on wire racks to cool.

SNOWY WHITE BREAD

Yield: 2 loaves
Prepare: 15 minutes
Rise: 1 hour
2-4 hours
1 hour
Bake: 45 minutes

Wouldn't we have loved to have had this recipe back in the days when making bread was a daily chore! This beautiful bread requires no kneading, and you can let the loaves rise almost at leisure. You'll be so proud of the results.

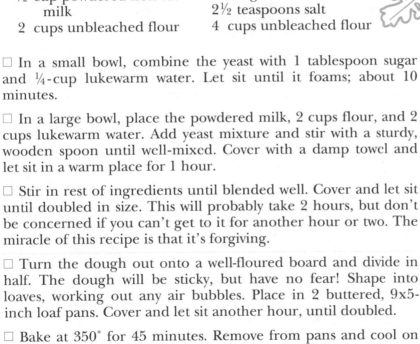

1 package dry yeast
1 tablespoon sugar
¼ cup lukewarm water
½ cup powdered non-fat milk
2 cups unbleached flour

2 cups lukewarm water
¼ cup sugar
3 tablespoons light vegetable oil
2½ teaspoons salt
4 cups unbleached flour

☐ In a small bowl, combine the yeast with 1 tablespoon sugar and ¼-cup lukewarm water. Let sit until it foams; about 10 minutes.

☐ In a large bowl, place the powdered milk, 2 cups flour, and 2 cups lukewarm water. Add yeast mixture and stir with a sturdy, wooden spoon until well-mixed. Cover with a damp towel and let sit in a warm place for 1 hour.

☐ Stir in rest of ingredients until blended well. Cover and let sit until doubled in size. This will probably take 2 hours, but don't be concerned if you can't get to it for another hour or two. The miracle of this recipe is that it's forgiving.

☐ Turn the dough out onto a well-floured board and divide in half. The dough will be sticky, but have no fear! Shape into loaves, working out any air bubbles. Place in 2 buttered, 9x5-inch loaf pans. Cover and let sit another hour, until doubled.

☐ Bake at 350° for 45 minutes. Remove from pans and cool on racks.

■ Note: You can easily double this recipe if you have a large enough mixing bowl.

INDIAN BREAD

Yield: 2 loaves
Prepare: 20 minutes
Rise: 1 hour
1 hour
Bake: 45 minutes

Although a few changes have been made through the many years to suit white man's tastes, the basic recipe is literally as old as the hills. It is also known as Anadama or Squaw's Bread, once a staple of many Indian tribes.

This is surprisingly good, and does not require much kneading. It's an absolute must with Planked Whitefish!

2 cups water	1 teaspoon salt
½ cup Indian meal (yellow corn meal)	1 cake of yeast (or 1 packet of dry)
2 tablespoons shortening	½ cup warm water
½ cup molasses	5-6 cups flour

☐ In a medium saucepan, bring 2 cups of water to a boil. Slowly stir in the Indian meal with a whisk, and remove from heat. Add shortening, molasses, and salt, mixing well. Pour into a large mixing bowl, and set aside to cool.

☐ Dissolve yeast in the warm water for 5 minutes. With a wooden spoon, beat into corn meal mixture alternately with enough flour to make a soft dough. Knead in rest of flour (you may not need the full 6 cups), until smooth.

☐ Place in a large, greased bowl. Cover with a damp towel and let rise in a warm place until double in bulk; about 1 hour.

☐ Turn out onto floured board and divide in half. Knead down and shape into 2 loaves. Place in 2 buttered, 9x5-inch loaf pans. Cover and let rise again until double; about 1 hour.

☐ Bake at 350° for 45-50 minutes. Set on wire racks until cool enough to remove from pans.

SWEET ENDINGS

delicate cakes, blue ribbon pies

Dear Bonnie,

We had a nasty storm yesterday... all day. No mail delivery. The snow really piled up, and the mill shut down.

It's beautiful today, though. The sun is shining and everything looks like Christmas cards. Children are out making angels in the snow. I wish you could see the Stand... or what there is of it. It's like a giant toadstool... sparkling white.

There may be nothing green outdoors; but our plants in the house are nice. Besides African violets in bloom, I have two pink impatiens left over from summer, and several red and green pepper plants that I potted and put in the side room... along with the parsley that I grow in the milk pail. Ruth dug up her geraniums to put in our basement for the winter, but they were blooming so nicely that we've kept them in a big box in the front window. I don't know how we're going to make room for the Christmas tree.

Did you know that it will be our 62nd wedding anniversary the day after Christmas? Ruth's making a Princess Daisy cake for us. I think back to when I was single... I swore I was going to marry someone from the south to avoid the cold. But I went 600 miles straight north with Maw! More about that later.

I'm too busy but it's fun. I owe lots of letters and have so many Christmas cards to send to all those wonderful friends. I'm making old-fashioned cookies for the neighbor children to decorate, and all sorts of Christmas cookies to pack up and mail to Jean and her family.

What are we having for Christmas dinner? First, Maw will open up the jug of dandelion wine he made last May, and we'll toast all our dear friends and family. Then he'll carve a big pork roast... the whole ham... so we can have hot pork sandwiches with gravy for left-overs! Of course, we'll have mashed potatoes, then apple scallop, beets with raisins, green beans with slivered turnips,... and mincemeat pie a la mode. I'll send you some of my recipes... see what you think.

Love and good luck and God bless you and yours,... have a real nice Christmas.

The Chards

226

COFFEE CHIFFON CAKE and
COCOA COFFEE ICING

Serves: 8-10
Prepare: 20 minutes
Bake: 1 hour

Light as a cloud and delicate in flavor, it can be served with just a dusting of powdered sugar, or turned into a celebration cake with Cocoa Coffee Icing.

1 tablespoon instant coffee granules
1 cup hot water
2 cups sifted all-purpose flour
1 tablespoon baking powder
½ teaspoon salt

6 eggs, separated
½ teaspoon cream of tartar
2 cups sugar
1 teaspoon vanilla
1 cup finely ground pecans or walnuts

☐ Preheat oven to 350°.

☐ Dissolve instant coffee in hot water, then set aside to cool. Sift together flour, baking powder, and salt. Set aside.

☐ In a large bowl, beat egg whites with cream of tartar until soft mounds form. Slowly beat in ½-cup of the sugar. Continue beating just until stiff peaks form. In another large bowl, blend egg yolks together then gradually beat in remaining sugar, then vanilla. Continue beating until thick and lemon-colored; about 3-5 minutes.

☐ With a wooden spoon, gently stir dry ingredients into egg yolk mixture in 3 parts, alternating with cooled coffee and ending with dry ingredients (with each addition, stir only until just blended). Lightly fold in ground nuts, then egg whites. Pour into ungreased, 10-inch tube pan. Bake 1 hour.

☐ Invert immediately to cool 1 hour before removing from pan. Then finish, if you wish, with the following *Cocoa Coffee Icing*.

2-3 tablespoons strong black coffee
3 tablespoons butter, softened

3 tablespoons cocoa
2 cups powdered sugar
¼ teaspoon salt

☐ Beginning with 2 tablespoons coffee, combine all ingredients and beat until smooth. Add up to 1 more tablespoon of coffee if necessary for right spreading consistency.

MATTIE's SPICE CAKE

Yield: 1 9-inch, 2-layer cake
Prepare: 25 minutes
Bake: 30-35 minutes

Light and delicately flavored, this old, old family recipe has made many a birthday just that much more special.

½ cup butter, softened
2 cups brown sugar
5 eggs, separated
2¼ cups sifted flour
1 teaspoon baking powder
¾ teaspoon baking soda
1 teaspoon salt

1 teaspoon cinnamon
¾ teaspoon ground cloves
½ teaspoon nutmeg
½ teaspoon allspice
1 cup sour milk or
   buttermilk*

☐ Preheat oven to 350°. Grease and flour 2 9-inch cake pans.

☐ In mixing bowl, cream together butter and brown sugar. Add egg yolks one at a time, beating each in well.

☐ Sift together dry ingredients. With a wooden spoon, gently stir in ⅓ of the milk, then ⅓ of the flour mixture, stirring only until incorporated. Repeat twice more.

☐ Beat egg whites until stiff but not dry. Fold into batter.

☐ Pour into prepared pans. Bake 30-35 minutes, just until cakes begin to loosen at edges and their centers spring back to the light touch. Cool completely on racks before removing from pans. Ice with Maple Syrup Frosting or the traditional 7-minute icing.

■ Note: *To sour the milk, add 2 teaspoons vinegar and let stand 5 minutes.

MAPLE SYRUP FROSTING

Prepare: 15 minutes

A satiny icing that will generously cover a 9-inch, 2 or 3-layer cake.

2 cups maple syrup
3 egg whites

⅛ teaspoon salt

☐ In a medium saucepan, boil syrup over medium-high heat, without stirring, until it will thread from a spoon (242°).

☐ Beat egg whites with salt until they are stiff but not dry. The moment the syrup is ready, beat into egg whites in a thin but steady stream.

TOFFEE NUTMEG CAKE

Serves: 12
Prepare: 25 minutes
Bake: 1 hour

Unforgettable when served with butter pecan ice cream.

3 cups sifted flour
1 pound light brown sugar
1 teaspoon baking powder
½ teaspoon salt
¾ cup butter, softened
½ cup finely chopped (but not ground) pecans
1 egg, lightly beaten
2-3 teaspoons freshly ground nutmeg
1½ teaspoons vanilla
1½ cups sour cream
1½ teaspoons baking soda
¾ cup coarsely chopped pecans

☐ Preheat oven to 350°. Grease and lightly flour a 9 to 10-inch tube pan with a removeable bottom.

☐ In a large bowl, using a pastry blender, combine flour, brown sugar, baking powder, and salt. Then blend in butter until mixture is crumbly.

☐ Combine 3 cups of this mixture with ½-cup finely chopped pecans. Place in bottom of tube pan, but do not pack down.

☐ Into remaining mixture, stir egg, nutmeg, and vanilla. Combine sour cream and baking soda, and add to mixture along with coarsely chopped nuts. Pour into tube pan.

☐ Bake 1 hour or until cake tester comes out clean.

☐ Cool on wire rack 15 minutes. Remove sides of pan and cool completely. Invert onto serving dish. Serve with butter pecan ice cream or whipped cream.

MAMA's PRUNE CAKE

Serves: 12
Prepare: 20 minutes
Bake: 45-60 minutes

Sometimes this is called "Surprise Cake" because no one is to know that it features prunes. I think it's a shame that prunes have to have such a wicked reputation. Here is a very moist and truly delicious cake that can change the minds of the most rigid prune-haters.

While the cake is still warm, drizzle with Buttermilk Glaze...or serve with Lemon Sauce...or place in shallow bowls and surround with Boiled Custard.

1 cup light vegetable oil	1 teaspoon cinnamon	
1½ cups sugar	1 cup buttermilk	
3 eggs	1 teaspoon vanilla	
2 cups sifted flour	1 cup chopped cooked	
2 teaspoons baking soda	prunes	
½ teaspoon salt	1 cup chopped pecans or	
1 teaspoon nutmeg	walnuts	
1 teaspoon allspice		

☐ Preheat oven to 350°. Thoroughly oil a Bundt pan or 9-inch tube pan.

☐ In a mixing bowl, cream together the oil, sugar, and eggs. Sift together the flour, baking soda, salt, and spices. With a wooden spoon, stir dry ingredients into egg mixture, alternating with buttermilk, just until mixed. Do not overbeat. Stir in vanilla, then fold in prunes and nuts.

☐ Pour into prepared pan and bake 45-50 minutes for a Bundt pan, 1 hour for a tube pan. (You may use a 9x13-inch baking dish, baking only 30-35 minutes.)

☐ Cool 10 minutes on a rack, then remove cake from pan. If icing with Buttermilk Glaze, do so while cake is still warm.

BUTTERMILK GLAZE

Prepare: 5 minutes

½ cup butter
½ cup buttermilk
1 cup sugar

1 tablespoon light corn syrup
1 teaspoon baking soda
1 teaspoon vanilla

☐ In a medium saucepan, melt butter then stir in remaining ingredients with a whisk. Boil 1 minute.

☐ While cake is still warm, prick with a fork then pour glaze over top, letting it drizzle down sides. (If cake has been prepared in a shallow baking dish, leave in dish, spreading glaze over top.)

PRIZE-WINNING APPLE CAKE

Serves: 12
Prepare: 10 minutes
Bake: 1 hour

This won first prize at the Ebenezer Sunday School Picnic. Kids in the kitchen love it because it is a throw-together cake and yet really good.

2 cups sugar
1¼ cups light vegetable oil
2 eggs
3 cups flour
1 teaspoon baking soda

1 teaspoon salt
2 teaspoons cinnamon
3 cups diced apples
1 cup chopped nuts
1 cup raisins (optional)

☐ Preheat oven to 350°.

☐ Believe this or not! Put all ingredients into one large bowl. Mix with your hands as you would a meatloaf, gently but thoroughly; do *not* use a spoon or mixer! Bake in an ungreased 9x13-inch pan for 1 hour. Cool before cutting.

APPLE WALNUT CAKE

Serves: 12
Prepare: 25 minutes
Bake: 1 hour

An honest-to-goodness, old-fashioned recipe that still outranks any so-called modern versions. It stays beautifully moist, and looks so pretty on a cake stand. We really like its Brown Sugar Frosting, but if you're short of time, sweetened whipped cream with a splash of sherry is very nice.

4 cups coarsely chopped or shredded, peeled apples	2 teaspoons vanilla
	2 cups sifted flour
	2 teaspoons baking soda
2 cups sugar	2 teaspoons cinnamon
2 eggs	1 teaspoon salt
½ cup vegetable oil	1 cup chopped walnuts

☐ Preheat oven to 350°. Grease and flour a 10-inch tube or Bundt pan.

☐ Combine apples and sugar, and set aside. In a large mixing bowl, beat eggs slightly, then beat in oil and vanilla. Sift together the flour, baking soda, cinnamon, and salt. Gently, but thoroughly, stir into egg mixture, then add walnuts and sugared apples.

☐ Pour into prepared pan and bake 1 hour.

BROWN SUGAR FROSTING

Prepare: 5 minutes

½ cup brown sugar	⅓ cup butter
½ cup white sugar	1 teaspoon vanilla
2 heaping tablespoons flour	½ cup chopped nuts
1 cup water	

☐ With a whisk, combine the sugars, flour, water, butter, and vanilla in a medium saucepan over medium heat. Stirring constantly, boil until slightly thickened. Cool, then add nuts. Drizzle over cake.

MANDARIN ORANGE CAKE

Prepare: 10 minutes
Serves: 12
Bake: 40 minutes

A most unusual cake...it has no shortening but is quite moist, and turns a rich, caramel color when baked. My neighbor describes it best..."It's a real good traveling cake."

2 eggs
2 cups sugar
2 cups flour
2 teaspoons baking soda
1 teaspoon salt

1 teaspoon vanilla
2 11-ounce cans mandarin
   oranges, drained
1 cup chopped pecans or
   walnuts

☐ Preheat oven to 350°. Grease a 9x13-inch baking dish or pan.

☐ Cream together eggs and sugar. Sift together flour, baking soda, and salt. Beat into egg/sugar mixture with a wooden spoon. Then stir in remaining ingredients until well-mixed.

☐ Pour into prepared pan and bake 40 minutes, or until center springs back to a light touch.

☐ Serve dusted with powdered sugar, and cut into squares. Pass a pitcher of rich cream to pour over, if you'd like.

■ Note: If you have a big sweet tooth, while cake is still warm spread with Brown Sugar Frosting (omitting nuts).

PINEAPPLE UPSIDE-DOWN CAKE with LEMON SAUCE

Serves: 8-10
Prepare: 20 minutes
Bake: 40-45 minutes

Arnie Hamel once told me that the only thing he's ever wanted passed on to him is the Bavarian china plate that his mother, Nellie (she's 94 this year!), used to serve Pineapple Upside-Down Cake on every other Sunday...his very, very favorite dessert.

Way, way back, when we were living at Huntley's lumber camp, this was our Sunday dessert...when we could afford it! We love it to this day, but I still think it tasted best baked in the wood stove in my old cast-iron skillet.

¼ cup butter
1 cup brown sugar
1 20-ounce can sliced pineapple
7-8 red or green maraschino cherries (optional)
3 eggs, separated
1 cup sugar
½ cup reserved pineapple juice
½ teaspoon vanilla
¼ teaspoon almond extract
1½ cups sifted cake flour
1 teaspoon baking powder
½ teaspoon salt

☐ Melt butter in a 9 to 10-inch heavy skillet with an oven-proof handle. Add brown sugar and stir over medium heat for a minute or so, until dissolved. Remove from heat.

☐ Drain pineapple, reserving ½-cup of the juice. Spread dissolved sugar mixture evenly over bottom of skillet, then fit in 7 or 8 pineapple slices. (Use any extra slices for another purpose.) Place a maraschino cherry in the center of each slice. Set aside while making cake batter.

☐ Preheat oven to 350°.

☐ Combine the egg yolks and sugar in a mixing bowl, beating well until light. Beat in reserved pineapple juice, and the vanilla and almond flavorings.

☐ Sift together flour, baking powder, and salt. With a wooden spoon or spatula, gently stir into mixing bowl just until incorporated.

☐ Beat egg whites until stiff but not dry. Gently fold into batter. Pour batter over pineapple and cherries in skillet. Bake 40-45 minutes, or until a toothpick tests clean.

☐ Cool 10 minutes. Run a knife around edge of skillet to loosen cake. Lay serving plate over skillet and invert. The cake should come out quite easily.

☐ Serve warm with Lemon Sauce or dollops of lightly sweetened, whipped cream.

■ Note: In place of pineapple, try fresh rhubarb or apples, or canned or fresh apricots, peaches, plums, blueberries or cherries.

LEMON SAUCE

Yield: 1 ¼ cups
Prepare: 5 minutes

This is nice over lots of good things...like gingerbread, fresh berries, apple cake. By tradition, it's made in the top of a double-boiler, but if you're good with a whisk you can do it in a saucepan.

4-6 tablespoons sugar	1 teaspoon grated lemon
1 tablespoon cornstarch	rind
1 cup water	¼ teaspoon vanilla
3 tablespoons butter,	2-3 drops lemon extract
softened	(optional)
1½-2 tablespoons lemon	Pinch of salt
juice	

☐ Combine sugar, cornstarch, and water in a saucepan. Stir constantly with a small whisk over medium to medium-low heat until mixture begins to clear and thicken.

☐ Remove from heat and immediately whisk in remaining ingredients, stirring until butter has blended completely.

PRINCESS DAISY CAKE

Serves: 10-12
Prepare: 20 minutes
Bake: 20-25 minutes

For years and years and years, this has been our cake for weddings and christenings…it's so light and elegant. Four batches will give you a 4-tiered cake with a 12-inch base to serve fifty.

Here's the recipe for <u>one</u> batch…what I do for birthdays for the girls in our family. Depending on the time of year, I wreath it in sweetpeas or daisies or Queen Anne's lace and wild asters, or crown it with one, perfect, hollyhock blossom.

1½ cups sugar
½ cup butter, softened
1 teaspoon vanilla
¼ teaspoon lemon extract
2½ cups sifted cake flour
2½ teaspoons baking
    powder

1 cup milk
4 large egg whites (reserve
    2 yolks for filling)
¾ teaspoon salt

☐ Preheat oven to 350°. I like to make 2 nice, high, 8-inch layers, but this recipe will be fine for 3 8-inch cakes or 2 9-inch. For whichever, cut circles of wax paper to fit the bottoms of the pans. Grease bottoms and sides of the pans, then fit in and grease papers.

☐ In a large mixing bowl, cream together sugar and butter until light and fluffy. Beat in vanilla and lemon extract. Sift together flour and baking powder.

☐ With a wooden spoon, stir in ⅓ of flour mixture just until blended, then half of milk, stirring only until blended. Repeat, ending with flour. (It is important to blend thoroughly but *not* overbeat.)

☐ Beat egg whites with salt until stiff but not dry. Gently fold into batter. Pour into prepared pans.

☐ Bake 20-25 minutes, or just until cakes begin to loosen from edges of pans. Cool completely on racks before removing to fill and frost.

LEMON FILLING

Yield: for 2-3 layers
Prepare: 10 minutes
Cool: 30 minutes

¾ cup sugar
2 tablespoons cornstarch
⅛ teaspoon salt
¾ cup water
2 egg yolks, slightly beaten

3-4 tablespoons fresh
  lemon juice
1 tablespoon butter
1 teaspoon grated lemon
  rind

☐ In a small saucepan, combine sugar, cornstarch, and salt. With a whisk, stir in water, egg yolks, and lemon juice until smooth. Cook over medium heat until thickened, stirring constantly. Remove from heat and stir in butter and lemon rind. Refrigerate until cool; about 30 minutes.

■ Note: Double recipe for a 4-tiered cake.

FLUFFY WHITE ICING

Yield: for 2-3 layers
Prepare: 10 minutes

Soft...so easy to swirl into pretty patterns. I like it for many different kinds of cakes, but it's perfect for Princess Daisy.

1 cup sugar
⅓ teaspoon cream of tartar
⅓ cup water
1 tablespoon lemon juice

2 large egg whites
1 teaspoon vanilla
¼ teaspoon lemon extract
  (optional)

☐ In a saucepan, combine sugar, cream of tartar, water, and lemon juice. Bring to a boil without stirring, and cook until it reaches the thread stage (242°).

☐ Meanwhile, beat the egg whites until stiff but not dry. When syrup is ready, pour steadily, in a thin stream, into egg whites, beating constantly. Add vanilla and lemon extract, and continue beating until mixture reaches spreading consistency.

DOUBLE CHOCOLATE POUND CAKE

Serves: 12
Prepare: 20 minutes
Bake: 1 hour, 20-30 minutes
Cool: 30 minutes

Our chocolate lovers give this 5 stars!

6 ounces semi-sweet bar chocolate (eating, not baking)
4 ounces milk chocolate
2 tablespoons water
1 cup butter, softened
2 cups sugar

4 eggs
2¼ cups sifted flour
¼ teaspoon baking soda
½ teaspoon salt
1 cup buttermilk
2 teaspoons vanilla

☐ Preheat oven to 325°. Grease and flour a bundt pan or 10-inch tube pan.

☐ Place the chocolate with the water in a medium saucepan. Melt over very low heat and set aside.

☐ Cream together the butter and sugar in a large mixing bowl. Beat in eggs, one at a time. Blend in chocolate.

☐ Sift together dry ingredients; then, with a wooden spoon, stir ⅓ into chocolate mixture just until blended. Stir in ½ of buttermilk until just blended. Repeat, ending with remaining ⅓ of flour mixture. Blend in vanilla.

☐ Pour into prepared pan, and bake 1 hour and 20 minutes, or until an inserted toothpick tests clean. Cool in pan on a rack for 10 minutes. Turn out onto rack and cool another 20 minutes. Place on serving plate, then pour Dark Chocolate Frosting over top while cake is still warm.

DARK CHOCOLATE FROSTING

Prepare: 5 minutes

This has just the right consistency for pouring, not spreading...thus, it has a lovely effect over angel food cake, too.

1 6-ounce package semi-sweet chocolate chips

2 tablespoons butter
2 tablespoons corn syrup
3 tablespoons milk

☐ In a small saucepan, melt chocolate chips with butter over low heat, stirring constantly with a small whisk. Stir in corn syrup and milk, beating until smooth. While still hot, pour over cake.

REAL LEMON PIE

Serves: 8
Prepare: 25 minutes
Bake: 25 minutes
5-10 minutes

Lemon lovers claim that this is the ultimate dessert...that lemon meringue pie cannot compare.

Pastry for a 2-crust, 8 to 9-inch pie (see next page)
1½ tablespoons sugar
1 teaspoon cinnamon or nutmeg
3 lemons

1½ cups sugar
3 tablespoons flour
6 tablespoons butter, softened
3 eggs
½ cup water

☐ Preheat oven to 400°.

☐ Roll out ½ of pastry. Cut out a 9-inch circle of dough, using the base of a 9-inch, deep pie plate as a guide, and place on an ungreased cookie sheet. Cut into 8 wedges.

☐ Combine sugar and spice, and sprinkle over wedges. Bake 5 minutes. Cool. Roll out remaining pastry and line pie plate, crimping edge.

☐ Grate yellow part of lemons' rinds. Peel, then slice lemons as thinly as possible, discarding seeds and any coarse pith.

☐ In a mixing bowl, cream together sugar, flour, and butter. Beat in eggs, then water. Stir in lemon slices and grated rind. Pour into prepared pie shell.

☐ Bake 25 minutes, then remove pie from oven. Using a metal spatula, quickly arrange baked pastry wedges on top of filling. Return to oven, then bake another 5-10 minutes for filling to set. Cool on rack, and serve at room temperature.

FOOLPROOF PIE CRUST

Yield: (see * below)
Prepare: 10 minutes

Don't use those cardboardy, commercial mixes. This is so quick and easy, and tender, and guaranteed not to fail. It's the best one I've come across in all my years of baking.

*For 9-inch pies, one recipe is enough for 4 single-crust or 2 double-crust and 1 single.

What dough you do not use can be kept in single-crust portions in the refrigerator for several days, or indefinitely in your freezer. If you have a micro-wave, each portion can be thawed in its plastic wrap in about 2½ minutes at the defrost power-level.

4 cups unsifted flour
1 tablespoon sugar
2 teaspoons salt
1¾ cups vegetable
    shortening**

1 tablespoon vinegar
1 egg
½ cup water

☐ In a large bowl, blend dry ingredients together with a fork. In a separate bowl, beat remaining ingredients together well. Stir into flour mixture with a fork until well moistened, then form into a ball with your hands. Chill if necessary for easier handling.

☐ For best results, use a lightly floured pastry cloth and rolling pin cover to roll out dough. Do not handle or roll your dough any more than necessary.

■ Note: **For richer pastries, you can replace ¼ cup of the vegetable shortening with soft butter.

RHUBARB CUSTARD PIE

Serves: 8
Prepare: 20 minutes
Bake: 40-50 minutes

Now you'll know why rhubarb is so often called pie plant!

3 cups thinly sliced
    rhubarb
2 tablespoons flour
1½ cups sugar

1 tablespoon butter, melted
3 eggs, separated
1 9-inch pie shell, unbaked
Cinnamon

☐ Preheat oven to 450˚.

☐ Place rhubarb in a mixing bowl. Combine flour and sugar, then stir into rhubarb along with melted butter. Beat egg yolks, and add to rhubarb. Beat egg whites until stiff but not dry. Fold into rhubarb mixture.

☐ Spoon into unbaked pie shell, and sprinkle with cinnamon. Bake at 450˚ for 10 minutes. Reduce heat to 350˚ and bake for another 30-40 minutes, until golden brown.

RHUBERRY PIE

Serves: 8
Prepare: 25 minutes

The color is gorgeous, and, if you don't tell what's in it, rhubarb haters will love it. It's great á la mode.

Pastry for a 2-crust, 9-inch
   pie (see index)
2½ cups fresh straw-
   berries, halved
2½ cups chopped fresh
   rhubarb

Grated rind of 1 orange
1½ cups sugar
3 tablespoons flour
2 teaspoons tapioca
3 tablespoons butter

☐ Preheat oven to 425˚. Prepare bottom crust for a 9-inch, deep pie dish.

☐ In a mixing bowl, gently but thoroughly combine remaining ingredients, except butter. Pour ½ of mixture into prepared pie shell. Dot with ½ of butter. Add rest of fruit and dot with remaining butter. Top with pastry that's been slit for steam vents.

☐ Bake at 425˚ for 15 minutes, then reduce temperature to 375˚ and bake another 30-40 minutes, or until lightly browned on bottom and bubbling in center. Cool on rack.

FRESH, FRESH PEACH PIE

Serves: 6-8
Prepare: 25 minutes
Chill: 3 hours

We can hardly wait for peach season to come, and here's a good reason.

9 medium-size peaches
  (or 6 large)
4 tablespoons cornstarch
1 cup water.
¾ cup sugar
¼ teaspoon almond
  extract

Pinch of salt
1 9-inch pie crust, baked
  and cooled (see index)
Garnish: sliced peaches,
  whipped cream, mint
  sprigs

☐ Slice 3 peaches (2, if large) into a blender, setting rest aside. Purée with remaining ingredients (except pie crust!) until smooth.

☐ Pour into a medium-size saucepan and cook over medium to medium-high heat, stirring constantly with a whisk, until it comes to a boil. Continue to cook, stirring, for another minute, until the purée is glossy and thickened. Cool.

☐ Thinly slice remaining peaches and stir into cooled mixture. Pour into prepared pie crust. Chill at least 3 hours.

☐ Garnish with sliced peaches and whipped cream...and how about a few sprigs of mint?

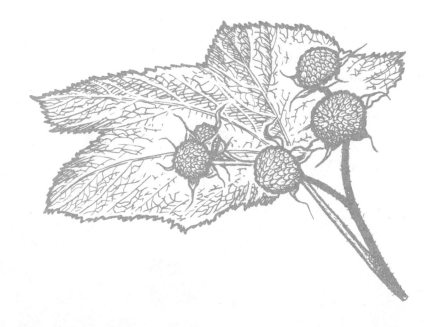

FRESH BERRY BERRY PIE

Serves: 8-10
Prepare: 20 minutes
Chill: 2 hours

Blueberries smothered in blueberries, then raspberries topping all, will give you one of the best desserts of many a summer eve.

4 cups fresh blueberries
  (note divisions in recipe)
½ cup sugar
2 tablespoons cornstarch
6 tablespoons water
1 tablespoon lemon juice

3-4 ounces cream cheese,
  well-softened
1 9-inch pie shell, baked
  and cooled*
1 cup fresh raspberries
Whipped cream

☐ In a medium saucepan, combine 2 cups of the blueberries with the sugar, cornstarch, and water. Bring to a boil and cook slowly until thickened, stirring constantly (about 2 minutes). Remove from heat, stir in lemon juice, then set aside to cool.

☐ Gently spread cream cheese on bottom of cooled pie crust. Stir 1½ more cups of blueberries into cooled berry mixture. Pour into prepared crust. Sprinkle the 1 cup raspberries over top, then remaining ½-cup blueberries. Chill completely (at least 2 hours).

☐ To serve, garnish with dollops of whipped cream.

■ Note: *This recipe is ideal for individual tarts. For tart or pie shells, for best appearance and least amount of shrinkage, prick the pastry with a table fork across the bottom and along sides, then bake at 425° for 10-12 minutes...just until golden brown. (See index for pastry recipe.)

OUR BLUEBERRY PIE

Yield: 1 9-inch pie
Prepare: 20 minutes
Bake: 45-60 minutes

This is our all-time favorite pie. The proportions of ingredients guarantee an unforgettable treat. Try the recipe for any berry pie, adjusting the sugar to the sweetness of the fruit.

The blueberries are luscious this year. Jean made two out-of-this-world pies. Makes me think of the time we went berry picking at Gilcrest. You couldn't move without stepping on blueberries, let alone sit!

1 generous quart of
   blueberries
2 teaspoons lemon juice
⅞ cup sugar
2 tablespoons plus
   1 teaspoon flour

½ teaspoon cinnamon
3-4 tablespoons butter
Pastry for a 2-crust, 9-inch
   pie (see index)
Sugar

☐ Preheat oven to 425°.

☐ Wash and clean blueberries of stems. Drain well, then place in a bowl and sprinkle with lemon juice. Combine sugar, flour, and cinnamon with a fork; then add to berries.

☐ Line a 9-inch, deep pie plate with half of pastry. Pour in half of berry mixture. Dot with half of butter. Top with rest of berries and then remaining butter.

☐ Roll out and cut rest of pastry into strips, ¾-inch wide. Lay over top of pie in lattice-fashion, then crimp edge. Lightly sprinkle with sugar.

☐ Bake at 425° for 15 minutes. Reduce temperature to 350°, and bake another 35-40 minutes; or until top and bottom crusts are nicely browned and center is bubbling.

☐ Simply wonderful served warm with scoops of vanilla ice cream.

GREEN TOMATO APPLE PIE

Serves: 6-8
Prepare: 25 minutes
Bake: 1 hour

I'll never forget everyone's surprise, especially my own, when one September I fixed our favorite apple pie recipe, but I used green tomatoes in place of some of the apples. It was so pretty, and just about the most delicious dessert one could ask for. Let me know if you don't think so, too!

It looks like we're going to have a glut of green tomatoes, but Marv loves them fried or in a pie. I'm always surprised how few people know how good they are.

Pastry for a 2-crust, 9-inch
    pie (see index)
2 cups thinly sliced green
    tomatoes
3 medium, tart apples
1 tablespoon lemon juice
½ cup sugar

½ cup brown sugar
2 tablespoons flour
1 teaspoon cinnamon
¼ teaspoon nutmeg
Pinch of salt
4 tablespoons butter
Sugar

☐ Preheat oven to 425°. Prepare bottom crust, fitting into pie dish.

☐ Thinly slice tomatoes, cutting slices in half, to measure 2 cups. Core and peel apples; thinly slice to match tomatoes. Toss tomatoes and apples in a large bowl with lemon juice. Combine dry ingredients and mix in lightly.

☐ Place ½ of fruit mixture in prepared pie shell. Dot with ½ of butter. Add rest of fruit and dot with remaining butter. Top with pastry that's been slit for steam vents, then crimp edge. Sprinkle with a little sugar.

☐ Bake at 425° for 15 minutes. Reduce heat to 350° and bake another 45 minutes.

☐ Serve warm, if possible...with some vanilla ice cream?!

CONCORD GRAPE PIE

Yield: 1 9-inch pie
Prepare: 30 minutes
Bake: 45-60 minutes

In the fall, sometimes we'll take our T-time out on the bench under the grape arbor...vines twisting everywhere, dripping with the blue-black fruit that makes our heads giddy with its fragrance. It comforts our souls. Our son, M.J., says it comforts his tummy! His favorite pie is grape.

4 cups Concord grapes	¼ teaspoon cinnamon
2-3 tablespoons butter	(optional)
1 tablespoon lemon juice	Pastry for a 2-crust, 9-inch
1 cup sugar	pie (see index)
3 tablespoons flour	Sugar
½ teaspoon salt	

☐ Preheat oven to 425°.

☐ Slit and pop grapes from their skins into a medium-size, heavy saucepan. Reserve skins.

☐ Simmer the pulp for 5 minutes, then press through a sieve to remove seeds. Combine the strained pulp with the reserved skins. Stir in butter to melt, then lemon juice. Combine sugar, flour, salt, and cinnamon; blend into grape mixture.

☐ Line a 9-inch, deep pie plate with half of pastry. Fill with prepared fruit. Top with remaining pastry that's been slit for steam vents. Crimp edges and sprinkle with a little sugar.

☐ Bake at 425° for 15 minutes. Reduce temperature to 350°, and bake another 35-40 minutes; or until crusts are browned and center is bubbling.

☐ Serve warm or at room temperature.

ALMA's PUMPKIN PIE

Serves: 8
Prepare: 20 minutes
Bake: 7-8 minutes
50-55 minutes

You'll never make a better pumpkin pie!

1 9-inch pie shell, unbaked (see index)
1½ cups cooked or canned pumpkin
⅔ cup brown sugar
1 rounded teaspoon cinnamon
½ teaspoon ground ginger
Dash each of ground cloves and nutmeg
½ teaspoon salt
2 eggs
1½ cups milk
½ cup light cream

☐ Preheat oven to 450°. Prick pie shell throughout with a table fork to help prevent puffing up while baking. Bake 7-8 minutes. Set on rack to cool while preparing filling.

☐ In a mixing bowl, whisk together remaining ingredients in order given. Pour into baked pie shell.

☐ Bake in lower third of oven at 450° for 5 minutes. Reduce heat to 350°, and bake 40 minutes, or until almost firm to the touch. Shut off oven, leaving pie in for 5-10 minutes. Don't get too firm, though. Cool on rack.

☐ Serve as is or top with lightly sweetened whipped cream and grated orange rind, or treat everyone to crunchy Penuche Topping.

PENUCHE TOPPING

Prepare: 5 minutes
Cool

¾ cup brown sugar
¼ cup butter, softened
¾ cup pecan halves
1 tablespoon milk

☐ Preheat broiler. Cream together brown sugar and butter with a fork. Stir in pecans and milk. Gently spread on cooled pumpkin pie.

☐ Broil *just* until tiny bubbles form. Remove immediately and let cool.

SOUR CREAM RAISIN PIE

Serves 6
Prepare: 25 minutes
Bake: 1 hour

Please take our word for it...when it comes to raisin pie, this recipe is top-notch!

1 cup raisins
Hot water
Pastry for a 2-crust, 8-inch
  pie (see index)
1 cup sugar
1 tablespoon flour

¼ teaspoon salt
1 egg, beaten
1 cup sour cream
1 teaspoon vanilla
Sugar

☐ Preheat oven to 400˚.

☐ Place raisins in a saucepan with enough hot water to cover, about 1 cup. Bring to a boil then remove from heat and let sit while you make your pastry for an 8-inch pie.

☐ Drain raisins. Combine sugar, flour, and salt; stir into raisins. Stir in beaten egg, then sour cream and vanilla. Pour into unbaked pie shell. Top with crust that's been slit for steam vents, crimping edge. Sprinkle with a couple teaspoons or so of sugar.

☐ Bake 15 minutes at 400˚, then 45 minutes at 350˚. Serve warm or cold with rich cream or ice cream.

SUGAR CREAM PIE

Serves: 6-8
Prepare: 10 minutes
Bake: 1 hour

This should be called "Nostalgia Pie." Big girls who were little girls two or more generations ago might recall sitting on kitchen stools, watching their mothers make pies, crossing their fingers that enough dough would be left to turn into sugar and cream tarts just for them.

To this day, it is still one of my favorite taste memories.

1 cup sugar
½ cup flour, minus
   1 tablespoon
2 cups heavy cream
½ teaspoon vanilla or a
   grating of nutmeg
   (optional)

1 9-inch pie shell, unbaked
   (see index)
3 tablespoons butter

☐ Preheat oven to 425°.

☐ Combine sugar with flour in a mixing bowl. Add cream and mix well. Add a flavoring of vanilla or nutmeg, if you wish, but I think it's just as good without it.

☐ Pour into pie shell and dot with butter. Bake 15 minutes. Reduce heat to 350° and bake 45 minutes more, or until the center is bubbly and thickened. If the edge of the crust begins to overly brown, cover it with strips of foil.

☐ Cool completely before cutting. If you wish, serve with fresh raspberries and/or sliced peaches.

PEANUT BUTTER PIE

Serves: 8
Prepare: 20 minutes
Chill: overnight

Wonderfully silky in texture, absolutely superb in taste...an unforgettable dessert.

1 cup graham cracker crumbs	3 tablespoons cocoa
Pinch of cinnamon	3 tablespoons flour
3½ tablespoons sugar	3 tablespoons melted butter

☐ Combine the above ingredients, mixing well, and press firmly into a 9-inch pie plate. Chill.

8 ounces cream cheese, softened	2 tablespoons melted butter
1 cup smooth peanut butter	1 cup heavy cream
1 cup sugar	1½ teaspoons vanilla

☐ Cream together cream cheese, peanut butter, sugar, and melted butter until smooth. Beat in cream and vanilla. Pour into chilled crust. Cover and chill at least 6 hours, preferably overnight.

3 ounces semi-sweet chocolate	¼ cup chopped peanuts
1½ tablespoons brewed coffee	

☐ Melt chocolate in a small saucepan; stir in coffee. Cool slightly, then quickly spread over chilled pie. Garnish with chopped peanuts, and chill until serving time.

SWEET ENDINGS

old-time desserts, and cookies, too

Bonnie dear,

I'm thinking of you today, as I do every day as a special friend. Hope you had a real nice holiday season with your family. The Christmas card you sent us said so much. The rabbit and the fox... and peace for the world. Sometimes I think we hear too much of things going on in the world. It's so nice here.

Winter has settled in. The ferry boats have stopped running from Mackinac Island, since the ice is forming in the Straits... they'll be berthed until spring. It's snowing like mad... just what it should do in January. I worry about the birds, though, and have put out all sorts of good things for them. We had a pair of cardinals at the feeder yesterday, but today they must be waiting out the storm.

A lot of men have been fox and coyote hunting. The snowmobiles are out in full force. I liked it better in the days when we just depended on our snowshoes. Lots of things were simpler then. For instance, who needed freezers? We just wrapped up the food and set it up high outdoors... let it freeze like a rock.

Days like this are perfect for reflecting at T-time on the years gone by... way, way back to when we were living in the lumber camp and what road there was was blocked by snow. My brother Charles Ratliff's wife was having a baby... we had to pull the doctor into camp on a little sled.

We were laughing about the time Jean was running down the bank at Taylor Creek. She was going so fast, she couldn't stop... right on into the freezing cold water. She still talks about it. Oh! And when Ruth was following her Dad over to Terry Fenlon's house. She was having fun stepping in his footprints in the snow, but he was pretending not to pay attention to her. She figured out how to get him... she started to yodel. He laughed and laughed.

And we still laugh when we think about it. We have so many little stories like that that make up our good memories. Just think! We've loved, lived, and laughed together for 62 years... and maybe cried a little. But they say there have to be some clouds to make a beautiful sunset!

Take care. Love 'ya,

Judy Chard.

BLINK-OF-AN-EYE
RHUBARB PIE

Serves: 6
Prepare: 10 minutes
Bake: 25-30 minutes

In just a couple blinks of an eye, you'll have a really good dessert...rather like a nice, crunchy, butterscotch brownie. It works with apples, too. Serve warm, topped with whipped or ice cream.

1 cup diced rhubarb
½ cup flour
1 teaspoon baking powder
¾ cup sugar

½ cup chopped pecans
   or walnuts
1 teaspoon vanilla
1 egg, lightly beaten

☐ Preheat oven to 350°.

☐ Place diced rhubarb in a medium-size bowl. Sift flour and baking powder over top. Add sugar, nuts, vanilla, and egg. Mix all together and spread in a buttered, 9-inch pie plate. Bake 25-30 minutes.

HOMEMADE PEACH
ICE CREAM

Yield: 1 quart
Prepare: 15 minutes
Freeze

Divinely delicious...crown with sliced peaches and/or fresh raspberries.

2 large eggs
¾ cup sugar
1½ cups sour cream

2 teaspoons vanilla
4 medium peaches, peeled
1 tablespoon lemon juice

☐ Beat eggs and sugar until light-colored and sugar has dissolved. Beat in sour cream and vanilla. Purée peaches in a blender or food processor with the lemon juice. Beat into sour cream mixture. Follow procedure for an ice cream maker, or see note.

■ Note: If not using an ice cream maker, pour the peach mixture into a shallow, glass baking dish. Freeze until half-frozen. Whirl in a blender or food processor (this helps eliminate ice crystals), then pour into a 1-quart mold or ice cream container. Lay plastic film on the surface of the ice cream, then tightly seal with a lid or foil. Freeze.

BROILED RASPBERRIES
and CREAM

Serves: 6
Prepare: 10 minutes
Bake: 3 minutes
Broil: 1 minute

Just a little variation of a wonderful theme...

4 cups raspberries*
1 tablespoon raspberry
    liqueur (or 1½
    teaspoons kirsch)

1 cup heavy cream
2 egg yolks
¼ -½ cup powdered sugar
1 teaspoon vanilla

☐ Preheat oven to 400°.

☐ Divide berries between 6 individual baking dishes. Sprinkle each with a ½-teaspoon liqueur. Place dishes on a cookie sheet.

☐ Whip cream until it forms soft mounds. Beat in egg yolks, and ¼ to ½-cup powdered sugar, depending on sweetness of berries. Add vanilla and continue beating for 1 minute. Pour over berries, proportionately.

☐ Bake in oven 3 minutes. Run under a broiler for a brief minute to brown the cream, keeping a *close* watch. Serve immediately.

■ Note: *Sliced strawberries are a nice substitution, or 2 cups of each combined.

To freeze whole berries, place them unwashed (if they aren't dusty or haven't been exposed to chemicals) on cookie sheets in single layers in your freezer. As soon as they are frozen, scoot them into plastic bags and seal well.

STRAWBERRY SHORTCAKES

Serves: 6 generously
Prepare: 10 minutes
Bake: 10 minutes

There are those who think that spongecake is the only true base for straw-berry shortcake, and then there are those of us who <u>really</u> know what's good! Here's the best recipe of all for biscuit-type shortcakes...tender, wonderful show-stoppers.

2 cups flour
2 tablespoons sugar
¾ teaspoon salt
1 tablespoon baking
    powder

4 tablespoons butter,
    softened
1 cup light cream

☐ Preheat oven to 450°.

☐ Sift together dry ingredients into a mixing bowl. Cut in butter with a pastry blender until mixture resembles fine crumbs. Pour in cream and mix gently with a fork until *just* blended.

☐ Drop 6 large spoonfuls of the batter onto an ungreased baking sheet. (At this point, you may cover with plastic wrap and refrigerate until a ½-hour or so before dessert time.)

☐ Bake at 450° for 10 minutes, or until puffed and lightly browned.

Softened butter for
    spreading
6 cups strawberries, sliced
    and sugared to taste

1½ cups heavy cream,
    whipped
6 gorgeous strawberries
    for garnish

☐ As soon as the biscuits are cool enough to handle, split and spread insides lightly with butter. Place bottoms on dessert plates, ladle sliced and sugared berries over all, then cover with tops. Crown each with a good dollop of whipped cream and a perfect strawberry. Serve immediately.

255

PEACH PINWHEELS

Serves: 6-8
Prepare: 30 minutes
Bake: 35-40 minutes

A peach shortcake with a different twist, and it can be made ahead except for baking.

1½ cups sugar
½ teaspoon cinnamon
½ teaspoon nutmeg

1¾ cups water
Grated rind of ½ lemon
½ cup butter

☐ Preheat oven to 425°.

☐ In a large saucepan, combine above ingredients and boil 5 minutes without stirring. Remove from heat; stir in butter, in pieces, until melted. Set aside to cool.

4 peaches
Juice of ½ lemon
2 cups flour
2 tablespoons sugar
2 teaspoons baking powder
1 teaspoon salt

½ cup vegetable
   shortening
¾ cup milk
Whipped cream or
   ice cream

☐ Peel and chop peaches. Add lemon juice and toss. Set aside.

☐ In a mixing bowl, sift together flour, sugar, baking powder, and salt. Cut in shortening until mixture becomes coarse crumbs. Add milk all at once, stirring with a fork just until a ball of dough is formed. Turn out onto a lightly floured board, and knead very gently only 2 or 3 times.

☐ Roll dough out to about 9x12 inches. Spread with peaches. Starting with long edge, carefully roll up in jelly-roll fashion. Cut into 1-inch thick slices and place in a buttered, 9x13-inch glass baking dish. (At this point, the dish may be covered and refrigerated for a few hours before baking.)

☐ Pour cooled syrup over top of pinwheels. Bake at 425° for 35-40 minutes. Serve warm with whipped cream or ice cream.

■ Note: Apples are a nice substitution for the peaches.

CARAMEL PEARS

Serves: 6
Prepare: 5-10 minutes
Bake: 15-20 minutes
1-2 minutes

This is so simple and so delicious, but uncommon in that you don't see it in recipe books. The recipe serves 6, but you may increase or decrease it proportionately, using a shallow casserole or individual ramekins. Can be prepared ahead except for baking.

6 ripe (but still firm) pears
Lemon juice (optional)
9 tablespoons sugar

6 tablespoons butter
12 tablespoons (¾ cup) heavy cream

☐ Preheat oven to 500° (that's right!).

☐ Peel, quarter, and core pears. If preparing ahead, toss pears in lemon juice to prevent darkening. Divide between 6 ramekins or arrange closely together in an ungreased, shallow baking dish (about 8x11-inch).

☐ Sprinkle pears generously with sugar; about 1½ tablespoons per pear. Dot each quarter with butter, to equal about 1 tablespoon per pear. Set aside until baking time.

☐ Bake, uncovered, 15-20 minutes, basting once or twice, until sugar is burned to a rich brown.

☐ Pour cream over top of pears; about 2 tablespoons per pear. Bake another minute or two, until cream has blended in. Serve while still hot.

■ Note: If serving in ramekins, place on napkin-lined plates.

BLACK CHERRY COBBLER

Serves: 6-8
Prepare: 20 minutes
10 minutes
Bake: 50 minutes

Northern Michigan's celebrated sweet black cherries are why one will see so many tourists driving our back roads in July. Every few miles, you can count on finding a little stand with a hand-lettered sign, "Washed Black Cherries Here!."

It's well-worth purple fingers to eat them by the handful or stew and pit them for a cobbler.

1 quart black cherries,
   unpitted

1½ cups boiling water
½ cup sugar

☐ Wash and remove stems from cherries. Drop into boiling water, adding ½-cup sugar. Cover and simmer until tender; about 7-10 minutes. Cool in juice.

1 cup reserved cherry juice
¼ cup sugar

1 tablespoon cornstarch
2 tablespoons butter

☐ Preheat oven to 400°. Pit cherries, reserving 1 cup juice, and place in an ungreased, 9x12-inch, shallow baking dish. Combine juice with sugar and cornstarch, and pour over cherries. Dot with butter. Bake, uncovered, for 20 minutes or until bubbling.

☐ See Purple Plum Cobbler for remaining ingredients and directions.

PURPLE PLUM COBBLER

Serves: 6-8
Prepare: 15 minutes
Bake: 50 minutes

Those velvety, purple plums of August and September are so beautiful set in a milk-glass bowl on our kitchen table, that it can take courage to put them into a cobbler...but well worth it.

1 cup sugar	6 cups pitted and quartered
1 tablespoon cornstarch	plums
¾ cup water	2 tablespoons butter

☐ Preheat oven to 400°. Mix together sugar, cornstarch, and water. Combine with plums. Pour into an ungreased, shallow, 9x11-inch baking dish. Dot with butter. Bake, uncovered, for 20 minutes or until bubbling.

1 cup flour	¼ cup vegetable shortening
1 tablespoon sugar	½ cup (on generous side)
2 teaspoons baking powder	sour cream
½ teaspoon salt	Heavy cream

☐ With a pastry blender, combine dry ingredients in a medium-size bowl, then cut in shortening until crumbly. Stir in sour cream with a fork until well-mixed.

☐ When plums have baked 20 minutes, drop dough by spoonfuls on top of bubbling fruit. Bake another 30 minutes, or until biscuits are lightly browned. Serve warm in shallow bowls, and pass a pitcher of cream. It's plum good!

APPLE BREAD PUDDING
with MAPLE CREAM

Serves: 4
Prepare: 20 minutes
Bake: 1¼ hours

This has to be the ultimate of bread puddings. It's easy and can be prepared a day ahead before baking.

3 apples, peeled and cored
2 tablespoons butter
¼ cup brandy
2 tablespoons dried currants
1½ teaspoons cinnamon
¼ teaspoon each ground cloves, nutmeg, ginger, and allspice
½ of a 1-pound baguette of French bread*
1 tablespoon sugar

☐ Thinly slice apples, cutting each slice in half. Melt butter in a medium skillet over medium-high heat. Add apples and remaining ingredients except bread and sugar. Cook about 10 minutes. Apples should be tender but still firm.

☐ Remove all crust from bread, then slice ¼-inch thick. *(Any bread of similar texture may be used, but keep pieces thin and less than 2 inches in diameter.)

☐ Butter an 8-inch, deep casserole, and sprinkle with 1 table-spoon sugar. Layer with half of the bread, then half of the apple mixture. Repeat. At this point, the dish may be set aside, covered, until baking time.

☐ The following topping may be prepared in advance, too:

½ cup flour
¼ cup butter, softened
3 tablespoons sugar
1 tablespoon cinnamon

☐ With your hands, combine the above 4 ingredients in a small bowl. Set aside.

☐ Shortly before baking time, preheat oven to 350°, and prepare the following custard:

2 whole eggs   ¾ cup sugar
3 egg yolks   1½ teaspoons vanilla
1¼ cups light cream

☐ With a whisk, lightly beat eggs and egg yolks in a mixing bowl. Whisk in cream, sugar, and vanilla. Pour over apple/bread mixture. Cover with reserved topping.

☐ Place casserole in a shallow roasting pan filled with 1 inch hot water. Bake 1¼ hours.

☐ Serve warm with the following delicious Maple Cream, which also can be made ahead.

We are so proud of our sugar maples. They are beautiful any time of year...lush green in summer, golden in the fall, black and handsome against deep snows, and then, in March or early April, so generous with their sap. When it is still well below freezing at night, but starts to warm up in mid-mornings with spring sunshine, Marv taps his favorite trees, the big old grand-daddies, to boil down the sap in the sugar shack.

MAPLE CREAM

Yield: 1¾ cups
Prepare: 10 minutes

1½ cups pure maple   ¼ cup brandy
    syrup   1 cup heavy cream, warmed

☐ In a saucepan, over medium-high heat, combine syrup and brandy. Cook, uncovered, until reduced about half or until the mixture has begun to darken; about 5-6 minutes. Whisk in warmed cream.

■ Note: The sauce may be reheated to serve warm, but do not boil.

THE-BEST-EVER
APPLE CRISP

Serves: 6
Prepare: 15 minutes
Bake: 50-60 minutes

It seems like a pretty grand statement to call this the best ever, but after tasting lots of others, it's true!

4 cups thickly sliced apples (pared or unpared)	¼ cup water
2 tablespoons lemon juice	Cinnamon
	Nutmeg

☐ Preheat oven to 350°.

☐ Spread apples in a buttered, shallow, 1½-quart baking dish. Combine lemon juice and water, and pour over apples. Sprinkle generously with cinnamon and lightly with nutmeg.

¾ cup flour	½ cup white sugar
½ cup brown sugar	¼ cup butter

☐ Work together above ingredients with fingers or pastry blender until crumbly. Spread over apples.

☐ Bake 50-60 minutes, or until apples are tender and topping is crisply browned. Serve warm with cream or ice cream.

INDIAN PUDDING

Serves: 4 to 6
Prepare: 5 minutes
Cook: 30 minutes
Bake: 1 hour

Serve warm with scoops of vanilla ice cream for a special winter's night. Easily prepared ahead and ever so good.

½ cup corn meal	3 cups milk
½ teaspoon salt	½ cup light molasses
½ teaspoon ginger	Vanilla ice cream or heavy cream
¼ teaspoon mace	
¼ teaspoon cinnamon	

☐ Preheat oven to 325°.

☐ In a large, heavy saucepan, combine corn meal, salt, ginger, mace, and cinnamon. Stir in milk with a whisk until smooth. Place over low heat and cook about 30 minutes, stirring often. Stir in molasses. Pour into a buttered, 1-quart, deep baking dish.

☐ At this point, the pudding may be covered and set aside on the counter or in refrigerator until baking time.

☐ Bake, uncovered, at 325° for 1 hour. Serve warm with ice cream or cream.

GINGER LEMON PUDDING CAKE

Serves: 8
Prepare: 10 minutes
Bake: 40-45 minutes
Cool: 30 minutes

Here's the perfect dessert for a simple autumn supper.

1⅓ cups flour
½ cup brown sugar, packed
3 teaspoons baking powder
1 teaspoon cinnamon
½ teaspoon ginger
½ teaspoon salt
½ cup water
¼ cup light molasses

¼ cup light vegetable oil
1½ cups boiling water
½ 6-ounce can frozen lemonade concentrate, thawed
½ cup brown sugar, packed
Whipped cream

☐ Preheat oven to 350°.

☐ In a mixing bowl, combine the flour, ½ cup brown sugar, baking powder, cinnamon, ginger, and salt. In a small bowl, combine the ½-cup water, molasses, and oil. Stir into dry ingredients. Turn into an ungreased, 8x8-inch, shallow baking dish.

☐ In a small saucepan, bring 1½ cups water to a boil. Stir in concentrate and brown sugar. Return to a boil, then pour carefully over batter in baking dish.

☐ Bake 40-45 minutes, until lightly browned at the edges. Cool 30 minutes. While still warm, serve with dollops of whipped cream.

BOILED CUSTARD

Yield: 2¼ cups
Prepare: 10 minutes

There's nothing new about this recipe; it's just that it's easily forgotten in these times of fancy desserts. It is so nice just by itself, served over fresh fruits or Prune or Raspberry Cake.

By the way, have you ever wondered why one calls it "boiled" custard when it must never be boiled?!

3 large or 4 medium egg
   yolks
¼ cup sugar
1 good pinch of salt

2 cups milk, scalding hot
   but *not* boiling
1 teaspoon vanilla

☐ Before placing over heat, slightly beat egg yolks with a whisk in a medium-sized, stainless steel saucepan.* Beat in sugar and salt, then scalding hot milk.

☐ Over medium to medium-high heat, continue to beat briskly with whisk until thick as cream, but do not allow to boil.

☐ Remove from heat and whisk in vanilla. Let cool to room temperature before refrigerating, periodically stirring with whisk.

☐ Can be served at room temperature or chilled.

■ Note: *Usually this is made in a double boiler to guard against curdling, but, if you use a whisk instead of a spoon and are conscientious about stirring vigorously, you should have no problems.

OLD-FASHIONED COOKIES

Yield: 10 dozen
Prepare: 15 minutes
Bake: 7-10 minutes

One of my customers gave me this. She said that it is a very, very old family recipe...treasured. You can add nuts, dates, candy, fruit, butterscotch or chocolate chips...whatever is on your shelf that appeals. You can ice them with a butter or powdered sugar frosting, or leave them plain. You just can't go wrong.

1 cup white sugar
1 cup brown sugar
1 cup butter (or
   shortening), softened
3 eggs
4 cups sifted flour

2 teaspoons baking powder
1 teaspoon baking soda
1 teaspoon salt
1 cup milk
1 tablespoon vanilla

☐ Preheat oven to 400°.

☐ In a large mixing bowl, cream together both sugars and butter. Beat in eggs.

☐ Sift together dry ingredients. Stir into bowl alternately with milk, then add vanilla.

☐ Drop by teaspoonfuls onto ungreased cookie sheets, about 2 inches apart. (You'll average 16-20 per sheet.) Bake 7-10 minutes, or until *just* beginning to brown. Do not over-bake. Remove from sheets while still warm.

JUNE's SUGAR COOKIES

Yield: 4 dozen
Prepare: 20 minutes
Bake: 10-12 minutes

Everyone looks forward to these...what sugar cookies are meant to be. Thus, we usually beg June to make a double batch.

½ cup sugar
½ cup powdered sugar
½ cup butter, softened
½ cup light oil
1 large egg
2 cups plus 2 tablespoons flour

½ teaspoon baking soda
½ teaspoon cream of tartar
¼ teaspoon salt
Sugar (¼-½ cup)

☐ Preheat oven to 375°.

☐ Beat together the two sugars, butter, and oil until creamy. Beat in egg.

☐ Combine flour, baking soda, cream of tartar, and salt with a whisk. Thoroughly blend into sugar and butter mixture.

☐ Place ¼-½ cup sugar in a small bowl. Shape dough into 1-inch balls and roll in sugar to coat. Place 3-4 inches apart on ungreased baking sheets. Using a small, flat-bottomed glass, flatten each ball to about ¼-inch thickness, dipping glass in the sugar each time.

☐ Bake until edges are lightly browned; about 10-12 minutes. Transfer cookies to racks to cool.

OATMEAL LACE COOKIES

Yield: 5 dozen
Prepare: 10 minutes
Bake: 6-8 minutes

When a child asks me for a baking lesson, this is the recipe I like to use. It couldn't be easier, and the cookies are as pretty as snowflakes...and she'll always go home so proud.

½ cup flour
½ cup sugar
¼ teaspoon baking powder
⅛ teaspoon salt
½ cup quick-cooking oats
2 tablespoons heavy cream
2 tablespoons light corn syrup
⅓ cup melted butter
1 tablespoon vanilla

☐ Preheat oven to 375°. Line a cookie sheet with foil and brush or spray lightly with oil.

☐ In a medium size bowl, combine flour, sugar, baking powder, and salt with a whisk. Stir in remaining ingredients with a fork.

☐ Using a ¼-teaspoon measuring spoon, drop batter onto cookie sheet 3 to 4 inches apart. Bake 6-8 minutes, until lightly browned. Let stand a few seconds before removing from sheet. Makes approximately 5 dozen, 2½-inch cookies.

☐ They will keep best if stored in tins.

ELEANORA's BUTTER NUT COOKIES

Yield: 9 dozen
Prepare: 15 minutes
Bake: 15 minutes

A delicate, wonderfully short cookie that is particularly nice for fancy occasions like weddings and ladies' teas...very easy to fix.

1 cup butter, softened
1 cup powdered sugar
1 teaspoon vanilla
½ teaspoon almond flavoring

1½ cups sifted flour
½ teaspoon baking soda
1 cup quick-cooking oats
1 cup walnuts, finely chopped

☐ Preheat oven to 325°.

☐ In a mixing bowl, combine butter and powdered sugar with a wooden spoon or sturdy beater, then add vanilla and almond flavoring. Sift together flour and baking soda. Mix in well, along with oats.

☐ Roll dough into small balls the size of a marble; about ¾-inch wide. Place chopped walnuts on a sheet of wax paper.

☐ Place balls on chopped nuts and flatten with a table fork to about 1½ inches. Slide each cookie off fork onto an ungreased baking sheet, walnut side up, about an inch apart. Bake 15 minutes.

Every time I bake cookies I can't help but think about the first batch I made for Marv right after we were married. I was so pleased about them...sugary and crisp. Well...he had just gotten his first pay check to support his bride, and what did that bride do but let it get stolen when she went down to the store. He got the news just as he was biting into one of my cookies. He was so mad (but I honestly don't think at me), that he started throwing cookies into the coal bucket, saying they were too crisp! To this day, whenever I make that recipe the girls say, "Here come Mom's coal-bucket cookies."

PEANUT COOKIES

Yield: 9-10 dozen
Prepare: 15 minutes
Bake: 8-10 minutes

A great little cookie...thin and crisp, but still wonderfully chewy.

1 cup butter, softened
1 cup brown sugar
1 cup white sugar
2 eggs
2 cups flour
1 teaspoon baking soda
1 teaspoon baking powder
1 teaspoon salt
1 cup cornflakes
1 cup oatmeal
1 - 1½ cups roasted
  peanuts

☐ Preheat oven to 325°.

☐ In a large mixing bowl, combine the butter, sugars, and eggs. Sift together flour, baking soda, baking powder, and salt. Stir into mixing bowl, along with remaining ingredients.

☐ Drop by teaspoonfuls, 2 inches apart, on ungreased cookie sheets. Bake 8-10 minutes. Remove from sheets while still warm.

CINNAMON TEA COOKIES

Yield: 8 dozen
Prepare: 30 minutes
Bake: 12 minutes

Not only are these good at "T-time", but a favorite on the Christmas tray.

1 cup butter, softened
¾ cup sugar
1 egg, separated
1 teaspoon vanilla
2 cups flour
4 teaspoons cinnamon
½ cup ground pecans
  or walnuts

☐ Preheat oven to 350°.

☐ In a large mixing bowl, cream together butter and sugar. Beat in egg yolk and vanilla. Combine flour and cinnamon, then blend in with a wooden spoon. Form into balls, using a ½-teaspoon as a measure.

☐ Beat the egg white only until frothy. Dip ½ of each ball in egg white then ground nuts. Place, dipped-side up, on ungreased cookie sheet, 1 inch apart. Bake 12 minutes.

MOLASSES COOKIES

Yield: 4-5 dozen
Prepare: 20 minutes
Bake: 8-10 minutes

I have a confession to make. After filling enough cookie jars over the years to stretch from here to the Soo, this is still the best molasses cookie I've ever tasted...but it came off the label of a Brer Rabbit Molasses jar!

¾ cup butter
1 cup sugar
1 egg
¼ cup light molasses
2 cups flour
2 teaspoons baking soda
1 teaspoon cinnamon
½ teaspoon cloves
½ teaspoon ginger
½ teaspoon salt

☐ Preheat oven to 375˚.

☐ Cream together butter and sugar. Beat in egg and molasses. Sift together remaining ingredients, then stir into molasses mixture.

☐ Form into 1-inch balls and place 2 inches apart on a greased or foil-lined baking sheet. Bake 8-10 minutes. (They will crack a little on top when done.)

LEONA's BUTTERSCOTCH COOKIES

Yield: 3-4 dozen
Prepare: 15 minutes
Bake: 6-7 minutes

Leona tells that this recipe came about by mistake one day, while she was trying to make butterscotch brownies. The brownies became cookies, and have been a favorite ever since. They are wafer-like and so-o-o delicious.

¼ cup butter
1 cup brown sugar
1 egg
1 teaspoon vanilla
½ cup plus 2 tablespoons sifted flour
1 teaspoon baking powder
½ teaspoon salt
½ cup finely chopped nuts

☐ Preheat oven to 350˚.

☐ Melt butter in a large saucepan. Stir in brown sugar until dissolved. Cool slightly. Beat in egg and vanilla.

☐ Sift together dry ingredients and stir into butter mixture along with nuts.

☐ Drop by teaspoonfuls on greased cookie sheets. Bake 6-7 minutes.

DOUBLE CHOCOLATE
CHIP SQUARES

Yield: 4 dozen
Prepare: 10 minutes
Bake: 25-30 minutes

There are lots of variations on this theme...but we've always had raves about ours. And it's so quick and easy for those last minute bring-a-batch-of-cookies assignments.

⅔ cup butter, melted
1 pound brown sugar
3 eggs
1 teaspoon vanilla
2¾ cups sifted flour
2½ teaspoons baking powder
½ teaspoon salt
1 cup coarsely chopped nuts
1 12-ounce package semi-sweet
   chocolate bits

☐ Preheat oven to 350°.

☐ In a large mixing bowl, combine melted butter and brown sugar. Add eggs, one at a time, beating well; then vanilla.

☐ Sift together dry ingredients. Add to mixing bowl, along with nuts and chocolate bits. Blend well.

☐ Pour into a greased, shallow roasting pan. Bake 25-30 minutes. When almost cool, cut into squares or bars.

CHOCOLATE DROP COOKIES

Yield: 4 dozen
Prepare: 30 minutes
Bake: 8-10 minutes

Guaranteed to be the first gobbled up at PTA meetings!

½ cup butter, softened
1 cup sugar
1 egg
2 ounces semi-sweet
   chocolate, melted
1½ cups sifted flour

1 teaspoon baking powder
½ teaspoon baking soda
¼ teaspoon salt
½ cup sour cream
1 teaspoon vanilla
1 cup chopped pecans

☐ Preheat oven to 350°.

☐ Cream together butter and sugar. Beat in egg. Sift together dry ingredients. Add alternately with sour cream to butter/sugar mixture. Stir in vanilla and nuts.

☐ Drop by teaspoonfuls onto greased cookie sheet. Bake 8-10 minutes. While cookies are still warm but not hot, spread with the following frosting.

1½ cups powdered sugar
2 tablespoons heavy cream
2 tablespoons butter,
   softened

1 ounce semi-sweet chocolate,
   melted

☐ Combine above ingredients with a fork until smooth.

CHOCOLATE PEANUT BUTTER GRAHAMS

Yield: 3 dozen
Prepare: 10 minutes
Chill: 15 minutes
Prepare: 5 minutes
Stand: 15 minutes

Somewhere between a cookie and a candy...an unforgettable experience for the sweet tooth.

22 graham cracker squares
   (1½ cups fine crumbs)
3 cups powdered sugar
8 ounces butter, melted
1 cup creamy peanut butter
1 12-ounce package semi-
   sweet chocolate chips

☐ Crumble graham crackers in a food processor or blender until fine crumbs. Combine with powdered sugar, blending well. (Depending on capacity, this may have to be done in 2 batches.)

☐ Combine in a large mixing bowl with melted butter and peanut butter, mixing well. Spread in an ungreased, 9x13-inch, shallow baking dish or pan, pressing firmly into an even layer. Smooth a sheet of plastic wrap or waxed paper evenly over surface.

☐ Place in refrigerator for 45 minutes, or freezer for 15 minutes (no longer), just to set up for easier spreading.

☐ Melt chocolate chips in a medium saucepan over very low heat, stirring constantly with a wooden spoon or heat-proof rubber spatula until smooth. Remove plastic wrap from graham mixture, then spread melted chocolate evenly over top.

☐ Let stand about 15 minutes for chocolate to firm up before cutting. Cut into 1 to 1½-inch bars or squares.

■ Note: These will keep a week or two, if refrigerated.

This is To Congratulate You
A Thought From Me To You!
About You!
You are full of Pep. You are n
To everyone. You don't Hate an
You are Good and sweet You
Are Like a Grandma To eve
Body. I Thank For Letting
me Spend The Night And The
Others Nights Too. And I
Thank You For Letting me cal
You Grandma Judy. More To come

274

CHOCOLATE CHIFFON COOKIES

Yield: 5 dozen
Prepare: 20 minutes
Bake: 45 minutes

The neighbor children call these "fairy cookies" because they are so dainty. When I make them for Christmas time, I press a pecan half into each one before baking.

1 cup butter, softened
1¼ cups powdered sugar
6 ounces German sweet
    chocolate, grated
1½ cups sifted flour
Pinch of salt
1 teaspoon vanilla
1 cup finely chopped pecans
Pecan halves (optional)

☐ Preheat oven to 250°.

☐ Combine butter and sugar, then stir in remaining ingredients (except pecan halves), blending well.

☐ Gently roll dough into 1 to 1½-inch balls, placing about 2 inches apart on an ungreased cookie sheet. Press a pecan half into each one, if you wish. Bake 45 minutes.

ND You Help THe
mmUNiTY A LoT Too.
iF THeRE is ANyTHINg YoU

like me to do. JusT SAy so.

BuT MosT imporTANT

THANKs FoR beiNg You

Love

SALLy

CHRISTMAS FRUIT COOKIES

Yield: 3 dozen
Prepare: 20 minutes
Bake: 8-10 minutes

Jewel-like cookies that capture the Christmas spirit...a delicious alternative to fruit cake.

½ cup butter, softened
1 cup brown sugar
1 egg
1⅓ cups flour
½ teaspoon baking soda
½ teaspoon salt
¼ cup buttermilk
1 teaspoon vanilla
¾ cup chopped pecans
¾ cup chopped dates
¾ cup chopped candied red cherries
½ cup chopped candied green pineapple
36 pecan halves

☐ Preheat oven to 350˚.

☐ Cream together butter and sugar. Beat in egg. Sift together flour, baking soda, and salt. Add alternately with milk to butter/sugar mixture. Stir in remaining ingredients except pecan halves.

☐ Drop batter, by teaspoonfuls, onto greased cookie sheet. Place a pecan half on top of each. Bake 8-10 minutes. Do not over-bake; the cookies should remain waxy, not dry.

These will keep nicely in tins.

BETH's CRACKERJACK POPCORN

Yield: 20 cups
Prepare: 15 minutes
Bake: 1 hour

Beth's house at Christmas time is a child's heaven...paper snowflakes on the windows, twinkling lights and flickering candles, cinnamon toast in the oven, the Advent calendar with sweet surprises...and always something fun to make for loving aunts and favorite teachers.

1 cup popcorn kernels
1-2 cups peanuts (or toasted
    almonds or pecans)*
½ pound butter
2 cups light brown sugar
    (well-packed)

½ cup light corn syrup
1 teaspoon salt
1 teaspoon baking soda
1 tablespoon vanilla

☐ Preheat oven to 200°.

☐ Pop popcorn kernels, to yield about 5 quarts. Divide between 2 ungreased, large, shallow roasting pans; then add nuts, dividing.

☐ In a large, heavy saucepan, melt butter, then stir in brown sugar, corn syrup, and salt with a wooden spoon. Stirring constantly, bring to a boil; then boil 5 minutes without stirring.

☐ Remove from heat, then immediately stir in baking soda and vanilla. Gradually pour over pop corn and nuts, mixing well.

☐ Bake 1 hour, stirring well every 15 minutes.

☐ Cool completely, then store in air-tight containers. This may be frozen.

■ Note: *Beth chops the nuts, in order to make it more difficult for little fingers to snitch them!

CREAMY OLD-FASHIONED CARAMELS

Yield: 200 pieces
Prepare: 45 minutes
(except cutting time)

This is the kind of recipe that you want to keep a secret...honestly, no commercial caramel can compare. It's Bea Allen's, and she found it in an old, old cookbook from a candy factory in Canton, Ohio, that was renowned at the turn of the century. She worked out the measurements for cooking on a home stove, and for years and years this has been her special gift to her many friends at Christmas time.

4 cups sugar
1 16-ounce bottle light
   Karo syrup
3 pints heavy cream
Butter the size of a walnut
   (about 2½ tablespoons)

1 tablespoon paraffin
   shavings
Pinch of salt

☐ Butter a shallow roasting pan or 2 9x13-inch glass baking dishes. Hook a candy thermometer on the edge of a heavy Dutch oven or kettle, then place the sugar, syrup, and 1 pint of the cream in the pot. Bring to a boil over high heat, stirring constantly with a truncated wooden spoon...one with a hole in its center is the best.

☐ When the thermometer reaches 236°, add another pint of cream, never ceasing to stir diligently. Add the last pint of cream when the temperature again reaches 236°.

☐ Continue cooking and stirring, until 242°. Immediately remove from burner, and stir in butter, paraffin, and salt. When blended in, pour caramel into prepared pan(s). Cool on a rack.

☐ When completely cooled, run a spatula or knife around edge of pan, then invert onto cutting board or marble slab. Cut into bite-size pieces. Wrap in small pieces of wax paper, twisting ends to seal.

☐ Tied up in plastic bags, the caramels will keep nicely for at least 2 weeks.

■ Note: We do not recommend doubling this recipe unless you have a very large kettle; then, plan on doubling the cooking time as well.

the FRUIT CELLAR

vinegars, pickles, and relishes

Dear Bonnie,

It's cold here this a.m. at 10:30. It's minus 8 degrees, but the sun is bright. There's blue sky and clean snow... the kind that squeaks when you walk in it.

The men came in for coffee to get warm. They are grading lumber out in the yard. I made some old-time doughnuts... did I send you that recipe? I got it out of a 1925 local church cookbook, and it's still good!

Well, the ice fishermen love this weather! You should see Hessel and Musky Bays,... honest-to-goodness shantytowns. They're catching perch, pike, and walleye. At night, closer in, you'll see the twinkling lights of lanterns where people are fishing without shanties, as late as they please. That's when you get rock bass... next to perch, our favorite fish.

There are more cross-country skiers every year using the channels and bays of the islands... must be like paradise for them. With the summer people gone, they have all that beauty to themselves... except for the deer, coyotes, beaver, mink and rabbits. (The squirrels, porkies, and raccoons are having their winter naps.)

Makes me think about how hard and long some of the past winters seemed to us. One year I cooked in a lumber camp for Sam Shields. The roads were so bad, we had to board the girls with Mrs. Wisner in Hessel so that they could get to school.

Once we had five riding horses. That was fun, but they would eat up all the profits during the winter. After three years, we gave up.

Lots of little rabbit tracks weaving across our snow. I'm trying to remember when they, the snowshoes, begin to shed their ermine coats to wear their summer brown.

It's been a long time since the hollyhocks have bloomed. Spring can't come too soon.

Love to all.
Your friend,
Judy Chard

PICKLED BABY ASPARAGUS
with TARRAGON

Yield: 5 pints
Prepare: 30 minutes
Process: 20 minutes

These are unique as appetizers, and work their way beautifully into relish or antipasto trays. They show-off as a very pretty gift.

4 pounds very thin, young asparagus	2 red bell peppers
3 cups white wine vinegar	1 medium onion
1 ½ cups water	5 teaspoons mixed pickling spices
3 tablespoons sugar	5 teaspoons dried tarragon
2 teaspoons salt	20 black peppercorns

☐ Wash 5 pint-size jars in hot, soapy water. Rinse, keeping hot in oven until ready.

☐ Wash asparagus. Trim ends so that stalks are ¾-inch shorter than jars. Set aside.

☐ Combine vinegar, water, sugar, and salt in a medium saucepan. Boil 10 minutes.

☐ Cut bell peppers into thin strips, and set aside.

☐ Cut onion in half *lengthwise*. Place each half cut-side down, then thinly slice. Line the bottoms of the jars with the onion.

☐ To each jar, add 1 teaspoon pickling spices, 1 teaspoon tarragon, and 4 peppercorns. Pack in asparagus spears, heads up, alternating with red pepper strips to give a striped effect. Be sure to leave ¾-inch headspace.

☐ Add boiling vinegar mixture to cover, leaving ½-inch headspace. Release any trapped air with a long, wooden skewer or pickling fork. Wipe rims of jars with a clean, damp cloth. Seal and process by water-bath method for 20 minutes (see index).

KEN's OLD-FASHIONED APPLE BUTTER

Yield: 6 pints
Prepare: 45 minutes
Bake: 6-8 hours

Leaving the skins on the apples and slow baking are what give this butter its rich color and flavor. It can be canned or frozen.

10 pounds tart apples
4-6 cups apple cider
3 cups sugar
2 teaspoons cinnamon

1 teaspoon ground cloves
½ teaspoon allspice
Juice of 2 lemons (optional)

☐ Preheat oven to 275°.

☐ Quarter apples and core, but do not peel. Place in a cooking pot with enough cider to cover. Cover and cook until tender; about 20 minutes. Press through a sieve or food mill; apple pulp should measure about 3 quarts.

☐ Stir rest of ingredients into apple pulp, then pour into a deep roasting pan. Bake, uncovered, stirring occasionally, until a rich, dark brown, and thick enough to mound in a spoon. This should take from 6 to 8 hours.

☐ If you wish to can the apple butter, see index for water-bath method, processing 10 minutes.

Mrs. Patrick's son-in-law brought us 1½ bushels of apples from Ohio. I'll have to do those up. He gave me the best recipe for apple butter. I'm sending it along to you.

BLUEBERRY BUTTER

Yield: 8 pints
Prepare: 15 minutes
Cook: 1 hour

A nice way to bring summer to your table throughout winter's months. Spread on buttered toast for a breakfast treat, or serve as a condiment with roast pork or lamb.

2 quarts fresh blueberries*
8 large, green, cooking apples
8 cups sugar

1 teaspoon allspice
1 teaspoon nutmeg
1 teaspoon mace

☐ Wash and drain blueberries; peel, core, and slice apples. Combine in a Dutch oven or pot with remaining ingredients.

☐ Bring to a boil, stirring. Lower heat and simmer 1 hour, stirring periodically, or until right consistency for spreading.

☐ May be stored in the freezer or canned. If the latter, see index for water-bath method, processing 10 minutes.

■ Note: *Frozen, sugarless blueberries may be used, but the flavor may not be so intense.

PIE PLANT CHUTNEY

Yield: 6 cups
Prepare: 15 minutes
Cook: 1 hour

We love this relish served with roast pork or wild duck and game, or poured over cream cheese as an appetizer with crackers. The sweet red pepper adds much to the color.

2 pounds rhubarb, cut in ½-inch pieces (6-7 cups)
1½ cups chopped onion
1 red bell pepper, coarsely chopped
1 orange, seeded and finely chopped (including rind)*
½ lemon, seeded and finely chopped (including rind)*

½ cup golden raisins
1 clove garlic, minced
1 cup sugar
1 cup brown sugar
1 cup vinegar
½ teaspoon cinnamon
¼ teaspoon ground cloves
¼ teaspoon cayenne pepper
½ teaspoon salt

☐ Combine all ingredients in a large, stainless steel saucepan. Cover and bring to a boil. Simmer gently for 1 hour or until mixture is thick enough to mound in a spoon.

☐ The chutney will keep up to 1 month in the refrigerator, or can be canned by water-bath method, processing 10 minutes (see index).

■ Note: *A food processor is handy for chopping the orange and lemon.

ROSY CRAB APPLE JELLY

Yield: 8-10 cups
Prepare: 30 minutes
Cook: 45 minutes
Strain: 4 hours plus

This has to be the loveliest of all jellies. Its nectar and fragrance are deliciously superb, and the redder-skinned the crab apple, the rosier the jelly...as if you have steeped its spring blossoms.

For crystal-clear jelly, strain the juices of the apples and lemons with care.

2½ pounds crab apples   Sugar
   (about 2 quarts)   Juice of 1-2 lemons,
Cold water   well-strained

☐ Wash and quarter apples. You can leave the cores, but remove all stems and any bruises or brown spots.

☐ Place in a large saucepan or pot with just enough cold water to cover. Cover the pan and cook over medium heat until the apples are very soft; about 45 minutes. Periodically stir and mash them.

☐ Ladle the fruit and juice into a dampened jelly bag (or a sieve lined with 2 layers of dampened cheesecloth), hung over a large bowl. Let the juice drip, without pressing, until it stops; at least 3 to 4 hours (or leave it overnight).

☐ At the end, you may gently press the bag, but you must be careful or you could end up with cloudy jelly.

☐ Measure the apple juice and pour into a large pan. For each cup of juice, add ¾-cup sugar. Stir until the sugar has dissolved, then add *strained* lemon juice to taste.

☐ Set the pan, uncovered, over high heat. Bring to a boil, and boil rapidly until it registers 220° on a candy/jelly thermometer. (If you are without a thermometer, test with a cold, dry, metal spoon. The jelly will be done when it leaves the spoon in a sheet instead of in droplets. Do not use the same spoon to retest unless it has been cleaned and is cold.)

☐ Immediately remove from heat. Skim away any foam and ladle into hot, sterilized, jelly jars. Leave ½-inch headspace, if sealing with paraffin, or ⅛-inch if using canning lids. Wipe the rims clean of any drips. Seal, cool, label, and store.

■ Note: To seal, I usually use paraffin, melting it in an old but clean coffee can, with its top squeezed to form a spout. I keep the can in a pan of simmering water, and first pour a very thin layer of wax over the hot jelly, making sure it covers all. If any bubbles form, I prick them with a toothpick. When the wax sets, I add another thin layer (about ⅛-inch).

CORNCOB JELLY

Yield: 3-4 ½-pint jars
Prepare: 15 minutes
Cook: 30 minutes
5 minutes

My niece gave me this recipe. She has more fun with it because everyone swears it's apple jelly.

12 bright red corncobs (field corn, scraped free of kernels)*	1 1¾-ounce package pectin
1½ quarts water	3 cups sugar

☐ Break cobs in half into a kettle. Add 1½ quarts water and boil for 30 minutes.

☐ Strain liquid to measure 3 cups. Pour into a medium-size saucepan. Add pectin and bring to a rolling boil. Add sugar, then boil 2-3 more minutes, or until jelly stage is reached. (Test by dipping a cold, metal spoon into syrup. It is done when syrup coats spoon well.)

☐ Pour into sterilized jars and seal.

■ Note: *City folks may need to know that "field" corn is what is grown for cattle and pigs to eat. The corn that people like does not have red cobs.

INDIA RELISH

Yield: 8 pints
Prepare: 30 minutes
Cook: 30 minutes
Process: 15 minutes

This method does not require that the vegetables sit in a brine overnight, and the apples are a unique addition.

12 medium-size green tomatoes
12 tart apples, peeled and cored
3 medium onions
2 red bell peppers
5 cups vinegar

5 cups sugar
3 teaspoons powdered ginger
1 teaspoon cayenne pepper
1 teaspoon turmeric
1 teaspoon salt

☐ Put all of the vegetables through a food grinder or processor until fine.

☐ Place the remaining ingredients in a large pot and bring to a boil. Add the vegetables, return to a boil, and simmer 30 minutes.

☐ While still hot, pack into clean, hot jars. Seal and process by water-bath method for 15 minutes (see index).

Green tomatoes are so pretty lined up on the window sill, reminding one of summer days passed. But I always have far more green tomatoes than I have window sills, so I pop them into the kettle with a few apples, and in no time have pretty jars of India relish.

ZUCCHINI PICKLES

Yield: about 8 pints
Prepare: 15 minutes
Stand: 3 hours
Prepare: 20 minutes
Process: 8 minutes

My niece, Shirley Dailey, knows an awful lot about cooking; so, if she says these are better than bread and butter pickles, then they are!

8 medium zucchini (4 quarts, cut up)
6 medium onions, sliced
1 green bell pepper, sliced
1 red bell pepper, sliced
2 cloves garlic, minced
⅓ cup coarse or non-iodized salt

Ice cubes
3 cups white vinegar
5 cups sugar
2 tablespoons mustard seed
1 teaspoon turmeric
½ teaspoon celery seed

☐ Slice zucchini to desired thickness, or quarter lengthwise then cut into 1-inch chunks. Combine with rest of vegetables, including garlic, and place in a stainless steel or porcelain pan. Cover with salt, then ice cubes. Let stand 3 hours. Drain, rinse, then drain again.

☐ Combine remaining ingredients and pour over well-drained vegetables. Bring to a rolling boil. Continue to boil while packing into hot, clean jars. Process in boiling water bath for 8 minutes (see index).

ZUCCHINI RELISH

Yield: 10-12 pints
Prepare: 20 minutes
Stand: overnight
Cook: 30 minutes

Knowing how a zucchini crop can do you in, my customers have been more than generous with their zucchini relish recipes...this one I like the best for its color as well as flavor. Children love it on their hamburgers and hot dogs.

12 large zucchini (to make 20 cups)	4 cups white vinegar
8 large onions (to make 10 cups)	8 cups sugar
⅔ cup salt	4 teaspoons celery seed
6 carrots, finely chopped	2 teaspoons dry mustard
3 green bell peppers, finely chopped	2 teaspoons turmeric
1 red bell pepper, finely chopped	2 teaspoons cornstarch
	1 teaspoon black pepper

☐ With a food grinder or processor, grind zucchini and onions. Stir in salt and let stand overnight. Drain and rinse well in cold water.

☐ In a large pot, combine remaining ingredients and bring to a boil. Stir in rinsed zucchini and onions. Cover, return to a boil, reduce heat, and simmer 30 minutes.

☐ To can, ladle hot relish into clean, hot jars. Seal and process by water-bath method for 15 minutes (see index).

☐ Otherwise, cool and store in refrigerator to keep for several weeks.

BLENDER CATSUP

Yield: 3 pints
Prepare: 30 minutes
Bake: 1½-2 hours

A snap to prepare, and a great way to use all those dead-ripe tomatoes when the garden seems to be running your life.

24 ripe, ripe tomatoes
  (about 9 pounds)
1 red bell pepper
1 green bell pepper
2 onions
1½ cups white vinegar

1½ cups sugar
1½ tablespoons salt
1½ teaspoons dry mustard
¾ teaspoon each allspice,
  ground cloves, cinnamon
¼ teaspoon cayenne pepper

☐ Preheat oven to 325°.

☐ Remove stem ends from tomatoes and quarter into a large bowl. Seed, then cut peppers into chunks or strips, and add to tomatoes. Quarter onions and mix in.

☐ In batches, purée vegetables with vinegar in electric blender. Pour into a large, deep roasting pan. Stir in remaining ingredients.

☐ Bake, uncovered, until mixture is reduced to half; about 1½ to 2 hours, depending on water content of tomatoes.

☐ Cool and store in the refrigerator for several weeks, or freeze. Or, to can, use water-bath method, processing 15 minutes (see index).

AUNT JANE's CHILI SAUCE

Yield: 18-20 ½-pints
Prepare: 45 minutes
Cook: 3 hours
Process: 15 minutes

Peaches and pears are the secret ingredients. Simply wonderful...a special gift for friends and neighbors at Christmas time.

30 ripe, average-size tomatoes	12 cinnamon sticks
6 peaches	1 tablespoon whole cloves
6 pears	1 quart vinegar
6 onions, quartered	3 cups sugar
3 green peppers, quartered	1 cup brown sugar
1 bunch celery, cut up	3 tablespoons salt

☐ Peel tomatoes by immersing in boiling water for 10 seconds or so, to loosen skins. Coarsely chop.

☐ Pit and core peaches and pears, but do not peel. Coarsely chop. Put onions, green peppers, and celery through a food grinder or processor.

☐ Break cinnamon sticks in half and tie up in cheesecloth along with cloves.Place in a large kettle, along with the vinegar, sugars, and salt. Bring to a boil.

☐ Add prepared fruits and vegetables, and return to a boil, stirring periodically. Reduce heat and let simmer, uncovered, until mixture has cooked down to desired consistency; about 3 hours. Stir from time to time; check seasoning.

☐ While still hot, using a wide funnel, ladle into clean, hot jars. Seal and process by water-bath method for 15 minutes (see index).

DAUGHERTY HERB VINEGARS

"Make them with dill, basil, mint, rosemary, tarragon, thyme, or whatever pleases you. With dill, it is important to use a lot of the weed as opposed to the head, although at least one flower will add the pretty touch.

"Stuffing the bottles is simple if you have a long pickling fork. If you wish to include garlic, use one large clove, cutting tiny slits in it to release the flavor. To anchor it to the bottom of the bottle, cut one larger slit and insert the stem of the herb.

"Use a distilled white vinegar of quality, Warming it (but do not overheat) before pouring into bottles. Do not cork until the vinegar has cooled. Then, if you'd like, dip the tops in warm sealing wax for an elegant look."

Jack Daugherty, one of our good summer friends, wrote down his method for bottling special vinegars. He said that he saves unique looking bottles throughout the year, then puts up his vinegars when fresh herbs are ready from the garden...dried herbs just don't give flavor. He has great fun with them for Christmas gifts.

WILD BERRY VINEGAR

Yield: 8-10 cups
Steep: 2-4 weeks

Wild blueberries, blackberries, or raspberries give exceptional flavor to vinegars. Sweeten the vinegar if you wish to use it in fruit salad dressings or sweet/ sour sauces for meats. For a wildly wonderful sauce for fish, follow the recipe for Mother's Mayonnaise, substituting blueberry vinegar and Dijon mustard.

4 pounds ripe berries (about 8 ½-pint baskets or 12 cups)	6 cups white vinegar Sugar (optional)

☐ Crush the berries (but do not purée), and place in a glass, stoneware, or stainless steel container. Pour vinegar over, and cover tightly. Let stand at room temp 2-4 weeks (longer the better for fuller flavor), shaking the container from time to time.

☐ After steeping period, strain the vinegar through a sieve lined with dampened cheese cloth, pressing to attain all liquid.

☐ If not adding sugar, pour through a funnel into sterilized bottles and cap. (For clarity, line funnel with filter paper.)

☐ If sweetening vinegar, measure and place in a stainless steel pan with about 1½ tablespoons sugar per cup of liquid (or to taste). Bring to a boil and simmer, uncovered, 5 minutes. Cool, strain again through cloth or filter paper, and bottle.

MOCK SALMON

Yield: 1 pint
Soak: 1 hour
Drain: 10 minutes
Prepare: 10 minutes
Pressure cook: 90 minutes

To many, canning fish may not have appeal, but in our part of the country the results are always appreciated. Fish such as mullet (suckers) or pike yield an excellent mock salmon for casseroles, salmon loaf, or patties, to be enjoyed when fresh fish isn't available. Here are the ingredients per pint.*

Clean, skinned, raw fish
Brine (see below)
1 tablespoon catsup

1 tablespoon light
  vegetable oil
1 teaspoon vinegar

☐ Cut fish into chunks. Soak 1 hour in a brine that has a ratio of 1 cup salt to 1 gallon water.

☐ Let fish drain for 10 minutes. Pack into clean, warm, pint jars, leaving 1-inch head space. To each jar, add the remaining ingredients. Use screw-cap lids, and screw down tightly.

☐ Process according to pressure cooker directions for 90 minutes at 10 pounds.

■ Note: *In order to destroy any existing bacteria, fish should *not* be canned in jars larger than 1 pint so that heat can thoroughly penetrate.

VENISON MINCEMEAT with CIDER

Yield: 10 quarts
Prepare: 30 minutes
Cooking: 1-2 hours

The original recipe has been in the Patrick family for too many years to remember. We've changed it just a little to suit today's tastes and ways of cooking.

3 pounds lean venison, cooked*
½ pound beef suet or butter
3 quarts chopped green apples (about 18 large)
3 pounds seedless raisins
1 pound currants
2 cups canned fruits with juice (i.e. cherries, plums, pineapple)

3 cups sugar
3 cup brown sugar
3 tablespoons cinnamon
1 teaspoon ground nutmeg
1 teaspoon ground cloves
¼ teaspoon allspice
2 teaspoons salt
¼ cup cider vinegar
1 quart apple cider

☐ Finely chop meat in a food processor or run through a meat grinder. If using suet, finely chop or grind. Combine with remaining ingredients in a large pot. Simmer, uncovered, stirring periodically, for 1 to 2 hours, or until apples have cooked down and it has become thick enough to mound in a spoon.

☐ Pack in sterile jars for canning by pressure cooker method, or cool and put in plastic containers to freeze.

■ Note: *To cook venison, place in a large pot, add ½-cup vinegar, and cover with water. Simmer, covered, until tender; about 3 hours.

CUPCAKES
for the BIRDS

Serves: countless hungry birds
Yield: about 4 quarts
Prepare: 15 minutes

Among our cold weather friends are the chickadees, nuthatches, woodpeckers, and jays that come to feast on the sunflowers. As winter deepens, and the cardinals, juncos, titmice, grosbeaks, and finches join the hungry crews, I make a big pot of this treat to help fill their tummies.

2 quarts water
1 cup butter, lard, or margarine
4 cups cereal (any combination of cornmeal, oatmeal, farina, Cream of Wheat, Roman Meal)

1 cup peanut butter (crunchy's best!)
1 cup chopped fruit (apples, raisins, currants, dates)
1 cup birdseed, chopped nuts, or sunflower seeds (optional)

☐ Bring water and butter to boil in a large pot. Slowly stir in cereal and cook until thick, anywhere from 5 to 15 minutes, depending on kind(s). Remove from heat and stir in peanut butter and fruit. Let cool before adding seeds or nuts.

☐ Spoon into small, non-metal containers. Store in refrigerator or freeze, using as needed.

■ Note: Whenever we have orange juice or half a grapefruit for breakfast, we save the empty rinds and store them in the freezer to fill with this bird pudding when the time comes. Also, children have fun patting it into pine cones to hang from trees.

We have the tallest sunflowers ever, this year...11½ feet! They'll be ready to be hung and dried for seeds when their petals have completely faded. I cut the flower heads, leaving a foot or two of stem and leaves, then tie string around a leaf joint and hang them upside down in a warm, dry place with good air circulation.

When the heads become dry and brittle, run your fingers over them to pop out the seeds. The seeds can be cracked and their kernels eaten raw, but it's easier to shell them after roasting in the oven. Just toss them, unwashed, in a touch of vegetable oil and lightly salt, then spread them out in a shallow pan and roast at 250° until crisp and brown, about 30-45 minutes.

WATER-BATH METHOD
for CANNING

You may wish to consult a cookbook that specializes in canning and preserving, but here are general instructions for the process that is used for pickles and relishes, sauces and condiments, fruits, and tomatoes.

☐ Equipment: jars, self-sealing vacuum lids, wide-mouth funnel, tongs, water-bath canner or deep kettle (at least 5 inches taller than jars) with canning rack and lid to fit, and cooling racks.

☐ Always thoroughly wash your jars and lids in hot, sudsy water or the dishwasher. Keep hot in your oven.

☐ Place rack in canner and fill halfway with hot water.

☐ Use a wide funnel for filling, keeping a clean towel at hand to wipe off any drips on rims of jars to ensure a tight seal. Prepared food should still be hot; fill only one jar at a time. Allow at least ¼-inch of space between food and top of jar.

☐ Screw lid onto jar tightly by hand, but if the lid buckles or bends, it is too tight.

☐ Place jar onto rack as soon as it is filled and sealed. Fit kettle with only as many jars as will allow water to still circulate between them. Pour hot water around them until measuring 1 to 2 inches over their tops. Cover kettle and bring to a full boil.

☐ Start counting processing time according to individual recipe, then immediately reduce heat until the water boils gently. (Higher altitudes will require longer processing times. If there is some question, check a canning cookbook.)

☐ When time is up, use tongs to remove jars to a cooling rack. Let jars cool, undisturbed, for 10-12 hours.

☐ Before storing canned foods, check their seals. After 12 hours, vacuum lids should be concave, and not giving when pressed. If there is any question, remove band and tip jar. If it stays on, it's sealed. Any jars that do not pass the test can be refrigerated and used within a week, or reprocessed in clean, hot jars.

☐ Store in a cool, dry, dark place for longest shelf-life.

EPILOGUE

Dear Bonnie:

I'm glad you can't see the Stand and the garden right now...they look so forlorn and desolate. For the most part though, it's been a beautiful winter, here in God's country.

We got word that one of our great-granddaughters is being married this spring...the first of that generation. Hard to believe.

Our family history is kept in our bible. Did you know that I was the oldest of three girls and had ten brothers? I was born Julia Beatrice Ratliff on August 2, 1905, and grew up in South Ironton, Ohio. I recall the flood of 1913 there, and how we all headed for the roof...the first floor ended up under water.

My Dad worked in the steel mill, but we had our own farm. We raised a lot of what we ate, even sorghum for molasses. We had a big house to keep clean...five, upstairs bedrooms. Everyone had to work. I remember my father cutting part of the legs off a table so that I could do the ironing.

How did I meet Marv? His family was originally from Sterling, Ontario. Then they homesteaded in Marlette, in the "thumb area" of Michigan, where he was born exactly three months after I was. Marv grew up there as a farmboy, then came down to Detroit to work in the auto industry.

That's where he met my brother...they shared an apartment. My brother brought him home for a visit. That was it...although my father wasn't too sure. He first thought Marv was a big-city boy, but of course he wasn't!

We were just twenty years old when we were married in 1925. Marv promised we'd go to Niagara Falls for our honeymoon. We did...twenty years later...by boat from Detroit to Buffalo. Best honeymoon anyone could have!

Our first daughter, Ruth, was born a year later, then Jean the following year. Then the Depression hit. Marv heard there was good work in the lumber camps in northern Michigan. Looking at it as an adventure, we four headed north in the spring in Marv's Whippet pick-up truck with our cookstove.

We first lived at Huntley's lumber camp, back of Rudyard. We'll never forget that first night there...stayed up all night shooing an army of mosquitoes off the girls.

"Number 59" was the railroad spur where we bought our supplies and picked up our mail...two houses and a one-room school. We would go for groceries by train...would load up a whole flatcar with $20 worth. In the winter, would melt icicles to wash clothes...used only a washboard and bar soap.

Then we rented a so-called "house" (we didn't want to think of it as a shack, but that's really what it was) on what was then the only real road between Trout Lake and Rudyard. We'll never forget when Marv's father came to visit us and shot a rabbit from the kitchen door at breakfast time.

We moved to Hessel in 1932 to the Walker farm, half-mile north of town. The Walkers owned the Hessel grocery store. The store's milk was right off their farm, as were the vegetables in the summer. Marv worked the farm, then in the winter also got a job on WPA. When his boss heard that he was getting $1 per day taking care of the cows on the farm, he lost his WPA job!

It was in 1934 when Marv saw this farm, an old, deserted homestead. It had a two-story, hewed-log house, a large barn and grainery, 21 apple trees, a good well, and 80 acres of land...he wanted it.

He had no money but he had made friends, one of them being Joe Fenlon, who owned the "big" store in Hessel. When Marvin told him he needed $250 to buy the place, Joe wrote him a check for the full amount and made out a mortgage. We were in business!

We put new floors and windows in the house. Marv made benches, a table, bed frames. I don't know what I would have done without my sewing machine. I made-over clothes for the girls...jumpers, blouses, underwear, insoles for shoes, mittens from discarded coats, vests...many things.

We paid Joe back.

But World War II came and we returned to Detroit to work in the factory, to save money to buy the 80 acres adjoining our farm that was owned by the Murray sisters.

We let another family move into our house while we were in Detroit. The day after New Year's, the house burned down. We had no insurance, so we stayed in Detroit until the war ended. I guess you could say I was like Rosie the Riveter...Marv worked just across the hall from me as a foreman. Seems like all our lives, we've never been far apart!

When we came home, we bought two army quonset huts (there were no building materials of any kind available), put them together, added a lean-to bathroom and kitchen, and went to work.

We bought 300 baby chicks, raising them in cages...keeping some for laying, butchering the rest for market. We cut saw logs and pulpwood, skidding logs with a horse named "Queen." We built a place in the woods for her and called it "Queen's Motel."

In 1947, our son, Marvin Jr. (or M.J., as we like to call him), came along...20 years after our second girl! We were so happy.

We then bought a block plant, making cement blocks from the sand in our field. Then we acquired the sawmill.

In 1960, we built our house. Marv made the blocks and cut the lumber for it. Several families paid us for their chickens and eggs by helping. How we love this home...and the Les Cheneaux!

Now I wonder what ever happened to the things that were so much a part of our daily life...castor oil, birds-eye diapers, the little potty beside the bed, the three-holer in the back yard (in the wintertime, o-o-o-ooo)...kerosene lamps and lanterns, the washboard or copper boiler to boil the clothes in, canning on a woodstove...we had no refrigeration, so everything had to be canned as soon as possible. Remember Fels Naptha and Octagon bar soap...rub the dishcloth over the soap to wash dishes...rub the soap onto the washboard to clean the clothes or cut it up into the washboiler? We didn't throw much away. Like we didn't have two bathrooms and four bedrooms...everybody had to snuggle. I think about how I pieced and quilted bed covers, and braided rugs, and made dolls from men's socks.

Marvin has made butcher blocks from our own lumber; also end tables, coffee tables...all sorts of things out of rare birdseye maple and mapleburls.

I think about how our four generations have sung in the choir at the Hessel Presbyterian Church, and all the times Ruth and I would sing for weddings and funerals, and when I taught Sunday School. Marv and I chaperoned the Cedarville High School seniors when they took their class trip to Chicago (and we danced to Guy Lombardo!).

I owned the restaurant and bake shop in the old feedstore next to McFee's in Hessel...I enjoyed that, but then Marvin needed a bookkeeper up here at the farm. I did that, the best I could, for a long time. I still write the checks but he checks on me when we get the bank statements!

I made my own white formal when I became Worthy Matron of Eastern Star. And that's another beautiful memory...being escorted by Marv Jr. through the "arch of roses," which was two long rows of pretty girls holding long-stemmed, red roses over us to form the arch.

I think about all the wonderful places we've been...like up to Lake in the Clouds and then on to Copper Harbor, where we had the feeling we were standing on the edge of the world, looking down on all those ore boats going through. They looked so tiny.

Lake Okeechobee in Florida, Swanee River, Las Vegas, Carlsbad Caverns, and California...always together.

And when we were visiting Jean and our grandchildren and great-grandchildren in Florida and ended up in the hospital at the same time. Marv was at one end of the place, and I at the other. We had both had surgery, but Marv's wasn't nearly so serious as mine.

He got very lonely, and one day spied a wheelchair that a nurse had left unguarded. You can guess the rest. He got in it and somehow found his way to my room. I said, "Who brought you here?" He said, "No one." I said, "Who gave you permission?" He said, "I ran away." Sounded just like a little boy.

He couldn't bend over nor could he stand up, and I couldn't roll over. But he held my hand, and I said, "I'll be better and go home with you. You'd better get back to your room before someone catches you."

With that touch of his hand, I got better. But...he saw seven ball games before I got out!

Thank you for letting me tell you so much about our beautiful life. It may not make a best-selling novel, but to us it's been the best of love stories. Now, back to today. We have tomato plants up...in the living room! We're going to order our seeds tomorrow for corn, beans, etc.

The first pair of robins showed up yesterday. They hung around the stand all day. Hope they decide to nest there. Marv heard geese overhead...it won't be too long before our spring is here.

I understand that you and your mother will be here in May. Let's take a walk in the woods together...when the warblers come.

We love you,

Judy Chard

INDEX

SPECIAL ACKNOWLEDGEMENTS

The Cedar Chest Cookbook
c/o Mrs. Glenn Rye
Hessel, Michigan 49745

Private Collection 1 & 2
Junior League of Palo Alto
555 Ravenswood Avenue
Menlo Park, California 94025

The Overlake School Cookbook
20301 N.E. 108th
Redmond, Washington 98053

Rave Revues Cookbook
Lakewood Center
P.O. Box 274
Lake Oswego, Oregon 97034

To order additional copies of
Hollyhocks & Radishes, enclose
check or money order for:

$13.95 per soft-bound cover
($15.95 Canadian)
$19.95 per hard-bound cover
($22.95 Canadian)
$2.00 shipping and handling

and send to:

Pickle Point Publishing
P.O. Box 4107
Bellevue, Washington 98009